MW00774134

The Making of the International Solar Alliance

The Making of the International Solar Alliance

India's Moment in the Sun

VYOMA JHA

OXFORD
UNIVERSITY PRESS

OXFORD
UNIVERSITY PRESS

Great Clarendon Street, Oxford, OX2 6DP,
United Kingdom

Oxford University Press is a department of the University of Oxford.
It furthers the University's objective of excellence in research, scholarship,
and education by publishing worldwide. Oxford is a registered trade mark of
Oxford University Press in the UK and in certain other countries

Published in the United States of America by Oxford University Press
198 Madison Avenue, New York, NY 10016, United States of America

British Library Cataloguing in Publication Data

Data available

Library of Congress Control Number: 2023944234

ISBN 978-0-19-888470-5

DOI: 10.1093/oso/9780198884705.001.0001

For Mamma and Papu

Acknowledgements

This journey of this book started alongside my doctoral journey at Stanford Law School. It would not have been possible to conceptualize and write this book without the supportive and dynamic academic environment in the JSD program at Stanford Law School, which provides exceptional training in empirical methods and encourages junior scholars to cross academic disciplines. First and foremost, I want to thank my advisors for their support and encouragement throughout my doctoral studies. Professor Janet Martinez has been a great mentor and a true champion of this research. Her enthusiasm from the time this was just an idea has been a real motivation. Our thought-provoking discussions and conversations over the years have helped me shape this book in its final form. I am so thankful for her mentorship and her friendship. Professor Saumitra Jha has been the most thoughtful reader, detecting every weak spot in my argument and encouraging me to sharpen my writing. I am truly grateful for his expert guidance on exploring the political economy implications to the study of law. Professor Deborah Hensler gave me the creative liberty to refine the contours of my doctoral project, without changing the direction and goals of my work. I am ever so grateful for her encouragement to write my doctoral dissertation as a book.

I would like to thank the team at Oxford University Press for making the publication of this book, an updated and revised version of my doctoral dissertation, possible. Special thanks to Dhiraj Pandey for his early support of the manuscript and for patiently answering all my questions through the different stages of the publication process. Thank you to the anonymous reviewers at Oxford University Press whose insightful comments helped strengthen the book. Although, of course, all errors and limitations are mine.

I wish to thank many outstanding scholars—seniors, colleagues, and friends—who have contributed immensely to developing the ideas presented in this book and my professional journey: Luis Bergolla, Silindile Buthelezi, Glenn Carroll, Pinaki Chakraborty, Abhinav Chandrachud,

Shih-Chun Chien, Doron Dorfman, Navroz Dubash, Lawrence Friedman, Arunabha Ghosh, Diana Guzman, Amalia Kessler, Phillip Lipsky, Diego Gil MacCawley, Rogelio Pérez-Perdomo, Mitch Polinsky, Lavanya Rajamani, Greg Shaffer, Richard Stewart, Alan Sykes, Arm Tungnirun, Allen Weiner, and Yoomin Won.

I would also like to acknowledge the financial support I received from Stanford Law School and the John M. Olin Program in Law and Economics for my fieldwork and participation in academic conferences. I have benefitted from many commentators and interlocutors at conferences such as the 2019 Annual Meeting of the Law and Society Association in Washington, D.C.; Institute for Global Law and Policy's 2018 Conference in Cambridge, Massachusetts; 2018 Annual South Asia Legal Studies Workshop in Madison, Wisconsin; 2018 American Society for International Law Midyear Meeting in Los Angeles, California; 2018 Annual Meeting of the Association on Law, Culture and Humanities in Washington, D.C.; and Stanford Program in Law and Society's 2017 Conference for Junior Researchers in Stanford, California. Some parts of this book have been previously published in *India Quarterly* (2022), in an article titled 'India and Climate Change: Old traditions, new strategies'; *Science Diplomacy Review* (2021), in an article titled 'Channeling the Sun: Ideas, Institutions and India's New Climate Diplomacy'; *Transnational Environmental Law* (2021), in article titled ' "Soft Law in a Hard Shell": India, International Rulemaking and the International Solar Alliance'; and *Trade, Law and Development* (2017), in an article titled 'Sunny Skies Ahead? Political Economy of Climate, Trade and Solar Energy in India'. My sincere thanks to the respective publishers for their permission to reproduce the previously published works.

This book has gained immensely from the deep and rich insights of those interviewed. My deepest gratitude goes to the senior government officials, diplomats, international public servants, civil society representatives, policymakers, and scholars I met—mostly in person and some virtually—over the course of the last few years. I remain indebted to all of them for generously giving their time and sharing their perspectives.

Thank you to my dear friends Ankana, Kartik, Vaishali, and Vivek for supporting me through these years. Thanks for always lending me your ear during the tough times, and sharing in the celebrations during the good ones.

This book would not be possible without the love and support of my family. I dedicate this book to the memory of my grandfather, Dr. P. N. Jha, whose life and service inspire me every day. My main reason to pursue a doctoral degree was to make up for the fact that I could never become a doctor like Dada. I am so thankful for the endless love and support from Dadi, Kaku, Kaki, and Shrinjay. Thanks also go to my parents-in-law, Nisha and Sury Kant, for their blessings and love. Rohit, my brother-in-law, thank you for always cheering on my efforts.

Rishi, my husband, thank you for being an equal part of this journey. Your love and patience, on good days and bad, has been my biggest strength and greatest joy. The start and end of this book marked a significant chapter in our lives, and I can't wait to find out what's next.

My brother, Viplav, thank you for being the wiser sibling and my voice of reason. Knowing that you are in my corner gives me the courage to do all that I do.

My parents, Ranjana and Ajay Jha, have helped me soar, and yet remain rooted. I am indebted to them for the unconditional love and unflinching support. This book is for them.

Contents

Tables and Figures

Tables

Figures

Abbreviations

BASIC	Brazil, South Africa, India, and China
BJP	Bhartiya Janata Party
BRICS	Brazil, Russia, India, China, and South Africa
CEEW	Council on Energy, Environment and Water
CII	Confederation of Indian Industry
CO_2	Carbon dioxide
COP	Conference of Parties
CSE	Centre for Science and Environment
G20	Group of 20
G77	Group of 77
GDP	Gross Domestic Product
GOI	Government of India
GW	Gigawatt
IAC	Interim Administrative Cell
IAS	Indian Administrative Services
IEA	International Energy Agency
IFS	Indian Foreign Services
INC	Indian National Congress
IRENA	International Renewable Energy Agency
ISA	International Solar Alliance
ISC	International Steering Committee
L&T	Legal and Treaties Division
LCR	Local Content Requirements
LOC	Line of Credit
MEA	Ministry of External Affairs
MNRE	Ministry of New and Renewable Energy
MOCI	Ministry of Commerce and Industry
MOEF	Ministry of Environment and Forests
MOEFCC	Ministry of Environment, Forests and Climate Change
MW	Megawatt
NAPCC	National Action Plan on Climate Change
NDA	National Democratic Alliance
NDC	Nationally Determined Contributions
NSM	National Solar Mission
OPEC	Organization of the Petroleum Exporting Countries

PIB	Press Information Bureau
PMO	Prime Minister's Office
PTI	Press Trust of India
PV	Photovoltaic
R&D	Research and development
TERI	The Energy and Resources Institute
TWI	Terrawatt Initiative
UN	United Nations
UNFCCC	United Nations Framework Convention on Climate Change
WTO	World Trade Organization

1

Introduction

Days before the start of the 2015 Paris Climate Conference (COP21), a BBC headline read: 'Can Paris climate talks overcome the India challenge?'[1] There was intense scrutiny on India's role in either securing or scuttling a global deal for climate action at Paris. Then United States (US) Secretary of State John Kerry, while praising China for its role in the climate talks, raised concerns about India: 'India has been more cautious, a little more restrained in its embrace of this new paradigm, and it's a challenge. ... We've got a lot of focus on India right now to try to bring them along.'[2] India, today, has a unique position in global governance: it is the fourth-highest emitter of carbon dioxide (CO_2) in the world after China, the United States, and the European Union; the second highest emitter of CO_2 among democratic countries; the fastest-growing major economy in the world; and yet it is home to the largest number of the world's poor. India continues to straddle an 'intriguing dual position in global climate politics'—on one hand, it is still a developing economy with a substantial poverty problem and low levels of historical and per capita emissions; while on the other, it is a large emerging economy that is under increasing pressure to address the global climate challenge.[3]

In this backdrop, on the first day of COP21, India and France jointly launched the International Solar Alliance (ISA) to boost solar energy for developing countries.[4] An alliance of 120 countries came together to support the Paris Declaration (Annex 1) on the basis of a shared

[1] J. Rowlatt, 'Can Paris climate talks overcome the India challenge?', *BBC News* (26 Nov. 2015), https://www.bbc.com/news/world-asia-india-34929578, accessed 15 Dec. 2022.

[2] D. Sevastopulo & P. Clark, 'Paris climate deal will not be a legally binding treaty', *Financial Times* (11 Nov. 2015), https://www.ft.com/content/79daf872-8894-11e5-90de-f44762bf9896, accessed 15 Dec. 2022 (subscription required).

[3] N.K. Dubash, 'The politics of climate change in India: narratives of equity and cobenefits', *WIREs Climate Change*, 4/3 (2013), 191–201.

[4] UNFCCC, 'International Solar Energy Alliance launched at COP21', *Newsroom* (30 Nov. 2015), https://newsroom.unfccc.int/news/international-solar-energy-alliance-launched-at-cop21, accessed 15 Dec. 2022.

The Making of the International Solar Alliance. Vyoma Jha, Oxford University Press. © Vyoma Jha 2023.
DOI: 10.1093/oso/9780198884705.003.0001

understanding that developing countries need technology, capacity building, and public finance to take solar energy to scale. A day before the launch, the Indian Prime Minister Narendra Modi, wrote an op-ed in the *Financial Times* urging the rich to take greater responsibility for climate change and reiterating that 'India will do its part for success in Paris.'[5] He went on to explain the decision to launch the ISA in these words:

> We are sharing our modest resources with the developing world, helping small island states and African nations with renewable energy. ... We should meet our need for clean energy and healthy habitats in a spirit of partnership, not put nations on different sides. India will work with governments, laboratories and industry to facilitate a natural transition to a clean energy era through affordable and accessible renewable energy.[6]

By late 2016, a little less than a year after the initial announcement, the Ministry of External Affairs (MEA) of the Government of India—India's foreign ministry—opened the Framework Agreement on the establishment of the International Solar Alliance for ratification (hereinafter Framework Agreement).[7] On 6 December 2017, upon the submission of instruments of ratification by fifteen countries, the ISA formally entered into force and acquired the status of a treaty-based international organization. In a year that witnessed multilateral climate negotiations weakening—particularly with the withdrawal of the United States from the 2015 Paris Agreement—the end was marked by a new, India-led treaty-based international organization becoming a legal entity.

Motivated by the lack of any specific international body to address the solar deployment needs of countries, the ISA was conceived by India as a coalition of 'solar-rich' countries to address their energy needs and aims to provide a platform to collaborate on addressing the identified gaps in solar deployment.[8] The 'solar-rich', or prospective ISA member countries

---

[5] N. Modi, 'The rich must take greater responsibility for climate change', *Financial Times* (29 Nov. 2015), https://www.ft.com/content/03a251c6-95f7-11e5-9228-87e603d47bdc, accessed 15 Dec. 2022.

[6] Ibid.

[7] See Annex 2 for the official text of the Framework Agreement.

[8] ISA, 'Working Paper on International Solar Alliance', *Media* (30 Nov. 2015), https://isolaralliance.org/media/press-release, accessed 15 Dec. 2022.

were identified as those located between the Tropic of Cancer and the Tropic of Capricorn, that is, countries geographically located for optimal absorption of the sun's rays (Annex 3). Crucially, most of them are developing countries with poor or no energy access; witness almost three hundred sunny days in a year; have large agrarian populations; and face major gaps in the potential solar manufacturing ecosystem.[9]

The ISA marks the first instance when the treaty-making process was led by India, and backed primarily by poor and developing countries in Asia and Africa. The ISA also witnessed an unusually quick ratification process—it took 386 days to enter into force from the day it was opened for signature.[10] Developing countries have typically not been at the forefront of international treaty-making, and the creation of the ISA invites empirical investigation and analysis. Interestingly, the ISA's prospective membership guidelines excluded countries like China or Germany, which are market leaders in solar and renewable energy, as 'solar-poor' countries.[11] Moreover, India has no perceivable competitive advantage in solar manufacturing or technologies, which begs the questions: what explains India's relative success in bringing together countries to form this new institution? What was the role of France in the creation of ISA? Why did India insist on a treaty structure for the new institution? Were any countries opposed to this? What are the transaction costs of bringing the 'solar-rich' countries vis-à-vis the 'solar-poor' countries on board?

Responding to these questions, this book explores the creation of the ISA as a treaty-based international organization. The core thesis is that India's leadership role in the creation of ISA marks an innovation in the structure of international organizations, which I describe as 'soft law in a hard shell'. I argue that the interests of the dominant actors driving the treaty-making process—in this case India's diplomats—explains the ISA's legal form and structure, wherein the institution uses the legal infrastructure of a treaty while relying on the social structure of participating actors for its future implementation. In this introductory chapter, I present the empirical puzzle that underlies this case study: why was ISA created

---

[9] Ibid.

[10] Compare this to similarly situated international organizations: the UNFCCC took 655 days and the International Renewable Energy Agency (IRENA) took 528 days to enter into force respectively.

[11] See Annex 3.

as a treaty-based international organization? I then make the case for adopting a political economy approach for this case study. In doing so, I situate this research within the broader international law and international relations scholarship. In the final section, I outline the roadmap of this book.

The Puzzle of the International Solar Alliance's Legal Form

International agreements generally have three core design elements: a formal treaty rather than soft law, mandatory dispute resolution procedures, and monitoring mechanisms.[12] The choices states make while drafting international agreements determine the force and credibility of their commitments.[13] A treaty, unlike a non-binding accord or a soft law instrument, is considered to be the most effective instrument for cooperation as it is more likely to induce compliance.[14] The ISA is a puzzling case as it does not contain any explicit or implicit compliance mechanisms, either by way of dispute resolution or monitoring mechanisms. It includes only one of the three elements mentioned earlier—a formal treaty, which in this case is the Framework Agreement.

On the face of it, the ISA has the makings of a 'climate club'—an exclusive group of 'solar-rich' countries geared towards cooperation on reducing the costs of finance and technology for the massive deployment of solar energy in member countries. According to one recent conceptualization of soft law instruments for climate change cooperation, a 'climate club' brings together groups of countries and non-state actors[15] to work on a specific climate issue.[16] Climate clubs typically start small

---

[12] A.T. Guzman, 'The design of international agreements', *European Journal of International Law*, 16/4 (2005), 579–612.

[13] Ibid.

[14] Ibid., at 597. See also C. Lipson, 'Why are some international agreements informal?', *International Organization*, 45/4 (1991), 495–538.

[15] Authority in world politics is diffused across multiple levels and diverse actors, and non-state actors are increasingly shaping the global response to the most pressing environmental problems. See J. Green, *Rethinking private authority: agents and entrepreneurs in global environmental governance* (Princeton, NJ: Princeton University Press, 2014).

[16] D.G. Victor, *Global warming gridlock: creating more effective strategies for protecting the planet* (New York: Cambridge University Press, 2011).

and build cooperation through incentives such as club goods (exclusive benefits to members), conditional commitments (promises of increased climate action provided others join the club), or side payments (monetary compensation for joining the club).[17] This club approach to climate diplomacy has stemmed in part from the extreme complexities associated with bargaining among the numerous and diverse countries involved in the United Nations Framework Convention on Climate Change (UNFCCC).[18] Yet, the ISA is not merely a small, informal coalition between enthusiastic countries. As of May 2021, the ISA operates under a formal treaty text that has 102 signatories, and has been signed and ratified by eighty-one member countries (Annex 4).

Some sceptics might also suggest that the ISA was simply a public relations exercise on India's part to announce something worthwhile at the Paris Climate Conference. If so, then India would have had limited success in driving the treaty-making process. It is conceivable that India would not have spent additional resources to set it up as a treaty-based organization if it was only meant to be a splashy announcement. More importantly, countries would not have ratified a treaty text if it did not further their material or strategic interests. But the ISA was not prematurely stopped in its tracks and became a legal entity following an intensive treaty-making process.

An added peculiarity of the ISA Framework Agreement is that there is no obvious mutual dependence among the prospective member countries. The 'solar-rich' countries, which form the bulk of the ISA's membership, are primarily poor and developing countries who need funding and access to technology to undertake large-scale solar energy deployment. Without any explicit provisions for financial or technology transfer in the Framework Agreement, it is difficult to understand why countries would perceive advantages to joining the agreement. Moreover, with no compliance mechanisms built into the treaty design, it would be difficult to ascertain the effectiveness of the international agreement going forward.

Why then did India insist on a treaty-based organization when the Framework Agreement did not contain any legal obligations for ISA

---

[17] D.F. Sprinz et al., 'The effectiveness of climate clubs under Donald Trump', *Climate Policy*, 18/7 (2018), 828–38.
[18] D.G. Victor, *The case for climate clubs* (Geneva: International Centre for Trade and Sustainable Development and World Economic Forum, 2015).

member countries? Some scholars have underscored the importance of trade-offs between form and substance in agreement design in order to grasp why states use or avoid legality.[19] An empirical inquiry into the political forces behind the treaty-making process would be needed in order to fully understand the trade-offs between form and substance in ISA's treaty design.

The creation of the ISA as a treaty-based organization is valuable as a case study because it has an empirical counterfactual in Mission Innovation. Launched on the same day as the ISA, on the sidelines of the Paris Climate Conference, Mission Innovation is an initiative to dramatically accelerate public and private global clean energy innovation, including doubling their current investments in the sector.[20] In spite of being announced on the same day and being carried by the same momentum and optimism of the Paris Agreement, both institutions have seen very different fates: Mission Innovation remains a global initiative of twenty-four countries and the European Commission,[21] while the ISA has turned into a treaty-based intergovernmental organization with eighty-one member countries. Are there any lessons in the understanding how or why the ISA acquired legal form? Does this case study offer fresh insights into India's role in contemporary international rule-making?

Scholars have long called for a 'dual interdisciplinary agenda' between international law and international relations, whereby international lawyers can ill afford to ignore available political science data on the world they seek to regulate.[22] More recently, legal scholars have adopted the

---

[19] K. Raustiala, 'Form and substance in international agreements', *American Journal of International Law*, 99/3 (2005), 581–614, 614. Raustiala argues that widespread preference for contracts in designing agreements weakens the substance and structure of multilateral agreements, particularly when states are uncertain about compliance costs. Thus, states might water down their commitments or weaken the monitoring systems in order to avoid non-compliance. In other words, the legality of the international agreement is achieved at the cost of weaker substantive obligations.

[20] UNFCCC, 'Mission Innovation—clean energy', *Newsroom* (30 Nov. 2015), https://unfccc. int/news/mission-innovation-clean-energy, accessed 15 Dec. 2022.

[21] Mission Innovation has been described as a 'nascent, immature venture', which seems to suffer from a level of duplication of existing institutions, such as the Green Climate Fund, Climate Technology Center and Network (CTCN), and WIPO GREEN. See M. Rimmer, 'Beyond the Paris Agreement: intellectual property, innovation policy, and climate justice', *Laws*, 8/1 (2019), 1–24, at 12.

[22] A.S. Burley, 'International law and international relations theory: a dual agenda', *American Journal of International Law*, 87/2 (1993), 205–39.

political economy approach in the study of international law,[23] with some urging international lawyers to focus on political economy in order to consider the role of law in the world's political and economic organization.[24] Van Aaken and Trachtman argue that it is important to analyse the 'why' questions when trying to analyse new developments around states cooperating and complying with public international law.[25] They write that

> any understanding of international cooperation through law must be infused with respect for the practical, State-based, political process by which formal cooperation occurs, and it must include a mechanism by which States would determine to create organizational structures which facilitate cooperation. It must develop a perspective on the interaction between multiple domestic political processes, and it must develop a theory of the creation of international organizations.[26]

It follows, then, that political economy is the study of the 'why' questions (why do we have laws, institutions, courts) by using as explanatory variables the 'who' (who are the actors—legislators, executives, judges, interest groups, countries, or international organizations—shaping international law) and 'what' (what motivates their preferences and/or constrains them—power, resources, institutions, laws, etc.).[27]

---

[23] A. Fabbricotti, ed., *The political economy of international law: a European perspective* (Cheltenham: Edward Elgar Publishing, 2016).

[24] D. Kennedy, 'Law and the political economy of the world', *Leiden Journal of International Law*, 26 (2013), 7–48.

[25] A. van Aaken & J.P. Trachtman, 'Political economy of international law: towards a holistic model of state behaviour', in A. Fabbricotti, ed., *The political economy of international law: a European perspective* (Cheltenham: Edward Elgar Publishing, 2016), 9–43, 10. Political economy is used in the national realm to understand political outcomes by identifying the interests of relevant actors and the institutions through which they pursue their interests, while international political economy applies in the international realm to understand the interaction between national politics and behaviour of states. See also, McNollgast, 'The political economy of law', in A.M. Polinsky & S. Shavell, eds, *Handbook of law and economics: volume 1* (Amsterdam: Elsevier Science Publishing, 2007), 1651–1738, 1654. Political economy of law has been understood as a branch of Law and Economics that applies positive political theory to study the development of law, that is, optimizing models of individual behaviour applied to political decision-making.

[26] Van Aaken & Trachtman, 'Political economy of international law: towards a holistic model of state behaviour', 22.

[27] A. Fabbricotti, 'Introduction', in A. Fabbricotti, ed., *The political economy of international law: a European perspective* (Edward Elgar Publishing, 2016), 1–8, 1.

Drawing on the political economy approach in the study of international law,[28] this case study asks 'why' the ISA was created as a treaty-based international organization? It proceeds to use the explanatory variables: 'who' were the main strategic actors driving the treaty-making process and 'what' motivated their preferences on legal form. In doing so, this book identifies the process (Chapter 3), politics (Chapter 4), and players (Chapter 5) behind the creation of this new international organization. By presenting an in-depth case study on the creation of the ISA, this book engages with different strands of international law and international relations scholarship.

With the growing focus on empirical legal research,[29] scholars have called for more studies looking at conditions under which international law is produced and has effects, including the actors and mechanisms involved.[30] According to Ginsburg and Shaffer, there are 'relatively few ethnographies of international law and organizations',[31] and there is a need to delink and investigate each step of the international legal process.[32] I argue that this case study offers a fresh perspective on 'how' international law is produced and highlights India's rising power[33] through the creation of a new international organization.

---

[28] T. Van de Graaf et al., 'States, markets and institutions: integrating international political economy and global energy politics', in T. Van de Graaf et al., eds, *Handbook on the international political economy of energy* (London: Palgrave Macmillan, 2016), 3–44; T. Van de Graaf & J. Colgan, 'Global energy governance: a review and research agenda', *Palgrave Communications*, 2/15047 (2016), 1–12; Van Aaken & Trachtman, n. 26; McNollgast, n. 26, 1654; Fabbricotti, 'Introduction'.

[29] P. Cane & H.M. Kritzer, eds, *The Oxford handbook of empirical legal research* (New York: Oxford University Press, 2010).

[30] T. Ginsburg & G. Shaffer, 'How does inter national law work?', in P. Cane & H.M. Kritzer, eds, *The Oxford handbook of empirical legal research* (New York: Oxford University Press, 2010), 753–84, 756. Ginsberg and Shaffer stress the importance of qualitative research in international law, especially to uncover the mechanisms and key actors involved, and identify three overarching questions for empirical legal research: (i) *why* international law is produced and invoked, focusing on the role of law in facilitating international cooperation; (ii) *how* international law is produced, focusing on the actors, institutions, mechanisms and processes involved in such production; (iii) *how* and under what conditions international law matters, in terms of affecting domestic law, the behaviour of states and other relevant actors.

[31] Ibid., 781.

[32] Ibid., 756. See also B. Simmons, *Mobilizing for human rights: international law in domestic politics* (New York: Cambridge University Press, 2009).

[33] Recent scholarship on India's foreign policy suggests that India is moving from being a 'rule-taker' to a 'rule-maker', especially in the context of global climate change, energy and trade governance. See generally, W.P.S. Sidhu, P.B. Mehta, & B. Jones, eds, *Shaping the emerging world: India and the multilateral order* (Washington, DC: Brookings Institution Press, 2013); T. Debiel & H. Wulf, 'More than a rule taker: the Indian way of multilateralism', in M. Hansel, R. Khan, & M. Levaillant, eds, *Theorizing Indian foreign policy* (London: Routledge, 2017), 49–68; N.K. Dubash, 'From norm taker to norm maker? Indian energy governance in global context',

The creation of the ISA must also be understood in light of the Paris Climate Conference. In 2015, after almost two decades of negotiations, the Paris Agreement reached a compromise between the legal form of the instrument as a whole and the legal character of the provisions.[34] The Paris Agreement is a legal instrument—a treaty under international law—but its provisions have varying degrees of normative force.[35] Therefore, the climate change negotiations at Paris sought to design a hybrid instrument with bottom-up elements to promote participation and a top-down process to promote ambition and accountability.[36] The dynamic interplay between the hard, soft, and non-law elements is a unique feature of the Paris Agreement,[37] and I explain that the creation and legal form of the ISA was heavily influenced by the realities of the multilateral climate change negotiations.

In the context of multilateral climate negotiations, almost all the studies related to India focus on the issue of 'position'.[38] But they reveal a gap in the understanding on whether Indian Prime Ministers have shaped or affected the negotiating position on climate change. Dubash and Rajamani contend that India's negotiating position has largely been defined within a

Global Policy, 2 (2011), 66–79; K. Hopewell, 'Recalcitrant spoiler? Contesting dominant accounts of India's role in global trade governance', Third World Quarterly, 39/3 (2018), 577–93.

[34] D. Bodansky, 2016. 'The legal character of the Paris Agreement' 25(2) Review of European, Comparative and International Environmental Law 142–50; L. Rajamani, 'Ambition and differentiation in the 2015 Paris Agreement: interpretative possibilities and underlying politics', International and Comparative Law Quarterly, 65/2 (2016), 493–514.

[35] L. Rajamani, 'The 2015 Paris Agreement: interplay between hard, soft, and non-obligations', Journal of Environmental Law, 28/2 (2016), 337–58.

[36] L. Rajamani, 'Understanding the 2015 Paris Agreement', in N.K. Dubash, ed., India in a warming world: integrating climate change and development (New Delhi: Oxford University Press, 2019) 205–21, 206.

[37] Rajamani, n. 35.

[38] Dubash, n. 3; K. Michaelowa & A. Michaelowa, 'India as an emerging power in international climate negotiations', Climate Policy, 12 (2012), 575–90; S. Sengupta, 'International climate negotiations and India's role', in N.K. Dubash, ed., Handbook of climate change and India: development, politics and governance (New Delhi: Oxford University Press, 2012), 101–17; A. Vihma, 'India and the global climate governance: between principles and pragmatism', The Journal of Environment & Development, 20/1 (2011), 69–94; J. Thaker & A. Leiserowitz, 'Shifting discourses of climate change in India', Climatic Change, 123/2 (2014), 107–19; A. Mohan, 'From Rio to Paris: India in global climate politics', Rising Powers Quarterly, 2/3 (2017), 39–61; N.K. Dubash, 'Of maps and compasses: India in multilateral climate negotiations', in W.P.S. Sidhu, P.B. Mehta, & B. Jones, eds, Shaping the emerging world: India and the multilateral order (Washington, DC: Brookings Institution Press, 2013), 261–79

foreign policy frame,[39] with relatively little evolution in domestic politics around climate change since the start of global climate negotiations.[40] However, by focusing on the spoken word of Indian Prime Ministers,[41] I argue that this case study reveals the first instance of an Indian Prime Minister actively shaping India's position on issues relating to climate change. Modi's leadership, in turn, marks an important geopolitical shift in India's foreign policy wherein climate change considerations—in this case solar energy—became a point for consideration to further India's strategic interests on the global stage.

Narlikar and Narlikar's book was a first-of-its-kind analysis of modern India's negotiating behaviour by rooting it in India's ancient bargaining techniques.[42] They unpack India's 'negotiating culture' and provide a framework to think about the role of culture and attitudes in framing negotiating positions.[43] I attempt to push this conversation further and argue that India's politico-legal culture plays into how it views and engages with international law. The lack or absence of lawyers has created a legal culture that is more political and less legalized. This broader politico-legal negotiating culture, I argue, explains India's embrace of multilateralism and motivation to steer ISA's treaty-making process. Narlikar and Narlikar also underscore the importance of coalitions for India's negotiating strategy and highlight its leadership on building coalitions, particularly with developing countries.[44] Although the ISA comprises mostly developing countries, this case study finds that India built new partnerships and alliances with developed countries as well. France was an important partner in launching and operationalizing the ISA. Japan, Australia, the Netherlands, the United Kingdom, and Italy too

---

[39] N.K. Dubash & L. Rajamani, 'Multilateral diplomacy on climate change', in D.M. Malone, C.R. Mohan, & S. Raghavan, eds, *The Oxford handbook of Indian foreign policy* (Oxford: Oxford University Press, 2015), 663–77.

[40] Ibid.

[41] Anandita Bajpai's recent work lays the groundwork for analysing the speeches and rhetoric of Indian Prime Ministers, providing a fresh perspective on secularism and market liberalization. Issues of climate change, notably, are entirely absent in this book. See A. Bajpai, *Speaking the nation: the oratorical making of secular, neoliberal India* (New Delhi: Oxford University Press, 2018).

[42] A. Narlikar & A. Narlikar, *Bargaining with a rising India: lessons from the Mahabharata* (New Delhi: Oxford University Press, 2014)

[43] Ibid.

[44] For instance, India's alliances with the global South such as Non-Aligned Movement (NAM), Group of 77 (G77), BRICS, BASIC, etc.

have signed on to the new organization. Therefore, this case study marks an important turn in India's diplomatic efforts to build a new coalition cutting across the developed and developing world.

There is a growing literature on global energy governance.[45] This case study complements other studies of international energy organizations.[46] While much of the early work on international energy cooperation focuses primarily on two organizations—the International Energy Agency (IEA)[47] and the Organization of the Petroleum Exporting Countries (OPEC)—global energy markets are changing and becoming entwined with concerns over climate change. As developing states become major sources of energy demand, the domestic politics within states will grow in importance.[48] Dissatisfaction with existing regimes could lead these states to seek alternative venues to secure energy supplies while also reinforcing their sovereignty.[49] Against this backdrop, the ISA offers a unique opportunity to examine the decision-making behind the creation of a treaty-based international organization focused on expanding solar energy in the developing world.

---

[45] A. Florini & N.K Dubash, 'Introduction to the special issue: governing energy in a fragmented world', *Global Policy*, 2/s1 (2011), 1–5; A. Florini & N.K Dubash, 'Mapping global energy governance', *Global Policy*, 2/s1 (2011), 6–18; R. Leal-Arcas & A. Filis, 'The fragmented governance of the global energy economy: a legal-institutional analysis', *The Journal of World Energy Law & Business*, 6/4 (2013), 348–405; Van de Graaf & Colgan, n. 28.

[46] A. Florini, 'The International Energy Agency in global energy governance', *Global Policy*, 2/s1 (2011), 40–50; T. Van de Graaf, 'Obsolete or resurgent? The International Energy Agency in a changing global landscape', *Energy Policy*, 48 (2012), 233–41; T. Van de Graaf, 'Fragmentation in global energy governance: explaining the creation of IRENA', *Global Environmental Politics*, 13/3 (2013), 14–33; J.D. Colgan, 'The emperor has no clothes: the limits of OPEC in the global oil market', *International Organization*, 68/3 (2014), 599–632.

[47] R.O. Keohane, 'International agencies and the art of the possible: the case of the IEA', *Journal of Policy Analysis and Management*, 1/4 (1982), 469–81. Keohane argues that while several international organizations are rule-making and rule-enforcing bodies, others' most important function is to serve as facilitators of agreement between governments. For example, the IEA's true value was as a participant in elite networks and a mobilizer of transnational coalitions.

[48] L. Hughes & P.Y. Lipscy, 'The politics of energy', *Annual Review of Political Science*, 16 (2013), 449–69.

[49] For a discussion on the concept of 'regime shifting', see L.R. Helfer, 'Regime shifting: the TRIPS agreement and new dynamics of international intellectual property lawmaking', *Yale Journal of International Law*, 29/1 (2004), 1–83; A. Ghosh, 'Seeking coherence in complexity? The governance of energy by trade and investment institutions', *Global Policy*, 2/s1 (2011), 106–19.

Research Design and Methods

This book, although based on a single case study, generates important insights for international legal and international relations scholars. For international legal scholars, this case raises important issues of treaty structure and the role of state and non-state actors in the treaty-making process. For international relations scholars, this case illustrates the role and behaviour of India as a rising power in global governance. I utilized a variety of methods to collect and interpret the data that informs the analysis in this book. Viewed as a whole, each of the methodological approaches has given me the opportunity to explore the creation of a new international organization from a broader socio-legal perspective, an aspect that is generally overlooked by international legal scholars. I hope that this discussion on the book's research design offers socio-legal scholars new insights on how to navigate the empirical turn in international legal scholarship.

The multi-pronged methodological approach that I have selected for this research has some distinctive advantages. First, the document analysis has allowed me to obtain a deep and contextualized understanding of the official process that led to the setting up of ISA. Second, the research interviews with key stakeholders in the creation of the ISA has provided an additional layer of granularity in understanding what happened behind the scenes. A significant limitation of this research could be the risk of bias having conducted interviews primarily with Indian stakeholders. Since I am interested in the creation of ISA within the broad construct of India's role in international rule-making, the perspectives offered by key Indian officials and stakeholders remain valuable. I have spoken to both French and American officials who provide an outsider's viewpoint on India's efforts behind the creation of the ISA. I must note that the document analysis has provided additional insights into statements/opinions of key stakeholders from countries other than India, thereby allowing a more comprehensive view of the overall process. Third, the political discourse analysis bolsters the key finding from the interview data about Modi's central role in pushing for the creation of the ISA, and goes on to ensure the reliability of the findings from the interview data.

Document Analysis

Qualitative document analysis is a good way to provide evidence of policy direction, legislative intent, understanding of perceived shortcomings or best practices in the legal system, and agenda for change.[50] With that in mind, I began the research with an in-depth coding and analysis of two sets of documents: (1) reports of the meetings of ISA's International Steering Committee (ISC); and (2) reports of the meetings of ISA's Interim Administrative Cell (IAC). The proceedings of all these early meetings have been captured in detailed reports, and are publicly available on the official ISA website. There were six meetings of the ISC between December 2015 and February 2018, and eight meetings of the IAC between February 2016 and March 2017. I coded the documents using the following keywords: 'motivation', 'objectives', 'activities', 'partners', and 'treaty text'.[51] I decided to rely on a qualitative document analysis in order to trace the procedural history, as well as understand the substantive issues and official narrative behind the creation of the ISA.

Elite Interviews

I was also interested in understanding how, in their own words, key stakeholders viewed the creation of the ISA. Therefore, I complemented the document analysis with semi-structured interviews. When selecting the individuals to be interviewed during the research process, I wanted to ensure that I capture a broad range of stakeholders across the policy-making spectrum so as to offer a cross-sectional analysis. Interviewees were selected through non-random purposive sampling technique. The interviews were designed to elicit the professional and expert opinions of relevant stakeholders in India who were closely involved in the treaty-making process. The interview questions were based on an open-ended and semi-structured protocol prepared in advance and focused on four

---

[50] L. Webley, 'Qualitative approaches to empirical legal research', in P. Cane & H.M. Kritzer, eds, *The Oxford handbook of empirical legal research* (New York: Oxford University Press, 2010), 926–50, 940.

[51] More information is on file with the author.

main frames: 'initiation', 'membership', 'treaty form', and 'location'.[52] The interviewees include: (1) senior officials of the ISA; (2) diplomats, or officers from the Indian Foreign Services (IFS), including two former Foreign Secretaries of India; (3) bureaucrats, or officers of the Indian Administrative Services (IAS); (4) senior-level members of think tanks and non-governmental organizations; (5) members of the private sector, industry, and media; and (6) other foreign[53] diplomats and officials.

I conducted twenty-three interviews across the summers of 2018, 2019, and 2020. All interviewees were promised anonymity, although some of them gave me express permission to use their names. However, given that several of the interviewees have held or are currently in high-ranking governmental or diplomatic positions, I decided to maintain the anonymity of the entire interview population. To quote them, I identify them by a general description of their role. The average interview lasted thirty minutes, and I took detailed handwritten notes during the meeting or phone conversation. In some instances, where I received permission to record the interview, I transcribed the audio recording on the same day.

I also drew from interviews I had conducted for an earlier research study that explored the political economy of the solar trade dispute between India and the US in December 2016.[54] This round of interviews, too, was based on a rigorous interview protocol designed to elicit the professional opinion of experts and relevant stakeholders in the field. The ISA's treaty-making process was in full swing at the time as the Framework Agreement had been opened for signature in November 2016. Although the focus of the interviews was on the solar trade dispute, all conversations mentioned the ISA in some form or another. The additional interview data allowed me to gain insights into the different stakeholders' impressions on the creation of the ISA. Therefore, given the time period of the interviews and the proximity of the interviewees to the subject matter of this research, the additional interview data could be considered as contemporaneous evidence on how different stakeholders viewed or participated in the creation of the ISA. Overall, I conducted interviews

---

[52] The interviews were conducted after approval of IRB Protocol by Stanford University's Research Compliance Office. More information is on file with the author.

[53] I interviewed a French diplomat and a former US official for this research.

[54] V. Jha, 'Sunny skies ahead? Political economy of climate, trade and solar energy in India', *Trade, Law and Development*, 9/2 (2017), 255–304.

with forty individuals, wherein I met five interviewees twice at different points of time. Annex 5 details the entire list of interviewees, while Table 1.1 presents the range of perspectives included in the interview population and the number of interviewees representing each perspective.

The handwritten and transcribed notes were organized and coded based on the four broad themes relied on during the interview process. I proceeded to complete a second round of coding using Dedoose—a web-based software for qualitative analysis. Following this second round of coding, I refined the codes to allow for more granular thematic groupings. During this round, I moved one step beyond the predecided codes and created codes around new themes emerging from the interview data. The interview data was finally coded based on the

Table 1.1 Snapshot of the Interview Population

Institution	Number and position of interviewees
Ministry of External Affairs	3 high-level former officials 2 mid-level current officials
Ministry of New and Renewable Energy	2 high-level former officials 3 high-level current officials
Ministry of Environment, Forests and Climate Change	3 high-level former officials 1 mid-level current official
Ministry of Finance	1 mid-level current official
Ministry of Commerce and Industry	3 high-level former officials 1 mid-level current official
Private sector, business actors, and foreign investors	1 Indian and 1 French solar energy entrepreneur 1 foreign investor representative 1 industry association representative 1 financial actor
Research and think tanks	4 heads of research organizations 3 high-level experts 1 mid-level expert 1 journalist
Lawyers and legal academia	2 lawyers 2 law professors
Foreign government officials	2 US officials 1 French official
Total	40

Source: Author's own analysis

following: 'motivation', 'India's leadership', 'geopolitics', 'process', 'legal form', 'goals', and 'future issues'. Sub-codes were developed under some of these categories: first, 'India's leadership' spawned the following sub-codes: 'Modi'[55], 'MEA'[56], 'MNRE',[57] and 'MOEFCC'[58]; second, 'process' was divided into 'pre-Paris' and 'post-Paris'; and third, 'legal form' led to two new sub-codes: 'treaty' and 'non-state actors'. The findings from the interview data are relied on for the overall analysis in this book, and find mention across all chapters.

Political Discourse Analysis

One of the key findings to emerge from the interview data was India's central role in the treaty-making process. Several interviewees attributed this to Prime Minister Narendra Modi's leadership on issues relating to solar energy and climate change. In fact, one of the climate negotiators who I interviewed specifically mentioned that I look at Modi's speeches to uncover the changing discourse on solar energy in India. This suggestion during the early interview process allowed me to segue into another methodological approach to reveal the full story behind the creation of the ISA. Did India's changing political systems affect climate policies and outcomes—in this case, both at the national level and in the international sphere? Did the arrival of Modi on the national scene really change the discourse on climate change, particularly the importance accorded to solar energy? Therefore, I decided to compare and contrast the speeches of two Indian Prime Ministers,[59] in a bid to ascertain whether India's changing domestic politics indeed marked a shift in the political discourse on solar energy.

This analysis is based on a comprehensive coding of the speeches of the Prime Minister at all domestic and international events. The texts of the

---

[55] Prime Minister Narendra Modi.
[56] Ministry of External Affairs.
[57] Ministry of New and Renewable Energy.
[58] Ministry of Environment, Forests and Climate Change.
[59] The main reason to code the speeches of the Prime Minister is that the Prime Minister's Office is responsible for setting the country's climate policy, as well as determining India's negotiating position during international climate change talks.

speeches were accessed through the official website of the Prime Minister of India and the Government of India's Press Information Bureau.[60] I chose to conduct this analysis across two time periods: 2008–10 and 2014–16 (see Table 2.1). The two data sets for analysis are: (1) speeches by Dr Manmohan Singh between 1 January 2008 and 31 December 2010; and (2) speeches by Narendra Modi between 15 August 2014 and 31 December 2016. It must be noted that Narendra Modi assumed office as Prime Minister on 26 May 2014, and his first publicly available speech as PM is dated 15 August 2014. As a result, the time period of analysis for Modi's speeches does not begin on 1 January 2014.

The choice of years is significant for two reasons: (1) there were two major multilateral climate talks within each time period—COP15 in Copenhagen in 2009 and COP21 in Paris in 2015; and (2) the ruling Indian government and Prime Minister was different during these two time periods—during the first phase, the ruling party was the Indian National Congress (INC) led by Dr Manmohan Singh; and during the second phase, the ruling party was Bhartiya Janata Party (BJP) led by Narendra Modi. The initial search registered a total of 336[61] speeches by Dr Manmohan Singh and 405 speeches by Narendra Modi.

Following this, I checked all the speeches for relevance to this study by checking it against the following keywords: 'climate', 'energy', 'solar', 're-newable', 'environment', 'development', and 'security'. The speeches were categorized under two colour codes: green (contains most keywords or contains some keywords but needs to be checked for context); and red (contains some or no keywords, but is completely out of context). The speeches coded green were checked for relevance in a second round of analysis, while those coded red were eliminated in this round. At the be-ginning of the second round, a total of 155 speeches by Dr Manmohan Singh and 113 speeches by Narendra Modi remained. In this round, the search had a few additional keywords in order to narrow down the rele-vance to the discourse around India's climate action/ambition and the

---

[60] Prime Minister Dr Manmohan Singh's speeches: https://archivepmo.nic.in/drmanmohansingh/all-speeches.php; Prime Minister Narendra Modi's speeches: https://www.pmindia.gov.in/en/tag/pmspeech/.

[61] The initial search yielded a total of 351 speeches, however the text of fifteen speeches was not available on the official website. As a result, the total number of speeches to be analysed was 336.

use of solar energy. The speeches were checked against the following keywords: 'climate change', 'solar energy', 'energy security', and 'International Solar Alliance'. This time, the speeches were again categorized under two colour codes: green (contains the additional keywords) and red (does not contain the additional keywords). At the end of this round, the total number of speeches for analysis by both Prime Ministers were 109 (Singh) and eighty (Modi) respectively.

Next, I qualitatively analysed the resultant sample to illustrate whether there were any shifts in the political discourse around issues of climate change and solar energy, particularly with the change in the Indian Prime Minister. The speeches were coded based on the question: What is the position of solar energy within the political discourse on climate change?

The software Dedoose was used to organize the coding, although the identification of the codes was based on a qualitative content analysis where each speech was read manually for context. The analysis was largely inductive; instead of focusing on the frequency of words, it tried to identify and examine the statements in their broader context to capture the meaning behind the statements. There were twenty-seven[62] distinct codes that were developed in the course of the analysis, and the codes with a similar underlying rationale were grouped together under one theme. The thematic findings from the political discourse analysis are discussed in Chapter 4. I also used a web-based reading and analysis tool, Voyant,[63] to generate data visualizations and supplement the qualitative discourse analysis.

Archival Data

The data-collection process also involved gathering archival materials and other relevant administrative data. There are two main sets of

---

[62] The codes (in no particular order) for analysis were: 'climate action'; 'historical responsibility'; 'equity'; 'development space'; 'domestic level action'; 'per capita commitment'; 'clean energy'; 'solar energy'; 'solar capabilities and applications'; 'climate justice'; 'technology transfer'; 'financial commitment'; 'foreign policy'; 'energy security'; 'energy access'; 'energy efficiency'; 'legal form'; 'energy partnership'; 'line of credit'; 'reframing coalitions'; 'global institutions'; 'Mission Innovation'; 'International Solar Alliance'; 'lifestyle argument'; 'cultural identity'; 'personal ambition'; 'symbolism'.

[63] https://voyant-tools.org/

archival data that I rely on for the book, and each piece of information has been valuable to add nuance to the broader story.

First, I collected data on the composition of Indian delegations at the international climate change negotiations over a two-decade period from 1995 to 2015. I accessed the online repositories of the UNFCCC and created a negotiator database in order to identify the key actors in India's negotiating teams over the years. The UNFCCC website contains participant information for each year's climate talks, that is, the Conference of Parties (COP),[64] and I extracted the necessary data on the Indian delegation for each of these years. In particular, I tried to identify the role of legal advisers, if any, within the Indian delegation over the years.

Second, I accessed the MEA Annual Reports to understand India's foreign policy stance on issues of climate change and energy security. These reports are publicly available on MEA's official website starting from the year 2000.[65] For the purposes of this book, I have studied the reports between the year 2000 and 2018. Other administrative data used in this book is based on publicly available sources and referenced whenever cited.

As a recently created organization, the ISA provides a window into the different stages in the life cycle of a treaty—pre-negotiation, drafting, negotiation, implementation, and possibly renegotiation. This book follows a case study approach,[66] in order to gain a comprehensive understanding of how and why the ISA was created as a treaty-based international organization. To do so, it narrows its focus on the ratification of the main treaty text—the Framework Agreement[67]—to illustrate the politico-legal issues during the creation of a new international organization, especially one backed by developing countries. For the purposes of this book, this would include the stages of pre-negotiation, drafting, negotiation, and signature in the life cycle of the treaty. Therefore, the time period of

---

[64] A few years' data (2002, 2006, and 2007) was unavailable on the UNFCCC official website and could not be obtained from alternate sources. However, these years are not crucial to the central analysis in this book, and I have proceeded with the analysis without taking these years into consideration.

[65] MEA (Government of India), *Annual Reports*, https://meacms.mea.gov.in/annual-reports.htm?57/Annual_Reports, accessed 15 Dec. 2022.

[66] R.K. Yin, *Case study research and applications: design and applications* (6th edition, Los Angeles: Sage Publications Inc., 2018).

[67] Framework Agreement on the establishment of the International Solar Alliance (ISA), Marrakesh (Morocco), 15 Nov. 2016, in force 6 Dec. 2017 (see Annex 2).

analysis is between mid-2014 (early inception of the idea) and December 2017 (ISA enters into force). I adopt a multi-method approach, relying on elite interviews, document analysis, political discourse analysis and archival data, to reveal the social and political life around the main legal text of the ISA. I present my main arguments and findings using three frames: process, politics, and players.

Process, Politics, and Players: Building Blocks of the International Solar Alliance

By taking a political economy approach to investigate the creation of ISA as a treaty-based organization, I find several competing issues, interests and institutions at play. Among them, India's role is front and centre, right from conceptualizing this new institution to driving the treaty-making process. India's interest in ISA stemmed from a variety of market and non-market factors. India had witnessed a dramatic fall in the price of solar energy and ramping up of solar targets at home, and sensed the potential to replicate its success story in other countries facing issues of energy access. Increasingly, also, India's development assistance to African countries included solar and renewable energy-related projects. There was a clear market opportunity to tap into the economic potential for solar energy in energy-starved parts of the world.

Meanwhile, approaching the Paris climate talks, India was under increasing pressure to show its commitment for a global climate agreement. Under Modi's leadership, in addition to showcasing its domestic climate actions, India was keen to take on a leadership role at the international level and carving a new international organization focused solely on solar energy offered the opportunity to do so. By framing the new grouping as an alliance of 'solar-rich' nations, India hoped to capture the interests of developing countries with problems of energy access but a high potential for solar deployment. In doing so, India also sought to reclaim the lost ground in climate talks over the last decade—from being alienated during negotiations to slipping into a non-dominant role among the various coalitions it was a part of.

Buoyed by Modi's personal ambition to lead on climate change, India's foreign policy displayed a new kind of economic diplomacy going into

Paris by re-energizing existing alliances, building new partnerships and driving the treaty-making process for a new international organization. The Paris Climate Conference provided an opportune moment to launch the new institution, as well as the perfect partner—France—to help steer the course towards such an institution. Although the French partnership appears to be rather organic given that they were the host country, there were several strategic reasons underlying France's decision to partner with India.

From the French perspective, India's participation was crucial to securing a global climate deal and partnering on the ISA was an easy 'give' in exchange for finalizing the Paris Agreement. Moreover, the French private sector was bullish on the prospects of driving a clean energy transition in the developing world. This gave the French government a new impetus to collaborate with India, which tied into its long-standing interest in strengthening its defence relationship with India. For India, meanwhile, the partnership with France provided a greater legitimacy to the efforts in bringing everyone to the table around the idea of ISA. France's vast networks and experience, particularly in the francophone countries, were also important to steer the early treaty ratification process. France also played a crucial role in giving an impetus to private sector and non-state participation in the ISA, which had implications for the treaty-making process and legal form of the ISA.

As a new kind of grouping not dominated by western powers, this case study challenges existing theories on the formation of international agreements and reveals how the interests of dominant actors can affect the legal form of an international agreement. The main argument in this book is that India's central role in the treaty-making process—driven primarily by Indian diplomats who were empowered by Modi's political leadership on climate change—was a crucial factor in determining the legal form of ISA. On the demand side, India was interested in leading the creation of a new international organization in an as-yet ungoverned space with unclear rules of engagement. By bringing together 'solar-rich' countries under the ambit of the ISA, India successfully steered the interests of these developing nations towards a common goal: to increase the deployment of solar energy and bring energy security to their people. On the supply side, however, it was easier to find consensus between countries when the international agreement did not contain legally binding provisions. The transaction costs of adding more countries and non-state actors were significantly reduced by keeping the treaty terms non-binding and flexible. Moreover, France's insistence on private-sector participation was another reason for India providing a leeway on treaty form by incorporating flexibilities in the treaty terms. The presence of non-state actors since the early days of the treaty-making process was further responsible for the flexibility built into the substantive provisions of the Framework Agreement, as well as the action-oriented profile of ISA. Ultimately, the ISA marks an innovation in international rule-making, which I describe as 'soft law in a hard shell', that is it uses the legal infrastructure of a treaty while relying on the social structure of participating actors for its future implementation.

This book begins with Chapter 2 on 'Political economy of solar energy in India' that sets the context for the creation of the ISA. It provides a background on climate policymaking in India, including an overview of the political and economic environment of solar energy in the country. Over the next few chapters, I explore the interconnections between the myriad factors underlying the decision to set up the ISA as a treaty-based international organization, and frame the empirical findings under three chapters: process, politics, and players. The rest of the book proceeds as follows: Chapter 3 on 'Process' provides a detailed analysis of ISA's treaty-making process and discusses the critical issues behind the creation of ISA as a treaty-based international organization. This chapter lays down the analytical framework for the book's main argument that the legal form of the ISA was a result of India's entrepreneurial diplomacy that took advantage of the political leadership's vision and India's strategic partnerships. Against the backdrop of the country's changing political leadership, Chapter 4 on 'Politics' focuses on the spoken word of two Indian Prime Ministers to identify the key shifts in the political discourse on solar energy. In particular, it highlights Prime Minister Modi's personal ambition to lead on the issue of climate change, as well as his vision for a new, India-led global alliance based on solar energy. Chapter 5 on 'Players' goes on to describe the main strategic actors—Indian diplomats—behind operationalizing the new institution. By tracing India's negotiating history and character at multilateral climate negotiations, this chapter illustrates how diplomacy sits at the core of India's international rule-making identity and how the broader politico-legal culture of India's diplomatic community was responsible for the choice of legal form of ISA. The final chapter (Chapter 6) summarizes the main findings and discusses some policy implications emerging from this case study on the creation of ISA as a treaty-based organization.

2

Channelling the Sun

Political Economy of Solar Energy in India

> *India is a tropical country, where sunshine is available for longer hours and in great intensity. Solar energy, therefore, has great potential as a future energy source.*
> —National Action Plan on Climate Change (MOEFCC 2008)

This chapter lays the groundwork for understanding the creation of the International Solar Alliance (ISA) as a new international organization. It traces the evolution of climate policymaking in India, with a particular focus on the interweaving of energy security and climate change concerns. By providing a detailed look at the significant markers of domestic climate policy, this chapter goes on to describe the role of solar energy within India's efforts to combat climate change. Against the backdrop of India's ambitious solar targets, the chapter also explores the long-standing solar trade dispute between India and the United States and its impact on the governance of solar energy in India. Ultimately, this chapter explains the Indian government's solar policy pivot from mid-2014, both at the national and international level.

The Foreign Policy Framing of Climate Change

In the early 1990s, from the start of the multilateral climate change negotiations under the United Nations Framework Convention on Climate Change (UNFCCC), climate change was treated as a foreign policy issue in India and fell in the domain of a handful of bureaucrats and diplomats.

The Making of the International Solar Alliance. Vyoma Jha, Oxford University Press. © Vyoma Jha 2023.
DOI: 10.1093/oso/9780198884705.003.0002

India's foreign policy, particularly through the Cold War, emphasized strongly on the principles of national sovereignty and non-alignment with either of the two major powers.[1] India was one of the leaders of the Non-Aligned Movement (NAM)—a grouping of states that are not formally aligned with or against any major power bloc. As a result India's foreign policy on climate change was guided by its traditional ideological and principle-based approach to multilateralism, and developing country concerns such as sovereignty, equity, and development.[2] Scholars have noted that the Indian government's initial positions during the climate negotiations served to protect India's sovereignty and preserve its development space.[3] The principle of 'common but differentiated responsibility', enshrined in the UNFCCC, has been at the core of India's strategy at the multilateral negotiations—the developing world argues that the historical responsibility to deal with climate change lies with the developed North and that they must take on a leadership role in addressing climate change.[4] This view was strongly endorsed by civil society observers in India as well, who famously noted that

the idea that developing countries like India and China must share the blame for heating up the earth and destabilizing its climate, as espoused in a recent study published in the United States (US) by the World Resources Institute (WRI) in collaboration with the United Nations, is an excellent example of environmental colonialism.[5]

[1] A. Mohan, 'From Rio to Paris: India in global climate politics', *Rising Powers Quarterly*, 2/3 (2017), 39–61, 47.

[2] M.G. Rajan, *Global environmental politics: India and the north–south politics of global environmental issues* (New Delhi: Oxford University Press, 1997); N.P. Rastogi, 'Winds of change: India's emerging climate strategy', *The International Spectator*, 46/2 (2011), 127–41, 129.

[3] A. Atteridge et al., 'Climate policy in India: what shapes international, national and state policy?', *Ambio*, 41/1 (2012), 68–77; S. Sengupta, 'International climate negotiations and India's role', in N.K. Dubash, ed., *Handbook of climate change and India: development, politics and governance* (New Delhi: Oxford University Press, 2012), 101–17; J. Thaker & A. Leiserowitz, 'Shifting discourses of climate change in India', *Climatic Change*, 123/2 (2014), 107–19; Mohan, n. 1.

[4] Rastogi, n. 2, 129.

[5] A. Agarwal & S. Narain, 'Global warming in an unequal world: a case of environmental colonialism', in N.K. Dubash, ed., *India in a warming world: integrating climate change and development* (New Delhi: Oxford University Press, 2019), 81–91, 81.

The dominant ideological narrative in India's negotiating position for over two decades has been on the issues of equity and differentiation.[6] India was instrumental in constructing and propagating the idea of 'differentiated responsibility' in the early years of the climate negotiations.[7] This principle creates a firewall between developed and developing countries, which has been the basis of India's reluctance to avoid any legally binding climate mitigation commitments.[8] As noted by then Prime Minister's Special Envoy on Climate Change, Ambassador Shyam Saran:

> therefore [due to historical responsibility], as the UNFCCC itself acknowledges, it is the developed countries who occupy the limited carbon capacity of the earth's atmosphere, who must achieve urgent and significant reductions in their emissions. It is for the reason of historical responsibility that in the UNFCCC, negotiated in 1992, it was agreed by consensus that emission reductions would only be required of the developed countries.[9]

Interweaving of Energy Security and Climate Change Concerns

India's foreign policy on energy, an area marked by continuity and change, has been driven primarily by the need to ensure access to energy resources. The large and real problems of insecure energy supply, led politicians to devote much attention to the need for 'energy security'. Historically, this has meant strong ties with the Gulf countries, from where India imports about two-thirds of its oil.[10] But the 2000s witnessed a turn towards a mercantilist approach, with India directly investing

---

[6] A. Vihma, 'India and the global climate governance: between principles and pragmatism', *The Journal of Environment & Development*, 20/1 (2011), 69–94, 78.

[7] C. Dasgupta, 'Present at the creation: the making of the framework convention on climate change', in N.K. Dubash, ed., *India in a warming world: integrating climate change and development* (New Delhi: Oxford University Press, 2019), 142–56; S. Sengupta, 'India's engagement in global climate negotiations from Rio to Paris', in N.K. Dubash, ed., *India in a warming world: integrating climate change and development* (New Delhi: Oxford University Press, 2019), 114–41.

[8] Rastogi, n. 2, 129.

[9] Vihma, n. 6, 78.

[10] N.K. Dubash, 'From norm taker to norm maker? Indian energy governance in global context', *Global Policy*, 2 (2011), 66–79, 73.

in energy resources in over thirty countries, including Angola, Libya, Nigeria, Sudan, Yemen, Venezuela, and the United States.[11] This can be seen through the overseas operations of ONGC Videsh Limited (OVL), the Government of India (GOI)'s main agent in its quest for equity oil and gas reserves.[12] One example is OVL's investment in an oil-based project, Sakhalin-I in Russia, which arose partly due to foreign policy backing.[13] In a bid to expand its sources of oil and coal, the Indian government has also made efforts to build long-term relations with Africa.[14]

In 2009, the GOI created the Energy Security Unit within the Ministry of External Affairs (MEA) with three main goals: to coordinate with other ministries; to support corporate entities in acquiring energy assets and striking strategic partnerships; and to facilitate transfer of technologies and to serve as an information node on energy security.[15] In the words of an adviser to the MEA, the aim of this unit has been to ensure 'uninterrupted supplies of energy to support economic and commercial activities necessary for the sustained growth of the economy'.[16] Therefore India's foreign ministry was in a position to considerably influence India's future foreign energy policy—it could favour securing energy supplies from countries with good political ties, while being cautious about energy investments in countries that could strain India's ties with other states.[17]

However, Carl et al argue that there is a wide gap between the theoretical imperative for a strategic energy policy and the GOI's ability to put such a policy into practice.[18] They point out a variety of domestic factors that overwhelm foreign policy aspects of energy, and leave the foreign policy apparatus with limited influence over what Indian firms do abroad.[19] They argue that energy security initiatives have had little

---

[11] Ibid. See also L. Norhona, 'Emerging economy resources needs and climate concerns: policy pressures and innovations', in E. Fritz, ed., *Developing country, emerging country, global player: India's route to responsibility* (Germany: ATHENA, 2010) 187–207.

[12] J. Carl, V. Rai, & D.G. Victor, *Energy and India's foreign policy* (Stanford, CA: Program on Energy and Sustainable Development, May 2008), 12.

[13] Ibid.; Dubash, n. 10, 68.

[14] Norhona, n. 11.

[15] Ibid. See also MEA, Annual Report 2009–10, https://mea.gov.in/Annual_Reports.htm?57/Annual_Reports, accessed 15 Dec. 2022.

[16] Dubash, n. 10, 74.

[17] D. Mistry, 'Domestic and international influences on India's energy policy', in S. Ganguly, ed., *Engaging the world: Indian foreign policy since 1947* (New Delhi: Oxford University Press, 2016), 425–47, 442–3.

[18] Carl, Rai, & Victor, n. 12, 40.

[19] Ibid.

impact due to two reasons: first, political fragmentation and uneven power sharing between the central and state governments; and second, weak administrative capacity of the GOI in the energy sector.[20]

Since the 2000s, one of the core narratives around Indian energy governance has been the interweaving of energy security and clean energy.[21] The first shift in Indian foreign policy on energy came by way of the 2006 India–United States Civil Nuclear Agreement. The highly publicized 2009 Indo–US nuclear deal was closely related to India's efforts to secure its energy future by winning international approval for its nuclear programme. In addition, the deal opened the door to accessing uranium supplies by allowing India an exception from the rules of the Nuclear Suppliers Group that prohibits sales of uranium to non-signatories of the Nuclear Non-Proliferation treaty.[22]

The second shift is seen through the entry of climate change in the narrative around energy security, which has had significant impact in terms of how energy was discussed and policy was institutionalized.[23] The addition of climate change to the energy narrative has forced India's foreign policy to pursue energy security objectives beyond bilateral and regional initiatives. This means engaging with the multilateral climate change negotiations under the UNFCCC process, as well as other broader forums like G20.[24]

Changing Geopolitics and India's Turn Towards Climate Policymaking

The gradual move of the international climate change regime towards a 'bottom up' architecture has exposed Indian energy policy to more external scrutiny. Thus making domestic actors take note of the linkages between India's internal and external energy policies.[25] India's official international negotiating position had been to stave off climate

---

[20] Ibid.
[21] Dubash, n. 10, 71–3.
[22] Ibid., 74.
[23] Ibid., 72.
[24] Ibid., 74.
[25] Ibid., 72.

mitigation commitments while preserving the space to grow domestically using conventional fossil fuels, particularly coal. But with increased international pressure for climate action through the G8/G20 process, India shifted the narrative by making a link between measures originally aimed at domestic energy security concerns and their global climate benefits.[26] It launched the National Action Plan on Climate Change (NAPCC), which rests on the concept of 'co-benefits', that is, measures that promote development while yielding co-benefits for addressing climate change effectively.[27] The new narrative combining energy security and clean energy opened the door for a 'co-benefits' approach to development, which included energy efficiency initiatives and promotion of renewables.[28] It provided the conceptual basis for India to preserve its 'development space' and make it clear that the primary motivation for any shift in energy trajectories would be tied to development, while climate change mitigation would remain a secondary concern.[29]

The global geopolitical context has changed considerably since the early 1990s when the UNFCCC was created. As a result, the geopolitics of the climate negotiations underwent a significant change by the time of the 2009 Copenhagen conference. There was an increased expectation on emerging economies to take the lead in influencing outcomes of global governance, which led to the formation of a new negotiating bloc—BASIC (Brazil, South Africa, India, and China).[30] In the early years of climate negotiations India identified with the Group of 77 (G77),[31] but over the years India played a key role in conceptualizing the BASIC bloc with other rapidly industrializing countries.[32] In addition, these emerging economies started having dialogues with the developed countries in other forums outside the UNFCCC process, such as the G8 + 5 Dialogue on Climate and Energy in 2008, the US-led Major Economies Forum on

---

[26] Ibid.
[27] MOEFCC (Government of India), 'National Action Plan on Climate Change', *Climate Change* (30 Jun. 2008), http://moef.gov.in/division/environment-divisions/climate-changecc-2/documents-publications/, accessed 15 Dec. 2022.
[28] A. Mathur, 'India and Paris: a pragmatic way forward', in N.K. Dubash, ed., *India in a warming world: integrating climate change and development* (New Delhi: Oxford University Press, 2019), 222–9, 225–7; Dubash, n. 10, 73.
[29] Dubash, n. 10, 72.
[30] Mohan, n. 1.
[31] Dasgupta, n. 7; Mohan, n. 1.
[32] Rastogi, n. 2, 131–2.

Energy and Climate in 2009, and the G20 conferences.[33] The increased pressure to take on climate commitments as a result of their changing economic status led to the first notable shift in India's climate position.

The first instance of a concrete national response around climate change emerged through the Prime Minister's Office (PMO) in 2007, with the creation of the Prime Minister's Council on Climate Change to coordinate national action for assessment, adaptation and mitigation of climate change. A multi-stakeholder body, the PM's Council on Climate Change was required to evolve a coordinated response to issues relating to climate change at the national level; provide oversight for formulation of action plans in the area of assessment, adaptation and mitigation of climate change; and periodically monitor key policy decisions.[34] It comprised twenty-six members, including the ministers from the MEA, Ministry of Environment and Forests (MOEF), Ministry of Finance, Ministry of Agriculture, Ministry of Water Resources, Department of Science and Technology and Ministry of New and Renewable Energy (MNRE); Deputy Chairman, Planning Commission; National Security Advisor; Chairman, Economic Advisory Council; and other climate change experts from varied backgrounds such as industry, academia, and civil society organizations. The Council was serviced by the PMO, and could obtain assistance as required from any Ministry/Department/ Agency of the government, especially the MOEF.[35]

In early 2008, the PM appointed Ambassador Shyam Saran—India's retiring foreign secretary—as the PM's Special Envoy on Climate Change to support the Council and to elaborate a National Action Plan on Climate Change (NAPCC).[36] This was a significant move leading up to the UN climate conference to be held in Copenhagen in December 2009. The Special Envoy's role was to lead the multilateral negotiations in which India was involved and to coordinate the national climate plan to make sure that the different efforts under it were harmonized.[37]

---

[33] Mohan, n. 1.

[34] PMO, *PM Council on Climate Change constituted* [media release] (5 Jun. 2007), https://archivepmo.nic.in/drmanmohansingh/press-details.php?nodeid=575, accessed 15 Dec. 2022.

[35] Ibid.

[36] I. Bagchi & N. Sethi, 'Saran is PM's envoy on climate change', *The Economic Times* (12 Mar. 2008), https://economictimes.indiatimes.com/news/environment/global-warming/saran-is-pms-envoy-on-climate-change/articleshow/2856831.cms?from=mdr, accessed 15 Dec. 2022.

[37] Worldwatch Institute, *Meeting Shyam Saran* [video] (2014), http://www.worldwatch.org/node/6078, accessed 15 Dec. 2022.

The NAPCC was the first deliberative process to put in place a domestic climate policy in India, which several scholars describe as being driven by global pressures.[38] The process was coordinated by the Special Envoy and ultimately provided the broad policy framework for required interventions on climate action and outlined priorities for mitigation and adaptation to be implemented through eight National Missions (Table 2.1). The NAPCC was envisaged to bring about a 'directional shift' in India's developmental pathway and rests on the concept of 'co-benefits' which is described as measures to 'promote … development objectives while also yielding co-benefits for addressing climate change effectively.'[39]

The core 'Missions' represent multipronged, long-term, and integrated strategies for achieving key goals in the context of climate change.[40] Operating on a strategic level are key line ministries that have been designated as the nodal ministry for the delivery of each of the eight 'Missions' under the NAPCC. Under the direction provided by the NAPCC, each of the nodal ministries was required to submit comprehensive mission documents detailing objectives, implementation strategies, timelines, and monitoring and evaluation criteria, to the PM's Council on Climate Change by December 2008. The MOEF, in turn, acted as the main coordinating entity under the NAPCC, as the comprehensive mission documents required that the nodal ministry liaise and coordinate its activities with the MOEF. Following the approval of the comprehensive mission documents by the PM's Council on Climate Change, the 'Missions' would await the final approval of the implementation framework by the Union Cabinet. It was only upon the final approval by the Union Cabinet that the required funding would be channelled into the 'Mission' through the budgetary outlays presented by the nodal ministries.

The process of creating the NAPCC was also marked with differences among the PM's Council on Climate Change. First, by suggesting any kind of domestic regulation India risked compromising its core stance on 'common by differentiated responsibility'. Second, there were differences

[38] N.K. Dubash & N.B. Joseph, 'Evolution of institutions for climate policy in India', *Economic & Political Weekly*, 51/3 (2016), 45–54; Rastogi, n. 23; A. Atteridge et al., n. 24; Sengupta, n. 24; Dubash, n.8.

[39] MOEFCC (Government of India), 'National Action Plan on Climate Change', *Climate Change* (30 Jun. 2008), http://moef.gov.in/division/environment-divisions/climate-changecc-2/documents-publications/, accessed 15 Dec. 2022.

[40] Ibid.

Table 2.1 India's National Action Plan on Climate Change

Mission	Nodal ministry	Salient features
National Solar Mission (NSM)	Ministry of New and Renewable Energy (MNRE)	NSM aims at increasing the share of solar energy in the total energy mix through development of new solar technologies.
National Mission for Enhanced Energy Efficiency (NMEEE)	Ministry of Power (MOP), Bureau of Energy Efficiency (BEE)	NMEEE seeks to upscale efforts to create a market for energy efficiency by creating a regulatory and policy regime that fosters innovative and sustainable business models to unlock this market.
National Mission on Sustainable Habitat (NMSD)	Ministry of Urban Development (MOUD)	NMSD attempts to promote energy efficiency in buildings, management of solid waste and modal shift to public transport, including transport options based on biodiesel and hydrogen.
National Water Mission (NWM)	Ministry of Water Resources (MOWR)	NWM aims at the conservation of water, minimizing wastage and ensuring more equitable distribution both across and within states.
National Mission for Sustaining the Himalayan Ecosystem (NMSHE)	Department of Science and Technology, Climate Change Programme Division (DST)	NMSHE aims at evolving management measures for sustaining and safeguarding the Himalayan glacier and mountain ecosystem.
National Mission for a 'Green India' (NMGI)	Ministry of Environment and Forests (MOEF)	NMGI focuses on enhancing ecosystem services and carbon sinks through afforestation on degraded forest land in line with the national policy of expanding the forest and tree cover to 33% of the total land area of the country.

Table 2.1 Continued

Mission	Nodal ministry	Salient features
National Mission for Sustainable Agriculture (NMSA)	Ministry of Agriculture (MOA)	NMSA would develop strategies to make Indian agriculture more resilient to climate change, new varieties of thermal-resistant crops, new credit and insurance mechanisms, and improving productivity of rain-fed agriculture.
National Mission on Strategic Knowledge for Climate Change (NMSKCC)	Department of Science and Technology (DST)	NMSKCC is intended to identify the challenges of, and the responses to, climate change through research and technology development and ensure funding of high quality and focused research into various aspects of climate change.

Source: National Action Plan on Climate Change (2008)

on whether the document was meant only for domestic purposes or as a signal to the international community.[41] While the NAPCC marked a turning point in India's engagement on the climate issue, it did not hint at any real shift in India's approach to the multilateral negotiations (a detailed discussion on India's role in the multilateral climate negotiations is in Chapter 5).[42] The core missions of the NAPCC, although developed in response to developments at the international stage, focused on India's domestic development needs.[43] Under the broad ambit of the NAPCC, the National Solar Mission (NSM)—India's flagship solar policy—was launched by the Government of India in January 2010 to create an

[41] Vihma, n. 6, 76–7.
[42] Rastogi, n. 2, 130.
[43] Atteridge et al., n. 3, 72.

enabling policy framework for the deployment of 22 gigawatts (GW) of solar power by 2022.[44]

A notable change in India's negotiating position came in the lead up to the Copenhagen conference in 2009.[45] India along with other BASIC countries announced voluntary targets to reduce the emissions intensity of its GDP by 20–25 per cent against 2005 levels by 2020. This was, in large part, attributed solely to the strong personality and worldview of then Environment Minister, Jairam Ramesh.[46] Although several commentators have argued that this shift was driven by a widening of domestic debates on the co-benefits approach to climate action.[47] Until then, India has consistently refused to take on any mitigation commitments, legally binding or voluntary. Environment Minister, Jairam Ramesh, called this 'per capita plus' and signalled his intention to change the 'narrative of India in climate change negotiations' even if it meant moving away from the traditional position.[48] It was met with major criticism by senior members of India's negotiating team who felt that this position compromised India's sovereignty and undid years of careful Indian negotiating strategy.[49] It was followed by a very public falling-out between the Minister, Jairam Ramesh, and the PM's Special Envoy on Climate Change, Ambassador Shyam Saran.

When viewed through the prism of India's foreign policy motivations, the shift at Copenhagen can be explained by three drivers: first, it strengthened India's claims for greater power in global governance by showing that it could shoulder the responsibility for solving global challenges like climate change;[50] second, it tried to minimize damage to its broader ambition of gaining permanent membership of the UN Security Council; and third, it came in the aftermath of blossoming Indo–US ties

---

[44] Government of India, Ministry of New and Renewable Energy, Resolution No. 5/14/2008-P&C, 'Jawaharlal Nehru National Solar Mission' (11 Jan. 2010), https://mnre.gov.in/resolution.

[45] Ibid.

[46] K. Michaelowa & A. Michaelowa, 'India as an emerging power in international climate negotiations', *Climate Policy*, 12 (2012), 575–90; N.K. Dubash, 'Of maps and compasses: India in multilateral climate negotiations', in W.P.S. Sidhu, P.B. Mehta & B. Jones, eds, *Shaping the Emerging World: India and the Multilateral Order* (Washington, DC: Brookings Institution Press, 2013), 261–79; Vihma, n. 6; Mohan, n. 1.

[47] Dubash, n. 46; Thaker & Leiserowitz, n. 3.

[48] Vihma, n. 6; Mohan, n. 1.

[49] Vihma, n. 6; Mohan, n. 1; Thaker & Leserowitz, n. 3.

[50] Mohan, n. 1; Rastogi, n. 2.

following the nuclear deal.[51] The emissions intensity targets announced before Copenhagen were particularly crucial because India agreed to undertake mitigation actions without any international financial support, which signalled that it understood and acknowledged its own responsibility and was ready to engage proactively.[52] It has also been said that India's move towards introducing greater flexibility in its negotiating position were driven by concerns of being isolated or sidelined during negotiations, and to seek broader geopolitical alignment, particularly with the United States and China.[53] Indian diplomats have engaged the Chinese over many years, signing a Memorandum of Agreement for cooperation on climate change in 2009 and attempting cooperation through the BASIC group.[54] In 2009, when China announced its target to cut the emissions intensity of its economy, India immediately followed with its own emissions intensity target.[55]

These tensions between the old focus on strategic autonomy and new directions in foreign policy was also evident in the 2011 Durban conference where India was 'caught between old arguments and allies such as the G77 and new realities and groupings such as BASIC'.[56] Following the departure of Jairam Ramesh as the Environment Minister, there was an attempt to reverse the shifts in India's climate policy in Durban and fall back on traditional arguments, which further led to India being isolated on the issue of legal form of the new climate agreement.[57] This issue will be discussed in more detail in Chapter 5 under the subheading 'Legal form and legal bindingness'.

[51] N.K. Dubash, 'The politics of climate change in India: narratives of equity and cobenefits', WIREs Climate Change, 4/3 (2013), 191–201, 193–4; Mohan, n. 1.
[52] Rastogi, n. 2, 131–2.
[53] With regards to India's ambition to join the 'high table' internationally, both the US and China will for instance have a major influence over India's attempt to gain permanent membership of the UN Security Council. Both have relationships to India's neighbours, particularly Pakistan and Afghanistan that cause some concern to India from a regional security perspective, while China and India are still also engaged in border conflict. Economically, the two are key trading partners of India. Moreover, US support was crucial for the realization of India's nuclear ambitions (with the conclusion of a US–India Civil Nuclear Agreement in 2008). Atteridge et al., n. 3, 70.
[54] Atteridge et al., n. 3, 70–1.
[55] Ibid.
[56] A. Hurrell & S. Sengupta, 'Emerging powers, North–South relations and global climate politics', International Affairs, 88/3 (2012), 463–84; Mohan, n. 22.
[57] Michaelowa & Michaelowa, n. 46; Thaker & Leiserowitz, n. 3.

A 'Modi'fication of India's Climate Policies

The most recent round of climate policymaking in India occurred while formulating the Nationally Determined Contributions (NDCs) before the COP21 in Paris in December 2015. At the time of the Copenhagen climate talks, India started with a substantially blank slate of climate policy; by the Paris climate talks, India showcased an array of actions on both mitigation and adaptation, at the national (federal) and state levels.[58] In June 2015, under the leadership of the new Prime Minister—Narendra Modi[59]—India set an ambitious domestic goal of achieving 175 GW of installed renewable energy capacity by 2022.[60] Of this, India's solar power capacity target was set at 100 GW by 2022, revised by five times its earlier goal of 22 GW of solar power by 2022.[61] According to India's NDC submitted to the UNFCCC, 40 per cent of its total power capacity is expected to come from renewable sources by 2030.[62] To put these numbers in perspective, the entire size of India's current installed capacity is 377 GW, of which renewable energy sources account for 91 GW.[63] In addition, the government is targeting nearly US$100 billion in renewable energy investments, including foreign direct investment, over the next five years under the 'Make in India' programme.[64] The rising profile of the

---

[58] N.K. Dubash & S. Ghosh, 'National climate policies and institutions', in N.K. Dubash, ed., *India in a warming world: integrating climate change and development* (New Delhi: Oxford University Press, 2019), 329–48, 338.

[59] On 16 May 2014 the Bhartiya Janata Party (BJP), led by Narendra Modi, won the general elections in India. The swearing-in of Narendra Modi marked the end of a two-term government led by the Indian National Congress and allies under prime minister of Dr Manmohan Singh. L. Mathew & A. Shah, 'Narendra Modi makes election history as BJP gets majority on its own', *Mint* (17 May 2014), https://www.livemint.com/Politics/vGyzihxgQEuYmzRmyRA1vN/Elect ion-results-2014-Counting-begins-as-Narendra-Modi-eyes.html, accessed 15 Dec. 2022.

[60] Press Information Bureau, 'Revision of cumulative targets under National Solar Mission' (17 Jun. 2015), http://pib.nic.in/newsite/PrintRelease.aspx?relid=122566, accessed 15 Dec. 2022.

[61] Ibid. This revised target of 100 GW will principally comprise 40 GW rooftop and 60 GW through large- and medium-scale grid-connected solar power projects.

[62] MOEFCC (Government of India), 'India's intended nationally determined contribution: working towards climate justice', *Climate Change* (1 Oct. 2015), http://moef.gov.in/division/environment-divisions/climate-changecc-2/documents-publications/, accessed 15 Dec. 2022.

[63] MOP (Government of India), 'Total installed capacity, power sector at a glance: all India' (31. Jan. 2021), https://powermin.gov.in/en/content/power-sector-glance-all-india, accessed 15 Dec. 2022.

[64] FDI up to 100 per cent is permitted in the renewable energy sector under the automatic route and no prior government approval is required. See Make in India (Government of India), 'FDI Policy', *Renewable Energy*, https://www.makeinindia.com/sector/renewable-energy, accessed 15 Dec. 2022.

renewable energy sector in the Indian energy framework must be understood in light of the twin urgencies that India continues to face: first, to
meet its energy requirements and ensure universal energy access to its
poor; and second, to reduce greenhouse gas emissions and adopt a low-
carbon pathway.[65]

By 2015, the Modi government had brought in a larger shift in the
Indian foreign policy agenda, especially as it wanted to be a leader in
global governance and stake its claim among other major powers in
global politics.[66] India's engagement with climate change was material to
its aspirations as a rising power.[67] It was important for India to not just
be part of the solution, but be *seen* to be part of the solution.[68] In Paris,
India's negotiating stance marked a complete departure from its previous
outings at international climate negotiations. India jointly launched the
ISA with France on the first day of COP21 and aggressively pushed for
expansion of its renewable energy programme. It also ratified the Paris
Agreement to help bring it into force, despite concerns that it would insist on developed countries first fulfilling their pre-2020 commitments
under the second phase of the Kyoto Protocol.[69] From being called 'obstructionist'[70] and 'difficult'[71] in climate negotiations, India was being
seen as playing a more constructive role in global climate policy.[72] India
was lauded for playing a bigger role in Paris and transitioning into an
'agenda-setter'.[73]

---

[65] V. Jha, 'India's twin concerns over energy security and climate change: revisiting India's
investment treaties through a sustainable development lens', *Trade, Law and Development*, 5/
1 (2013) 109–49; A. Ghosh, 'Governing clean energy subsidies: why legal and policy clarity is
needed', *BioRes*, 5/3 (2011), 2–4.

[66] A. Narlikar, 'India's role in global governance: a Modification?', *International Affairs*, 93/1
(2017), 93–111; S. Saran, 'India's contemporary plurilateralism', in D.M. Malone, C.R. Mohan,
& S. Raghavan, eds, *The Oxford handbook of Indian foreign policy* (Oxford: Oxford University
Press, 2015), 623–35.

[67] N.K. Dubash, 'An introduction to India's evolving climate change debate: from diplomatic
insulation to policy integration', in N.K. Dubash, ed., *India in a warming world: integrating climate change and development* (New Delhi: Oxford University Press, 2019), 1–28, 2–3.

[68] Ibid., 3.

[69] A. Mohan & T. Wehnert, 'Is India pulling its weight? India's nationally determined contribution and future energy plans in global climate policy', *Climate Policy*, 19/3 (2019), 275–82.

[70] U. Mathur & G.C. Varughese, 'From 'obstructionist' to leading player: transforming India's
international image', in D. Michael & A. Pandya, eds, *Indian climate policy: choices and challenges*
(Washington, DC: The Henry L. Stimson Center, 2009), 43–8.

[71] Vihma, n. 6.

[72] Mohan & Wehnert, n. 69; Michaelowa & Michaelowa, n. 46; Mohan, n. 1.

[73] Saran, n. 66; Mohan, n. 1.

India's diplomatic positioning at the Paris conference has been described as a paradigm shift as it 'provided India with an opportunity to showcase a new diplomatic configuration, reflective of the new reality in which it is a stakeholder both in the traditional developing world, the G77, and in the large economies, the G20'.[74] I pick up this discussion in Chapter 5 where I illustrate how India's diplomats and climate negotiators, empowered to strike deals by the new political leadership, steered the course towards a new international organization. In establishing the ISA, India sought out developing countries as its primary members and beneficiaries of a common solar future, but also reached out to developed countries as partners to help achieve the ISA goals. Ultimately, the creation of the ISA reveals India's diplomatic success in capturing an issue-specific governance area,[75] as well as straddling the G77 and G20 blocs in enabling the formation of a new intergovernmental organization.[76]

The Promise and Embrace of Solar Energy in India

India, today, ranks fifth in the world in total installed renewable energy power capacity after China, the US, Brazil, and Canada.[77] It also ranks fifth in total installed solar energy power capacity after China, the US, Japan, and Germany.[78] In November 2020, renewable energy capacity in India was at 136 GW, almost 36 per cent of India's total installed generation capacity. India aims to increase this to over 200 GW by 2022, which would exceed its 175 GW target stated under the NDC.[79]

---

[74] A. Mathur, 'India and Paris: a pragmatic way forward', in N.K. Dubash, ed., *India in a warming world: integrating climate change and development* (New Delhi: Oxford University Press, 2019), 222–9, 228–9.

[75] A. Ghosh, 'Making sense on its own terms: India in the HFC and aviation negotiations', in N.K. Dubash, ed., *India in a warming world: integrating climate change and development* (New Delhi: Oxford University Press, 2019), 230–249, 243.

[76] Mathur, n. 74, 228–9.

[77] IRENA, *Country rankings*, https://www.irena.org/Statistics/View-Data-by-Topic/Capacity-and-Generation/Country-Rankings, accessed 15 Dec. 2022.

[78] Ibid.

[79] A. Koundal, 'India's renewable power capacity is the fourth largest in the world, says PM Modi', *The Economic Times* (26 Nov. 2020), https://energy.economictimes.indiatimes.com/news/renewable/indias-renewable-power-capacity-is-the-fourth-largest-in-the-world-says-pm-modi/79430910, accessed 15 Dec. 2022.

Indian policy interest in solar power dates back to the 1980s, with several pilot projects operating at different scales over two decades. With only about 0.4 per cent of the world's known oil reserves, India has historically been an international price taker in the markets for oil and coal. As a result it is vulnerable to significant geopolitical shocks and risks. This situation came into focus following the global oil crisis, and remains a dominant concern in India's energy planning. Providing access to energy in a reliable manner has been the central pillar shaping the energy landscape in India, including the renewable energy landscape.[80] The Department of Non-Conventional Energy Sources (DNES)—a first of its kind in the world—was set up in 1982.[81] However, the high prices remained a major impediment to the large-scale deployment of solar as compared to conventional power sources such as coal.[82]

Globally, the early 2000s saw a significant rise in renewable energy deployment through public incentives such as subsidies, feed-in tariffs (FITs), and R&D investments, which fostered economies of scale and made solar cells more affordable. Between 2009 and 2018, the cost of solar electricity plummeted by 88 per cent, making solar photovoltaic (PV) the second-cheapest energy source after fossil fuels.[83] Solar power deployment in India did not occur in a meaningful way until 2009. The small scale of deployment prior to 2009 can be broadly divided into two phases: pre-2005 and 2005–9. The pre-2005 period in the solar energy sector was mainly policy-driven and focused on some academic, R&D, and small-scale demonstrations. The DNES, which turned into an independent ministry in 1992—Ministry of Non-Conventional Energy Sources (MNES)—funded several pilot projects that explored solar-power applications within India, particularly decentralized, rural installations. Although the motivation to explore solar energy applications stemmed from the promise of demonstrating a localized, indigenous energy source, there was a lack of a strategic approach by the government.

[80] A. Chaudhary, C. Krishna, & A. Sagar, 'Policy making for renewable energy in India: lessons from wind and solar power sectors', *Climate Policy*, 15/1 (2014), 58–87, 74–5.

[81] K. Chawla, 'Drivers, apparatus, and implications of India's renewable energy ambitions', in D. Scholten, ed., *The geopolitics of renewables* (Amsterdam: Springer, 2018), 203–27; Chaudhary, Krishna, & Sagar, n. 80., 63–4.

[82] Chaudhary, Krishna, & Sagar, n. 80., 71.

[83] A. Legrain & J. Pham-Ba, *Well below two cents* (Paris: Terrawatt Initiative, Jun. 2020), 66–70.

The period saw neither scale-up of solar deployment nor domestic industry creation within the solar sector.[84]

The period from 2005 to 2009 saw a boom in the international market for solar power; as a result Indian policymakers began to take the solar sector more seriously as a tool for energy access and energy security. In 2006, the MNES was renamed as the Ministry of New and Renewable Energy (MNRE). There were central government policies aimed at rural deployment of solar energy. At the same time, due to the increasing global demand, some Indian firms—Moser Baer and Tata BP Solar—set up manufacturing plants. This sectoral growth was halted by the global slump in solar installations following the economic crisis of 2007–8, leaving Indian manufacturers stranded with significant unrecovered installations.[85]

The drivers for renewable energy in India have evolved over time: energy security in the 1980s after the oil shock, energy access in the post-liberalization India of the 1990s, and ultimately climate change and diplomatic implications of negotiation positions in the target-setting era of the 2010s.[86] Following the launch of the NAPCC, the National Solar Mission (NSM) was launched in January 2010. Around this time, to encourage the development of a solar industry within the country, the government introduced a domestic content requirement (DCR) for solar projects funded through the NSM. These provisions, however, were the subject of a trade dispute between India and the US at the World Trade Organization (WTO). Both the Panel and the Appellate Body ruled against India and held that these provisions violated global trade rules by imposing mandatory DCRs on solar power producers.

The Making of the Trade Dispute Over India's Solar Policy

In the absence of a legal framework for the promotion of renewable energy under the UNFCCC, renewable energy policies of countries have

---

[84] Chaudhary, Krishna, & Sagar, n. 80., 71.
[85] Ibid.
[86] Chawla, n. 81.

been the subject of several legal challenges under international economic law. Dispute settlement, especially through adjudication at the WTO or before an Investor-State Dispute Settlement tribunal, has brought issues of competitiveness and protectionism to the forefront instead of the climate mitigation potential of renewable energy policies. FITs, which have emerged as a popular policy tool to incentivize the uptake of renewable energy and secure global competitive leadership in green technologies,[87] are at the heart of such international economic disputes. Characterized by three key elements—guaranteed electricity purchase prices, guaranteed grid access, and a long-term contract—FITs for renewable energy often incorporate 'local content' or 'domestic content' requirements which mandates a certain percentage of goods used in the production process of renewable energy projects to be sourced locally.[88] The policy choice for local content requirements (LCRs) garners political support on the promise of 'green jobs' and long-term economic competitiveness,[89] however they share a controversial relationship with the WTO with the legality of such support schemes coming under the scanner. They are being challenged for violating the principle of national treatment, as well as a provision under the Agreement on Subsidies and Countervailing Measures (SCM Agreement) that expressly prohibits subsidies contingent on the use of LCRs.[90]

[87] R. Stewart et al., 'Building blocks for global climate protection', *Stanford Environmental Law Journal*, 32 (2013) 341–92.

[88] M. Wilke, *Feed-in tariffs for renewable energy and WTO subsidy rules: an initial legal review* (Geneva: International Centre for Trade and Sustainable Development, 2011).

[89] J. Kuntze & T. Moerenhout, *Local content requirements and the renewable energy industry— a good match?* (Geneva: International Centre for Trade and Sustainable Development, 2013); S. Stephenson, *Addressing local content requirements in a sustainable energy trade agreement* (Geneva: International Centre for Trade and Sustainable Development, 2013); J. Lewis, 'The rise of renewable energy protectionism: emerging trade conflicts and implications for low carbon development', *Global Environmental Politics* 14/4 (2014) 10–35, 11.

[90] Article III:4 of the General Agreement on Trade and Tariff (GATT) reads: 'The products of the territory of any contracting party imported into the territory of any other contracting party shall be accorded treatment no less favourable than that accorded to like products of national origin in respect of all laws, regulations and requirements affecting their internal sale, offering for sale, purchase, transportation, distribution or use. The provisions of this paragraph shall not prevent the application of differential internal transportation charges which are based exclusively on the economic operation of the means of transport and not on the nationality of the product.'. Article 2.1 of the Agreement on Trade-Related Investment Measures (TRIMs) reads: '1. Without prejudice to other rights and obligations under GATT 1994, no Member shall apply any TRIM that is inconsistent with the provisions of Article III or Article XI of GATT 1994.'

Renewable energy-related disputes tend to blur the traditional North–South divide witnessed in trade disputes as both developed and developing countries are adopting similar renewable energy policies with a potential of upsetting international trade or investment rules and are equally vulnerable to challenge under international economic regimes.[91] Crucially, India's solar policy—NSM—became the subject of a WTO dispute initiated by the US owing to certain provisions on LCRs (*Indian Solar* dispute).[92] Both the Panel and the Appellate Body ruled against India and held that it violated global trade rules by imposing mandatory LCRs on solar power producers.

The NSM came on the heels of India's National Action Plan on Climate Change (NAPCC). During the formulation of the NAPCC, the primary objective was to announce India's position on climate action. The NAPCC process was driven by the aim to find options for the use of energy in a manner that optimizes the energy mix in the country. The NAPCC provides that a National Solar Mission will be launched 'to significantly increase the share of solar energy in the total energy mix while recognizing the needs to expand the scope of other renewables and non-fossil options'.[93] The NAPCC identifies solar energy as 'an extremely clean form of energy generation with practically no form of emissions at the point of generation'.[94]

The creators of the initial solar policy envisaged that it would 'lead to energy security through the displacement of coal and petroleum'.[95] To quote a senior IAS official, who was at the Ministry of Environment, Forests and Climate Change (MOEFCC) during the creation of the NAPCC, 'manufacturing was a distant objective and secondary at that time, the fundamental push (for the NSM) came from the fact that India needed to move towards renewables'.[96] A senior energy expert who

[91] M. Wu & J. Salzman, 'The next generation of trade and environment conflicts: the rise of green industrial policy', *Northwestern Law Review*, 108 (2014), 401–74.

[92] Panel Report, *India—certain measures relating to solar cells and solar modules*, WT/DS456/R (Feb. 24, 2016), http://www.wto.org/english/tratop_e/dispu_e/cases_e/ds456_e.htm; Appellate Body Report, *India—certain measures relating to solar cells and solar modules*, WT/DS456/AB/R (16 Sept. 2016), http://www.wto.org/english/tratop_e/dispu_e/cases_e/ds456_e.htm [hereinafter *Indian Solar* dispute].

[93] MOEFCC (Government of India), 'National Action Plan on Climate Change', *Climate Change* (30 Jun. 2008), http://moef.gov.in/division/environment-divisions/climate-changecc-2/documents-publications/, accessed 15 Dec. 2022.

[94] Ibid., at 20.

[95] Ibid.

[96] Participant 16, interview with author, 14 Dec. 2016.

advised the Government of India during the NAPCC process affirms that India's initial policies on climate change, including the NSM, were not a domestically driven initiative, but were rather purely driven by external demand, that is, the Copenhagen Climate Change Conference. The document was created for the external world in order to outline India's position and commitments on climate action, and was not motivated by a domestic manufacturing agenda.[97]

Following the launch of the NAPCC, a sub-group within the Prime Minister's Council on Climate Change was tasked with coming up with the 'nuts and bolts of the solar policy'.[98] At this stage, it was decided that one of the policy elements of the NSM would be the public procurement of 1000 MW of solar power through NTPC Limited[99]—an Indian Public Sector Undertaking and India's largest power utility. The Ministry of New and Renewable Energy (MNRE), the nodal ministry for the implementation of the NSM, was responsible for all future guidelines and policies on solar energy.

Under the NSM, in order to facilitate grid connected solar power generation, the MNRE through NTPC Ltd entered into long-term Power Purchase Agreements (PPAs) with solar power developers to purchase the solar power generated by them, providing a guaranteed rate for a twenty-five-year period. Following the purchase, NTPC Ltd would resell the electricity to downstream distribution utilities, which would ultimately sell it to the final consumer.[100] Solar photovoltaic (PV) projects are developed primarily across two technologies: solar crystalline silicone and solar thin-film. The guidelines issued by MNRE for the selection of solar PV projects under the first phase of the NSM made it mandatory for all projects based on crystalline silicon technology to use the modules manufactured in India, while solar PV projects based on thin-film technologies were kept outside the purview of government procurement of solar power. At the time, the government decided not to apply the LCR rule to thin-film technologies since there was only one player in the

---

[97] Participant 37, interview with author, 14 Dec. 2016.
[98] Participant 36, interview with author, 6 Dec. 2016.
[99] Formerly known as National Thermal Power Corporation.
[100] For a detailed discussion on the facts of the case, please see ¶7.1 to 7.14 of the *Indian Solar dispute*, Panel Report, n. 74, 31–5.

domestic market for thin-film technologies and it would have given them the monopoly.[101]

Misplaced Motivation

According to one government official, who was closely involved in the creation and implementation of the NSM, the initial motivation for LCRs came from the Mission Document which provided the basis for MNRE's thrust on local manufacturing.[102] However, according to another MNRE official, this was a case of 'misplaced motivation' as it was thought that there was no way forward on achieving the solar targets without a local manufacturing capability.[103] He noted that solar was never considered a 'strategic' energy choice for the country for there was never a vision within the MNRE to go beyond targets and create a full value chain around solar energy. Another interviewee noted how this move merely indicated the ruling government's socialist and self-reliant bent of mind and seemed impervious to the fact that there had been no local development in solar manufacturing up until then.[104]

According to some interviewees, a crucial factor to be noted is that the scale of domestic solar manufacturing was very limited. The LCR measures were applicable only on 1000 MW of the total 22,000 MW target for solar power. Therefore, the government was merely looking at LCRs as an opportunity to not let the domestic solar manufacturing industry die down in the face of global competition. Moreover, LCRs would have increased the manufacturing costs under all circumstances and the government procurement appeared to be mere 'tokenism';[105] this view was backed by many of the interviewees, who noted that there was very little evidence to show the presence of a strong domestic industry lobby in favour of the LCR rule. Instead, the LCR rule seems to have been instituted at the behest of a single bureaucrat who believed that local manufacturing was essential to achieve the solar targets.

---

[101] Participant 39, interview with author, 14 and 16 Dec. 2016.
[102] Ibid.
[103] Participant 13, interview with author, 8 Dec. 2016.
[104] Participant 24, interview with author, 6 Feb. 2017.
[105] Ibid.

A policy expert who has followed the progress of the NSM closely attests to the fact that when the solar policy was formulated, the notion of LCR was not thought through as having trade implications. Simply put, it was a technical ministry which came to a 'fairly heuristic' conclusion that if there was a national target, then a part of it should be developed at home.[106]

The overwhelming view within the MNRE was that a localization provision would help develop the local industry by creating a manufacturing base and allowing them to keep up to date with development in technology.[107] Government officials in the Ministry of Commerce and Industry (MOCI), however, recall that the MNRE continued with the LCR measure despite contrary advice from them. As a senior official of the Indian Administrative Services (IAS), who was formerly in the MOCI noted:

India was not inclined to be wiped away in manufacturing of solar industry. It wanted to retain that base, knowing fully well that it was not competitive. Clearly it had no large scope, but it wanted that small space for its own industry. This whole dimension of 'green jobs' related to this litigation—I doubt anyone has said it. How many jobs would 10 or 20% LCR even create? Solar power projects creating jobs is a different issue, but the LCR in itself was not promoting this. I don't think jobs were ever a driving force behind this. It was entirely about wanting to keep doing something in solar energy as it was an important space for India.[108]

Several interviewees across policy think tanks, civil society, and the industry agreed that the idea of 'green jobs' was a complete afterthought. On the question of the inclusion of LCRs in the NSM to promote 'green jobs', one interviewee said that he would be 'surprised' if there was a strategic explanation for the LCRs based on generating more jobs in the economy.[109] Neither the NAPCC, nor the Mission Document emphasized job creation as a primary objective of the solar policy; even if these documents did mention solar manufacturing capability, the overwhelming view among the interviewees is that the notion of domestic

---

[106] Participant 4, interview with author, 16 Dec. 2016.
[107] Participant 30, interview with author, 14 Dec. 2016.
[108] Ibid.
[109] Participant 28, interview with author, 12 Dec. 2016.

solar manufacturing was a complete myth. For the domestic solar manufacturing to have become a success, the government needed pre-established (and successful) semiconductor and manufacturing policies. Without that, many of the interviewees argued that there was no way to turn India into a manufacturing hub for solar energy.

From a legal perspective, it seems easy to argue that the LCR was geared towards enhancing India's solar manufacturing capacity and jobs, but several interviewees were sceptical about the solar manufacturing sector driving the economy. In order for the LCR measure to be an effective tool for protecting and promoting the local industry, most of the interviewees said that India needed pre-existing research and development in solar manufacturing. As it stood, the LCR rule was providing an incentive structure based on what one or two companies were doing. According to one interviewee, 'a long-term stake will come when a country has also invested in manufacturing as well as in believing that it is a part of the economy.'[110] In this case, it appears that India had neither demonstrated a manufacturing capacity nor pushed for LCRs on the grounds of creating and adding 'green jobs' to the local economy.

Token Protectionism

Following the first phase of the NSM, it was realized that several companies had bypassed the LCR rule and opted for the cheaper thin-film technologies. As a result, the Indian market for solar PV projects differed greatly from the global norm for it skewed heavily towards thin-film technologies and away from crystalline silicone technologies, which was the opposite of global norms. One of the driving forces for the use of thin-film technologies was the US EXIM Bank's financing obligations: concessional finance for solar power developed at low interest rates, but contingent on the use of US-manufactured thin-film cells and modules.[111] It was only at this point, at the end of the first phase of NSM, that several players realized that India had the potential to become a 'big market' for solar.

---

[110] Participant 36, n. 98.
[111] Participant 39, n. 101.

For the second phase of the NSM, in order to correct the imbalance in technology diffusion, the government decided to extend the LCR rule to thin-film technologies as well. Under this revised policy, two Indian companies ended up being the main beneficiaries of the government's support measures: Moser Baer and IndoSolar. Following this move, the US alleged that the LCR rule was in violation of WTO rules. At this point, one of the available options for India was to dismantle the LCR rule within the NSM. According to a majority of interviewees the Commerce Ministry advised the MNRE to remove the LCR rule for a variety of reasons: (1) it was legally untenable under the WTO rules; (2) almost 90 per cent of the components being used by the domestic manufacturers were being imported; (3) the rule covered only 1000 MW of solar power generation and did not add to the rhetoric of building a strong solar manufacturing landscape; and (4) other Indian states, such as Gujarat, were successfully pursuing solar policies without imposing similar LCR rules. Yet, the LCR measure remained in place.

A strong justification of the LCR rule continued on the understanding that it would be covered under the government procurement exception; according to several interviewees, the widespread belief within the government was that the measure would qualify as government procurement. Within the bureaucratic circles there was a prevailing view that the LCR methodology had been applied with some success in the past, especially in the automobiles sector and that it could similarly ride through a WTO challenge in the solar energy sector. As a senior IAS officer noted, it is a matter of 'finding the right balance between promoting the industry through lawful means and through means that can stand the test of law'.[112] As a trade lawyer noted:

Not every country designs every policy thinking of WTO implications. You often take a call that you want to have a policy for whatever other reasons you may have. And indeed, when it gets challenged, you tackle it as and when it comes. WTO rulings are prospective in nature and you can try to achieve what you can it the time the dispute plays out. Perhaps, it was thought that since most countries are adopting similar policies [LCRs in renewable energy policies], it [the NSM] is unlikely

[112] Participant 16, n. 96.

to be challenged. But once Canada (FIT) was challenged it became anybody's guess who would be next.[113]

Still, many interviewees were of the view that it would have been easier to defend the LCR measure if (1) there had been investment in creating a domestic industry via research and capital and (2) there was a fully fledged solar landscape supporting the domestic industry. According to one interviewee, if the above had indeed been the case 'we should have gone ahead and tried to protect them, drag for time till the industry finds its feet. We should have done it shamelessly. But not for such a silly thing—when 90 per cent of the value of the products was being imported, what 'local industry' are we trying to protect?'[114]

New Government, New Lens on the Solar Policy

The solar dispute ended up as a reflection of the dichotomy in India's thinking on the issue of LCRs, which had got exacerbated with the transition in the political set-up after the 2014 general elections. The new government came up with an ambitious power-generation programme and looked at the issue of local manufacturing in a completely new light. The new Prime Minister, Narendra Modi, had a strong solar agenda and backed it with a strong manufacturing focus.[115] As a result, the perspective on the solar trade dispute completely changed with the change in ruling party. The earlier government's arguments on technology continuity and maintaining a small manufacturing base was superimposed by the new government's ambitious solar targets. According to one interviewee, the new government's insistence on defending the LCR rule was 'a contrarian approach' given its revamped solar targets.[116] Thus, there

---

[113] Participant 33, interview with author, 8 Dec. 2016.

[114] Participant 26, interview with author, 9 Dec. 2016.

[115] PIB, *Revision of cumulative targets under National Solar Mission* [media release] (17 Jun. 2015), http://pib.nic.in/newsite/PrintRelease.aspx?relid=122566, accessed 15 Dec. 2022; PIB, *Prime Minister to launch 'Make in India' initiative* [media release] (24 Sep. 2014), http://pib.nic. in/newsite/PrintRelease.aspx?relid=109953, accessed 15 Dec. 2022; PIB, *'Make in India' programme* [media release] (24 Jul. 2015), http://pib.nic.in/newsite/PrintRelease.aspx?relid=123 724, accessed 15 Dec. 2022.

[116] Participant 30, n. 107.

was a clear conflict between the two policies as the huge demands generated by the high ambitions of the new government would not have been met with more expensive locally manufactured equipment. This further complicated a crucial issue from India's point of view: energy security.

The prevailing line of thought among the solar power developers has been that the LCR measures raise the costs of raw materials and that it is preferable to choose the cheapest available materials, even if it means importing them is the viable option. But, the intellectual view on this issue could be very different from the business view; according to one interviewee:

A critical consideration for a country is whether it wants to incentivize entrepreneurs/industry for energy security as a user (where they could import cheap parts from other countries and have no domestic manufacturing capability) or as a producer and user (create a domestic manufacturing base that would also provide jobs).[117]

The business view always remains geared towards the cost competitiveness of such an enterprise; but in order to engage people into the benefits of climate change, it becomes imperative to promise job creation and wealth generation. In light of this, several interviewees were critical of the American stance of taking India to the WTO. According to one:

I hold the US more accountable, or responsible for the way it (dispute, emphasis added) played out. I think there was an element of inflexibility, where India was being used to 'set an example' or as a 'flag' to other potentially larger trade partners who could actually impact US competitiveness. Indian manufacturers were barely going to make a dent (to US competitiveness, emphasis added).[118]

There is little evidence to suggest that the LCR rule was politically motivated and inserted in the NSM as a concerted effort to protect the 'infant' domestic industry or to create 'green jobs'. Interviewees across the government and civil society believe that in order to achieve a long-term

---

[117] Participant 24, n. 104.
[118] Participant 4, n. 106.

stake for solar power in the country it would be necessary to invest in local manufacturing so as to create a full-service ecosystem around solar energy; however, most of them were quick to add that there was no such broad policy objective guiding the inclusion of LCRs in the NSM. According to several interviewees the early inclusion and implementation of such a protectionist measure within the NSM was an act of mere tokenism enacted to benefit only a handful of companies that occupied a very small share in the wider solar energy landscape in India. Against the backdrop of the new government ramping up the country's solar energy targets and providing a major thrust for manufacturing in India, the ill-advised LCR policy found a new set of defenders. The reason, most of them agreed, for the protracted solar trade dispute was the different perspective with which the new government viewed the LCR policy.

New Government, New Lens on the Trade Dispute

The MOCI is India's nodal ministry for all matters relating to trade policy and the WTO. The MNRE is the nodal ministry in charge of the National Solar Mission. The MOEFCC, meanwhile, is responsible for India's engagement with the international climate change regimes under the UNFCCC.

The dispute (Figure 2.1) officially began in February 2013, when the United States requested formal consultations with India at the WTO. Under the WTO regime, if the mandatory consultations fail to produce a satisfactory settlement within sixty days, then the complainant may request adjudication by a Panel.[119] In February 2014, a year later, the United States requested supplementary consultations with India. This second round of consultations, ultimately, led to the creation of the Panel in April 2014. Interestingly, after the first round of consultations between the two countries, India had filed a request for information with the WTO Committees on Subsidies and Countervailing Measures and Trade-Related Investment Measures in April 2013. India sought

---

[119] Understanding on Rules and Procedures Governing the Settlement of Disputes art. 4.7, Apr. 15, 1994, Marrakesh Agreement Establishing the World Trade Organization, Annex 2, 1869 U.N.T.S. 401.

information from the United States with respect to LCRs in specific renewable energy-sector subsidy programmes in the states of Delaware, Minnesota, Massachusetts and Connecticut.[120] However, India did not raise a formal counter-challenge at the WTO until 9 September 2016,[121] exactly a week before the Appellate Body's final decision in the *Indian Solar* dispute.

The primary motivation for the United States Trade Representative (USTR) to initiate the WTO dispute against India was to create a level playing field for American solar cells and module manufacturers in India's solar market. The request for consultations was meant to raise concerns over some protectionist measures in India's solar policy and to ensure that it was not being discriminatory towards goods from the US. Although the issue touched upon different facets, including India's solar ambitions forming the basis of its climate commitments, the USTR was only tasked with 'enforcing international trade rules'.[122] The basis for launching a WTO dispute against a country rests on USTR's 'open door policy', which allows aggrieved stakeholders to come with concerns over a foreign country's measure.[123] In this case, there was intense domestic lobbying in the United States to bring a WTO dispute against India's solar policy. In June 2013 John Smirnow, the Vice President of the Solar Energy Industries Association (SEIA) testified before the US Congress on India's use of LCR in its solar policy, which discriminates against US solar exports and provides an unfair competitive advantage to India's domestic solar manufacturers.[124] His testimony, in part, read: 'Our only hope is that the U.S. government's recent decision to initiate WTO dispute settlement proceedings against the LCR will eventually cause India to reverse course.'[125]

[120] Committee on Subsidies and Countervailing Measures, Minutes of the Regular Meeting Held on 22 April 2013, WTO Doc. G/SCM/M/85 (5 Aug. 2013).

[121] Request for consultations by India, *United States—certain measures relating to the renewable energy sector*, WT/DS510/1 (9 Sep. 2016).

[122] Participant 40, interview with author, 27 Jan. 2017.

[123] Ibid.

[124] Committee on Energy and Commerce, *A tangle of trade barriers: how India's industrial policy is hurting U.S. companies* (27 Jun. 2013), http://docs.house.gov/Committee/Calendar/ByEvent.aspx?EventID=101056, accessed 15 Dec. 2022.

[125] Ibid.

2010
- **11 January**: Launch of the National Solar Mission
- **25 July**: Ministry of New and Renewable Energy Guidelines for Selection of New Grid Connected Solar Power Projects, Batch-I

2011
- **24 August**: Guidelines for Selection of New Grid Connected Solar Power Projects, Batch-II

2012
- **December**: Ministry of New and Renewable Energy, National Solar Mission: Phase II—Policy Document

2013
- **6 February**: Request for WTO consultations by the United States
- **20 March**: First round of consultations between the two countries

2014
- **10 February**: Supplementary request for consultations by the United States
- **20 March**: Second round of consultations between the two countries
- **14 April**: Request for establishment of Panel by the United States
- **22 May**: Directorate Gerernal of Anti-Dumping & Allied Duties issues Final Report of anti-dumping investigation concerning imports of solar cells
- **23 May**: WTO Panel created
- **24 September**: Panelists confirmed
- **12 October**: Timetable for the Panel adopted

2015
- **3–4 February**: First meeting of the Panel with parties
- **4 February**: Panel session with third parties
- **28–9 April**: Second meeting of the Panel
- **9 June**: Panel issued descriptive part of report
- **24 July**: Interim report of the Panel
- **28 August**: Final Panel Report sent to parties
- **12 December**: Paris Agreement adopted

2016
- **24 February**: Panel Report circulated to WTO Members
- **20 April**: India notified the intent to appeal certain issues of law under the Panel Report
- **4–5 July**: Oral hearing of the appeal
- **9 September**: Request for WTO consultations by India
- **16 September**: Final Report of the Appellate Body

Figure 2.1 Timeline of the WTO Dispute and Related Developments

The US had raised concerns over the use of LCRs in India's solar policy well before the launch of the formal consultations at the WTO, particularly during the India–US Trade Policy Forum. The testimony of Mr Smirnow also indicates that the US government first tried to establish a collaborative dialogue with India regarding the use of LCRs and requested formal consultations before the WTO as a last resort effort to get India to drop the use of such protectionist measures.[126]

Several interviewees were of the view that the dispute was motivated squarely by trade interests and the American desire to get into the Indian solar market. As one interviewee remarked: 'Who's bothered about other countries [about LCRs within their renewable energy policies]? It [this dispute] is because of the size of the Indian market for the next 20–30 years.'[127] Some others felt that the dispute was not necessarily targeting India's solar ambitions, rather it was fundamentally a 'symbolic dispute' undertaken to send a signal that such a policy cannot be replicated in other sectors.[128] In addition, several interviewees suggested that the anti-dumping investigation initiated by Indian authorities against American solar cells and modules cannot be disregarded when trying to uncover the 'big picture' behind this WTO dispute.

Against the backdrop of the WTO dispute brewing between the two countries, India had initiated an anti-dumping investigation against imports of solar cells and modules from China, United States, and Malaysia in November 2012. The Directorate General of Anti-dumping & Allied Duties (DGAD) proceeded to initiate this investigation at the behest of Indian solar manufacturers who complained that solar cells and modules were being dumped into India by exporters from these countries. In May 2014, the DGAD ruled in favour of the domestic solar manufacturers and recommended an anti-dumping duty on solar cells and modules from China, United States, and Malaysia.

Although the complaint was brought before the DGAD by domestic solar manufacturers, there was a distinct divergence in the views held by the solar manufacturers and the solar power developers in India. While the manufacturers pushed for the imposition of anti-dumping duty, the public opinion held by the developers was that an anti-dumping duty would increase the prices of developing solar power projects due to more expensive imports.

Furthermore, the final decision of the DGAD came on 22 May 2014, five days before the new government took office. On 26 May 2014, there

[126] Ibid.
[127] Participant 26, n. 114.
[128] Participant 33, n. 113.

was a change in the Central Government and the National Democratic Alliance (NDA) led by the Bhartiya Janata Party came to power.[129] With the change in government the prevailing view of the developers found favour with the new government that decided not to impose the anti-dumping duty on solar cells and modules.[130] Although the local solar manufacturing industry had won their case before the DGAD, the NDA government took a strong position to not support the imposition of the anti-dumping duty as it would have considerably raised the price of solar power in the country. Around the same time, the government met with representatives of the domestic solar manufacturing industry who agreed to not press for anti-dumping duty if they were given a certain assured market.[131] Therefore, the government continued with its decision to not impose anti-dumping duty on solar cells and modules, including on imports from American manufacturers, and proceeded to revise India's solar targets from 22 GW to 100 GW of solar power by 2022.[132] As one of the interviewees noted:

Finance Ministry in its wisdom did not impose the (anti-dumping) duty. We don't have the capacity to make solar cells or modules in the country; we have to buy it from outside. If we were to impose an anti-dumping duty just to protect an alleged domestic industry, where 90% of components itself are being imported, power costs would have risen and the expansion of solar energy would have suffered. Finance Ministry made the right decision—they have to look at national interest rather than the interest of a particular domestic industry which is calling for protection.[133]

[129] Express News Service, 'Narendra Modi takes oath as India's 15th Prime Minister', *The Indian Express* (26 May 2014), http://indianexpress.com/article/india/politics/live-narendra-modi-swearing-in-ceremony-today-may-26/, accessed 15 Dec. 2022.

[130] Special Correspondent, 'India not to impose anti-dumping duty on solar panels: Nirmala', *The Hindu* (10 Sep. 2014), http://www.thehindu.com/business/Economy/india-not-to-impose-antidumping-duty-on-solar-panels-nirmala/article6397475.ece, accessed 15 Dec. 2022; Press Trust of India, 'Govt drops anti-dumping duty on solar panel imports from US, China', *Business Standard* (10 Sep. 2014), http://www.business-standard.com/article/pti-stories/india-not-to-impose-anti-dumping-duty-on-solar-panels-nirmala-114091000659_1.html, accessed 15 Dec. 2022.

[131] Participant 39, n. 101.

[132] Press Information Bureau, 'Revision of cumulative targets under National Solar Mission' (17 Jun. 2015), http://pib.nic.in/newsite/PrintRelease.aspx?relid=122566, accessed 15 Dec. 2022.

[133] Participant 26, n. 114.

The two countries had been discussing the LCR provisions under the NSM prior to the formal WTO consultations. In fact, the MOCI had flagged the issue of WTO incompatibility of certain measures within India's NSM well before the initiation of the formal dispute. As a trade lawyer noted:

> The way policymaking works (in India, emphasis added), even before any policy is put forth in the public domain, it is vetted by other ministries. The Commerce Ministry had always been very clear that there will be a WTO compatibility issue. Especially when Canada got challenged, they were very clear in their advice. The basic elements of interministerial work are present; no one does anything in isolation. There is always a debate and discussion and awareness of possible risks to go forward and to decide how to attack it.[134]

Despite receiving contrary advice from the MOCI, the MNRE continued defending the provisions on LCRs. Now the basis for defending the measure, however, was to assure a small market for the faltering domestic industry. Since the government had decided to suspend the levy of anti-dumping duty, the MNRE's insistence on LCRs was merely to assure a small market to the domestic players who were 'in a very bad shape'.[135] Although the domestic solar manufacturers wanted a much larger percentage of LCRs, the MNRE's main objective was to keep the prices of solar power low and to open the solar energy market in order to sustain the broader goals of the NSM.

India's defence of the LCR measure got further complicated with the transition in the political set-up after the 2014 general elections. As one interviewee recalled:

> The new government came with an ambitious power generation program and looked at the issue of local manufacturing in a completely new light. The new Prime Minister had a strong solar agenda, and backed it with a strong manufacturing agenda. As a result, the perspective on the solar trade dispute completely changed with the change in

---

[134] Participant 33, n. 113.
[135] Participant 39, n. 101.

government. The earlier government's arguments on technology continuity and maintaining a small manufacturing base was superimposed by the new government's ambitious solar targets. As a result, the new government's insistence on defending the LCR rule was a contrarian approach given its ambitious solar targets. There was a clear conflict between the two policies as the huge demands generated by the high ambitions of the new government would not have been met with higher cost locally-manufactured equipment.[136]

The commonly held view among several interviewees was that India would not have won the case at the WTO and India's insistence to contest the case at the WTO made little strategic sense. The WTO Panel, unsurprisingly, ruled against India and held that the LCRs in the NSM were in violation of WTO rules. The Panel circulated its final report to the parties on 27 August 2015; however, the final report was published only in February 2016. According to several interviewees, the only reason for the delay in the publication of the Panel Report was because the parties were still taking to each other and had requested for the Panel Report to not be published. Between August 2015 and February 2016, there were a series of bilateral talks between the Indian Power Minister, Mr Piyush Goyal and the USTR in order to settle the dispute and arrive at a deal which could sidestep the judgment of the Panel; these discussions took place over several video and phone-in conferences. Interviewees who were privy to these conversations agree that this was an 'informal process' or a 'backdoor effort' on part of the two governments to mutually settle the dispute before the Panel Report was published.[137]

Crucially, one of the most significant aspects during this phase was the sidelining of the MOCI. After circulation of the Panel Report, the Power Minister, Mr Piyush Goyal, is said to have convened a closed-door meeting with trade lawyers to seek their opinion on how the NSM could be covered by the government procurement exception. India's main thrust during these negotiations was that it did not impose anti-dumping duties on American solar cells and modules with the expectation that the

---

[136] Participant 30, n. 107.
[137] Participant 35, interview with author, 14 Dec. 2016. Participant 25, interview with author, 28 Jan. 2017.

US would not proceed with the dispute at the WTO. In order to settle the dispute, India was ready to remove the TRIMS-inconsistent provisions as long as its public utilities could procure locally made solar cells and modules. As part of the negotiated settlement, India agreed to change its policy but did not want the final Panel Report to be published. The US, on the other hand, stressed that it had initiated the dispute on the ground that it is a matter of principle and insisted on the circulation of the Panel Report in spite of arriving at a mutually agreeable solution. Ultimately, the bilateral talks appear to have broken down on the question of publishing the Panel Report. Once the Panel Report was published, it was only a matter of time before India went into appeal.

Although India had identified similar LCRs within renewable energy support programmes in the United States in 2013, it not raise a counter-challenge at the WTO until September 2016. As one respondent puts it: 'India not a major exporter to the United States—so why bother? Independently this case would have never gone to the WTO, so the tit-for-tat complaint never made any sense.'[138]

Within the government, the understanding was that even though the US measures don't impact Indian exports, it could have pursued the counter-challenge as an 'in principle' dispute. As a result, it had begun the process of examining the rules and building a case as far back as 2013–14. However, one of the main reasons for not bringing a formal complaint against the US was the political undercurrents between the two countries. In 2013, it was the diplomatic row over the arrest of an Indian diplomat, Devyani Khobragade, in New York that made matters tense between the two countries. In 2014, it appears that with a new government in power, India did not want to strain its relations with the US by raising a trade dispute. Further in 2016, there was additional debate over whether India should bring a formal dispute against the US, especially since the US had supported India in the wake of the Uri terror attacks. As one interviewee noted: 'This always happens with the United States. They bring a case based purely on trade interests, whereas for India it is never primarily trade interests but the larger geopolitical issues that determine whether a WTO dispute will be brought against the US.'[139]

[138] Participant 25, n. 137.
[139] Participant 35, n. 137.

India's Solar Policy Pivot

Although India lost the solar trade dispute at the WTO, there weren't any political repercussions for two reasons: first, internally, there is an understanding that India is not geared towards manufacturing, at most it could be a hub for assembly; and second, there is a strong public opinion in India that the price of solar energy is low largely because of cheap imports. As a result, the WTO ruling was immaterial for India as it didn't change the status quo. Several stakeholders agreed that removing the provisions on LCRs would not detract India from achieving its solar targets and that they could be achieved in a much more cost-effective manner through cheaper imports. Therefore, the solar power-generating sector was 'very happy' for the 'level playing field'.[140] The forecast for the solar-manufacturing sector was not as bright. The immediate impact of the WTO decision and phasing-out of the LCRs has been on Indian solar manufacturers. According to one interviewee, the WTO ruling has 'destroyed ambitions of domestic manufacturers, ruined their expansion plans and left them bleeding'.[141] The two companies who had invested in setting up a fabrication and assembly plant, Moser Baer and IndoSolar, have lost out the most. According to another interviewee, these companies had begun scaling down on manufacturing and pivoted their business models towards generation of clean energy.[142]

India has failed to generate a domestic solar manufacturing industry, and its industrial productivity in this sector remains far below that of the dominant player, China.[143] With its ambitious high-capacity installation targets, and in the aftermath of the WTO dispute against its solar policies, India has inadvertently chosen to become a consumer rather than a producer of new energy technologies. On the other hand, in pursuance of its clean energy ambition, China has squarely positioned itself as a producer and market leader of low-carbon energy technologies.[144] One of the biggest dilemmas facing India's solar programme is that 80 per cent

---

[140] Participant 26, n. 114.

[141] Participant 34, interview with author, 8 Dec. 2016.

[142] Participant 24, n. 104.

[143] S. Shidore & J.W. Busby, 'One more try: The International Solar Alliance and India's search for geopolitical influence', *Energy Strategy Reviews*, 26 (2019), 100385.

[144] S. Joshi & L. Powell, *India: energy geo-politics* (New Delhi: Observer Research Foundation, Oct. 2018), 27–9.

of the solar panels are from China or Chinese-owned companies based elsewhere.[145]

An intriguing aspect, then, of India's role in the creation of the ISA is the inherent weakness (or lack thereof) of domestic manufacturing capacity in the solar space. It neither has China's manufacturing capacity of solar panels nor does it possess the financial prowess to unilaterally subsidize the production of solar panels that would drive down prices around the world.[146] Unlike China's Belt and Road Initiative, India is also limited in its ability to offer financial inducements to other countries to embrace solar power.[147] An interviewee highlighted the dichotomy in India's leadership on ISA and the lack of competitiveness in solar manufacturing: 'You're coming up with it [the ISA], but manufacturing is missing in India. It's your money, your alliance, but the Chinese will sell panels to them [ISA member countries].'[148]

The government, however, had a clear ambition of reaching its ambitious clean energy goals and did not want the provisions on LCR to act as a constraint in reaching this goal. Against the backdrop of the *Indian Solar* dispute, India demonstrated a solar policy pivot both at the national and international levels.

On the national level, as the *Indian Solar* dispute progressed, there was a clearer understanding of the WTO incompatibility of the LCR measures within the Indian policymaking circles. During the bilateral talks between Piyush Goyal and the USTR, one of the focal negotiating points was on the issue of treating the challenged LCR measure as government procurement. These consultations, however, did not lead to any settlement between the parties. After the adverse WTO ruling, India, on its part, began the effort of dismantling the LCR measure and finding two alternatives for domestic solar manufacturers: one of the ways is through government procurement for the defence and railway sectors; the second is by creating a demand-pull incentive in the domestic solar manufacturing sector through the 'Make in India' programme, which allows up to 100

[145] S. Jai, '70% duty on solar imports: how serious is China dominance in Indian market?', *Business Standard* (12 Jan. 2018), https://www.business-standard.com/article/economy-policy/70-duty-on-solar-imports-how-serious-is-china-dominance-in-indian-market-118011100565_1.html, accessed 15 Dec. 2022.
[146] Shidore & Busby, n. 143.
[147] Ibid.
[148] Participant 7, interview with author, 6 Dec. 2016.

per cent of foreign direct investment in the renewable energy sector. As one of the interviewees remarked: 'One of the major positives from the dispute is that the government understood the value of solar and started thinking of ways to absorb electricity from solar.'[149]

In order to move away from the prospect of importing all its clean energy equipment, the government appears inclined towards turning India into a $100 billion market for clean energy through the 'Make in India' programme. 'Make in India'—with its greater emphasis on innovative financing, low-cost loans, multilateral and bilateral finance negotiations— could work to create a demand-pull incentive, thus bringing in more players into the domestic manufacturing market. Moreover, it allows for 100 per cent foreign direct investment in the solar energy sector, which creates a level playing field for foreign solar manufacturing companies. With this initiative, the government is attempting to create a competitive manufacturing environment and improve the ease of doing business in India.[150] One of the interviewees argued that 'Make in India' can complement the entire process of achieving solar targets in a WTO compliant way.[151] Another described how India is finally moving towards positioning itself as a market post the WTO decision, but that the 'irony or tragedy of the situation is that (we) became embroiled in a unnecessary dispute'.[152] As a senior government official puts it: 'The WTO dispute serves as a lesson for policymakers that it needs to find innovative measures to support and strengthen the domestic industry, which is a definitely a need considering the scale of the (solar) targets.'[153]

On the international level, India took a lead role in the creation and operationalization of the ISA. According to several interviewees, the Paris Agreement doesn't deal with renewable energy, particularly solar energy; consequently, the ISA is motivated by a desire to bring countries together in an effort to identify the kind of technologies as well as the research and development needed to push towards the deployment of solar energy globally. According to one interviewee, 'the ISA could be used as a means of

[149] Participant 34, n. 141.
[150] Participant 31, interview with author, 18 Dec. 2016.
[151] Participant 29, interview with author, 13 Dec. 2016: 'The WTO decision is not a blow to India's solar ambitions. It is a little bit of redirection, which says that your goal is okay, but just do it this way.'
[152] Participant 13, interview with author, 8 Dec. 2016.
[153] Participant 16, n. 96.

recalibration on part of developing countries to set rules.'[154] In addition, India vociferously argued for ISA to be a treaty-based international organization. While the dispute does not have a perceivable role in the creation of ISA, it evidences a stronger commitment shown by India to take the lead on solar norm-making. It is difficult to establish a correlation between the solar trade dispute and India's lead role in the creation of ISA, but it could be argued that it served as a trigger for India's efforts to take its ambitious domestic solar targets to a global level through the platform of the ISA. A global partnership on a collaborative platform that includes 'all the countries between the two tropics' could provide additional legitimacy to India's domestic goals. According to one interviewee: 'ISA is a way to find a global aggregation and convergence towards a global target for solar. Currently, India has domestic targets but we hope to extend it into the international arena.'[155]

Ultimately, there are some distinct factors driving India's lead role in the creation of the ISA. First, India's large domestic markets and energy-related actions could drive down the prices for certain products, such as high-efficiency air conditioners, HFC-free refrigerators, solar appliances, or electric vehicles. The low-cost solutions created for Indian markets could have distinct advantages for ISA member countries and be readily transferable to other developing country contexts in Africa, Southeast Asia, and Latin America. Second, the Indian model of scale-up solar, which includes creating an enabling environment for both utility-scale solar plants and off-grid distributed solar energy, could be an attractive idea to organize other countries around.[156]

A third, all-important, factor is Modi's emphatic embrace of solar energy. As the Chief Minister of Gujarat, Modi was an early proponent of solar energy.[157] The Gujarat government had launched its solar policy in 2009, well before the announcement of the NSM by the Centre in January 2010. In 2010, while he was still the Chief Minister of Gujarat, Modi launched a book on climate change that outlined vision on achieving a low-carbon economy and the issue of climate justice.[158] In this book,

[154] Participant 26, n. 114.
[155] Participant 16, n. 96.
[156] Shidore & Busby, n. 143.
[157] Chaudhary, Krishna, & Sagar, n. 80.
[158] HT Correspondent, 'Kalam to release Modi's book on climate change', *The Hindustan Times* (21 Dec. 2010), https://www.hindustantimes.com/books/kalam-to-release-modi-s-book-on-climate-change/story-a2M5P48BiAWYvrT8d3JYrM.html, accessed 15 Dec. 2022.

Modi emphasized the need for convergence of economy, energy, and ecology, in order to take care of the poor and future generations in the journey towards sustainable development. He proposed a 'paradigm shift' on climate change, calling for active development and dissemination of clean energy technologies.[159]

The state of Gujarat aimed to install 500 MW of solar power by 2014. In April 2012, when the Charanka solar park—Asia's largest solar park[160]—was inaugurated in Gujarat, the state had achieved an installed capacity of 605 MW ahead of the 2014 target date. It was then, speaking at an event dedicating the Charanka solar park to the nation, that Modi first expressed his vision for a new grouping of nations with high solar power potential: 'There are different league of nations like OPEC and others. A league should be formed among the nations which get more sun rays. India should play a prominent role into the formation of such a league and step up its R&D to lead those nations.'[161]

Interestingly, in the same speech, Modi stated that he had spoken to then Prime Minister Manmohan Singh on the need for forming such an association of countries and India taking on such initiatives.[162] Certain areas in the world have a much greater potential to 'harvest' sun light than others because the number of sun hours in the world is higher each month or because the sun shines with a greater intensity.[163] This early idea to bring these 'solar-rich' nations together as a new bloc, ultimately took form as the ISA under Modi's leadership as Prime Minister.

Over the course of the next few chapters, this book presents the empirical findings and arguments using three frames—process (Chapter 3), politics (Chapter 4), and players (Chapter 5)—in order to explain the

---

[159] N. Modi, *Convenient action: continuity for change* (Gurgaon: Lexis Nexis, 2015).

[160] DNA Correspondent, 'Asia's largest solar park inaugurated in Patan', *DNA* (31 Dec. 2010), https://www.dnaindia.com/india/report-asia-s-largest-solar-park-inaugurated-in-patan-1488 351, accessed on 15 Dec. 2022.

[161] FWire, 'India should take initiatives to form league like OPEC: Modi', *Firstpost* (19 Apr. 2012), https://www.firstpost.com/fwire/india-should-take-initiatives-to-form-league-like-opec-modi-281550.html, accessed 15 Dec. 2022.

[162] Agencies, 'India should take initiatives to form league like OPEC: Narendra Modi', *The Indian Express* (19 Apr. 2012), https://indianexpress.com/article/news-archive/web/india-sho uld-take-initiatives-to-form-league-like-opec-narendra-modi/, accessed 15 Dec. 2022.

[163] D. Criekemans, 'Geopolitics of the Renewable Energy Game and Its Potential Impact upon Global Power Relations', in D. Scholten, ed., *The Geopolitics of Renewables* (The Netherlands: Springer, 2018), 37–73.

making of the ISA. The book's central argument is that the creation of the ISA as a treaty-based international organization illustrates a new kind of Indian economic diplomacy, which buoyed by the political vision marks the first deliberate instrument of India's foreign policy on climate change and energy.

3

Process

India, International Rule-Making, and the International Solar Alliance

> *The International Solar Alliance represents a new kind of flexible multilateralism.*
>
> —Former Indian diplomat (Participant 21, interview with author, 26 Jul. 2018)

This chapter examines the creation of the ISA—a new international organization led by India and backed primarily by developing countries—from the inception phase until it became a legal entity. Official documents and wide-ranging interview access provide data that offers insights into the treaty-making process. This chapter analyses the politico-legal issues behind the scenes in order to explain the creation of ISA as a treaty-based international organization. It lays down the analytical framework for the book's main argument that the legal form of the ISA marked an innovation in the structure of international organizations that is best described as 'soft law in a hard shell': it uses the legal infrastructure of a treaty while relying on the social structure of participating actors for its future implementation. Empirical evidence suggests that three factors explain the treaty structure of the ISA: first, India's lead role in driving the treaty-making process; second, the early involvement of non-state actors in implementation; and third, the value of legal form for developing countries.

On 30 November 2015 the ISA was launched as a joint initiative of India and France during the UN climate talks in Paris. The ISA was envisaged as multi-country partnership organization with membership from solar-resource-rich countries between the two tropics,[1] and aims 'to

---

[1] ISA, 'Working paper on International Solar Alliance', *Media* (30 Nov. 2015), https://isolaralliance.org/media/press-release, accessed 15 Dec. 2022.

The Making of the International Solar Alliance. Vyoma Jha, Oxford University Press. © Vyoma Jha 2023.
DOI: 10.1093/oso/9780198884705.003.0003

NDIA, INTERNATIONAL RULE-MAKING, AND THE ISA   65

provide a platform for cooperation among solar-resource-rich countries, through which the global community, including governments, bilateral and multilateral organizations, corporations, industry, and other stake-holders, can contribute to help achieve the common goal of increasing the use and quality of solar energy in meeting energy needs of prospective ISA member countries in a safe, convenient, affordable, equitable and sustainable manner.'[2] At the launch event, India and France issued the Paris Declaration (Annex 1) with the stated objectives of reducing the cost of finance and technology of solar deployment, formulating financial instruments and mobilizing investment into solar power generation, and paving the way for good technologies for solar generation and storage.[3]

It was initially proposed that the governance structure would consist of an assembly, a council, and a secretariat. However, it was subsequently decided that the detailed and final structure of the ISA would be subject to member countries' deliberations and suggestions.[4] In this regard, two provisional bodies played a critical role in shaping the governance structure of the ISA: the International Steering Committee (ISC) and the Interim Administrative Cell (IAC).

In order to realize the stated goals, the Paris Declaration put forth a decision to create the ISC to provide 'necessary guidance, direction and advice' to establish the alliance and it was kept open to interested countries.[5] The first meeting of the ISC was held on 1 December 2015, a day after the launch event. The major ideas and opinions to emerge from the inaugural meeting were that the ISA should: (1) find a niche for itself; (2) avoid duplication of efforts; (3) undertake tangible projects and programmes over time; and (4) leverage and promote private sector involvement.[6] These were the guiding principles for the ISC's work between December 2015 and February 2018. There were a total of six ISC meetings, with each meeting being attended by representatives from participant countries

[2] ISA, background, https://isolaralliance.org/about/background, accessed 15 Dec. 2022.
[3] UNFCCC, 'International Solar Energy Alliance launched at COP21', Newsroom (30 Nov. 2015), https://newsroom.unfccc.int/news/international-solar-energy-alliance-launched-at-cop21, accessed 15 Dec. 2022.
[4] ISA, n. 1.
[5] Ibid.
[6] ISA, 'Report of the First Meeting of the International Steering Committee', Steering Committees (Paris, 1 Dec. 2015), https://isolaralliance.org/about/steering-committees, accessed 15 Dec. 2022.

and observer organizations. The work of the ISC was completed at its final meeting on 20 February 2018, a few weeks prior to the ISA's Founding Conference in March 2018.

Another key decision to emerge from the inaugural ISC meeting was the constitution of the IAC, with an overarching aim to facilitate the establishment of the ISA and ensure its transformation from a *de facto* to *de jure* body, that is, a legal, intergovernmental organization.[7] The IAC was set up within Government of India's Ministry of New and Renewable Energy (MNRE) and was responsible for the interim management of the ISA.[8] In doing so, the IAC's mandate was to: (1) finalize the Framework Agreement in consultation with member countries; (2) initiate action for implementing activities from India's contribution to the ISA; (3) engage in discussions with institutions and international organizations, and explore prospects for collaboration; and (4) firm up an action plan for the ISA in consultation with member countries.[9] The IAC would cease to exist once the ISA enters into legal force.[10] The IAC remained in operation for a little over a year, with a total of eight meetings between February 2016 and March 2017.[11] The meetings were attended by the members of the IAC,[12] representatives of other countries, and special invitees, including representatives from multilateral organizations, non-governmental organizations, financial institutions, and the private sector.

On 15 November 2016, about a year since the ISA's launch, the Government of India opened the Framework Agreement (Annex 2) for

---

[7] ISA, 'Constitution of the Interim Administrative Cell of the International Solar Alliance to facilitate establishment of ISA from *de facto* to *de jure* status', *Steering Committees* (29 Jan. 2016), https://isolaralliance.org/about/steering-committees, accessed 15 Dec. 2022.

[8] Ibid.

[9] ISA, 'Report of the first meeting of the Interim Administrative Cell of the International Solar Alliance', *Steering Committees* (New Delhi, 10 Feb. 2016), https://isolaralliance.org/about/steering-committees, accessed 15 Dec. 2022.

[10] See n. 7.

[11] The IAC was re-designated as the interim secretariat of the ISA in the sixth IAC meeting. See ISA, 'Report of the sixth meeting of the Interim Administrative Cell of the International Solar Alliance', *Steering Committees* (New Delhi, 14 Jun. 2016), https://isolaralliance.org/about/steering-committees, accessed 15 Dec. 2022.

[12] The core membership of the IAC comprised of the Chairman (Secretary, MNRE) and the Convener (Dr P.C. Maithani, Director, MNRE). Other members of the IAC were the nominated representatives from the Ministry of External Affairs (MEA), Ministry of Environment, Forests and Climate Change (MoEFCC), Ministry of Finance, Solar Energy Corporation of India (SECI), National Institute of Solar Energy (NISE), National Institute of Wind Energy (NIWE), National Institute of Bio-Energy (NIBE), and the Indian Renewable Energy Development Agency (IREDA).

Table 3.1 First Fifteen Countries to Ratify
the Framework Agreement

S.No.	Country	Date of ratification
1.	France	24 Apr. 2017
2.	Nauru	22 May 2017
3.	Mauritius	27 May 2017
4.	India	28 Jun. 2017
5.	Niger	25 Sep. 2017
6.	Fiji	25 Sep. 2017
7.	Tuvulu	25 Sep. 2017
8.	Ghana	16 Oct. 2017
9.	Seychelles	16 Oct. 2017
10.	South Sudan	16 Oct. 2017
11.	Somalia	18 Oct. 2017
12.	Mali	22 Oct. 2017
13.	Bangladesh	22 Oct. 2017
14.	Comoros	1 Nov. 2017
15.	Guinea	6 Nov. 2017

Source: Author's own analysis

signature during the COP-22 in Marrakesh, Morocco. The ISA identified 121 prospective member countries (those falling between the Tropics of Cancer and Capricorn), which are also members of the United Nations, to join the Alliance by signing and ratifying the Framework Agreement (Annex 3). On 6 December 2017, 30 days after the submission of instruments of ratification by fifteen countries (Table 3.1), the Framework Agreement formally entered into force and ISA acquired the status of an international organization.[13] As of May 2021, the ISA has ninety-four signatory countries and seventy-five ratifying countries.[14]

The Framework Agreement has a total of fourteen articles. ISA members take coordinated actions through ISA's work programmes and

---

[13] PIB, *ISA to become a treaty-based international intergovernmental organization tomorrow* [media release] (5 Dec. 2017), http://pib.nic.in/newsite/PrintRelease.aspx?relid=174097, accessed 15 Dec. 2022.

[14] ISA, 'Member countries', *Membership*, https://isolaralliance.org/membership/countries, accessed 15 May 2021. See also, Annex 5.

activities launched on a voluntary basis, aimed at better harmonizing and aggregating demand for, inter alia, solar finance, solar technologies, innovation, research and development, and capacity building.[15] While the membership was kept open to countries lying fully or partially between the two tropics, UN member countries that were located beyond the tropics were invited to join the ISA as 'Partner Countries'.[16] Moreover, other regional or international organizations that have potential to help the ISA achieve its objectives could join the ISA as a 'Partner Organization'.[17] The United Nations, including its organs, were identified as ISA's 'Strategic Partner'.[18]

While the ISA has been promoted as a treaty-based international organization, it maintains a stance that it will *not* duplicate or replicate the efforts of other international organizations in the renewable energy sector.[19] Rather it aims to establish networks and develop synergies with them and supplement their efforts in a sustainable and focused manner.[20] Since its inception the ISA has signed joint declarations with Partner Organizations, which include a variety of non-state actors such as multilateral and regional developments banks, climate-related agencies, and financial institutions.[21] In addition, the ISA also has Corporate Partners that include Indian energy-related agencies and foreign investors.[22]

Ultimately, the ISA's governance structure consists of an assembly and a secretariat.[23] Going forward, the seat of the ISA shall be in India.[24] The Government of India will support the ISA by hosting its secretariat for an initial period of five years and thereafter it is expected to generate its own resources and become a self-financing entity.[25] The

---

[15] Article II of the Framework Agreement, *Guiding principles.*

[16] Article VII of the Framework Agreement, *Member and partner country status.*

[17] Article VIII of the Framework Agreement, *Partner organization.*

[18] Ibid.

[19] In particular, International Energy Agency (IEA), International Renewable Energy Agency (IRENA), Renewable Energy and Energy Efficiency Partnership (REEEP), Renewable Energy Policy Network for the 21st Century (REN21), United Nations bodies, bilateral organizations, etc.

[20] ISA, n. 2.

[21] See Table 3.2.

[22] See Table 3.3.

[23] ISA, *Governance*, https://isolaralliance.org/governance/first-assembly, accessed 15 Dec. 2022.

[24] The ISA is currently headquartered in Gurugram, India. See, Article XII of the Framework Agreement, *Seat of the ISA.*

[25] Article VI of the Framework Agreement, *Budget and financial resources.*

first assembly of the ISA was held on 3 October 2018 in New Delhi, India.[26]

One of the stated goals of the ISA is to reduce the costs of finance and technology for immediate solar deployment.[27] Interestingly, however, the Framework Agreement imposes no targets or legally binding obligations on member countries for either financial or technology transfers. Instead, the ISA aims to be a facilitator of technology, knowledge, and finance.[28] ISA's collaborations with various transnational actors appear to be put in place mainly to leverage the technical expertise, financial capacity, and global networks of its Partner Organizations in order to scale up solar energy deployment in member countries. India's insistence, then, on the ISA being a treaty-based international organization raises questions on its motivation to steer the treaty-making process. What are the reasons for ISA's present legal form especially when the treaty text contains no binding legal commitments on countries? If the ISA member countries will take actions on a 'voluntary basis' then isn't ISA better-described as soft law?[29] Why open the Framework Agreement for signature and ratification by other countries when the bulk of the work is expected to be implemented by non-state actors?

This chapter breaks down the treaty-making process in order to unpack the reasons behind the choice to make ISA a treaty-based international organization. Through a combined analysis of the empirical data from official ISA documents and elite interviews, the ISA's procedural history can be traced back to two phases, which are best described as the pre-Paris and post-Paris phases of treaty-making. The pre-Paris phase, or the period of conceptualization, lasted from June 2014 to November 2015. The post-Paris phase, or the period of operationalization, lasted from December 2015 to March 2018.

---

[26] It was attended by representatives of thirty-eight countries that have ratified the Framework Agreement, forty-one observer countries that have either signed or yet to sign the Framework Agreement, and 57 partner organizations and special invitees. See, ISA, 'Report of the first assembly of the International Solar Alliance', *Governance* (National Capital Region, 14 Jan. 2019), https://isolaralliance.org/governance/first-assembly, accessed 15 Dec. 2022.

[27] The Paris Declaration states that countries '[s]hare the collective ambition to undertake innovative and concerted efforts with a view to reducing the cost of finance and cost of technology for immediate deployment of competitive solar generation assets in all our countries and to pave the way for future solar generation, storage and good technologies adapted to our countries' individual needs.' See, UNFCCC, n. 3.

[28] ISA, n. 2.

[29] Article II of the Framework Agreement, *Guiding principles*.

Pre-Paris: Period of Conceptualization

This period marks the prenegotiation stage, a principal function of which is to build trust between parties.[30] The sequencing of prenegotiation is highly context dependent, but domestic politics can significantly affect the ordering of the stages of prenegotiation.[31] In this case, the prenegotiation stage of the ISA must be viewed in light of India's motivation to cement its global leadership and establish its seriousness on climate action. As a consequence, India was squarely in the driver's seat during the process of 'getting to the table', which was marked by two crucial elements: first, India's recognition of the fast-evolving state of the world on solar energy and the leadership gap it sought to fill at the international level; and second, the identification of France as a potential partner and bringing other interested allies on board.

State of the World on Solar Energy and India's New Leadership Role

This is not the first time a developing country has floated the idea of an international organization, although it is the first time India has taken this kind of initiative. According to several interviewees, the reasons behind this move cannot be looked at independently from the international climate change negotiations under the United Nations Framework Convention on Climate Change (UNFCCC). Many interviewees, who have been involved with climate change negotiations, noted that they had become prolonged and fractious, with India losing its influence

---

[30] W. Zartman, 'Prenegotiation: Phases and Functions' in J.C. Stein, ed., *Getting to the table: The process of international prenegotiation* (Baltimore, MD and London: Johns Hopkins University Press, 1989) 1–17, 13–14.

[31] Prenegotiation matters for several reasons both when the parties get to the table and when they do not. First, it provides the participants with significant opportunities for learning, both about themselves and others. Second, it permits the participants to learn about the preconditions for and possibilities of both a negotiated agreement and an alternative management of their relationship. Finally, the process of 'getting to the table' is inherently valuable and significant irrespective of the outcome of the negotiating process, as the learnings could have consequences for the management of the larger relationship between the parties. See, J.C. Stein, 'Getting to the table: The triggers, stages, functions and consequences of prenegotiation', in J.C. Stein, ed., *Getting to the table: The process of international prenegotiation* (Baltimore, MD and London: Johns Hopkins University Press, 1989) 239–68, 251.

on rule-making and being perceived as a spoiler during negotiations.[32] According to them, within the developing country block, China had become far more influential than India.[33] Traditionally, India's stance during climate change negotiations was driven by idealistic positions in international diplomacy. However, with ISA PM Modi wanted to shift this status quo and have India take a leadership position in climate diplomacy. According to one interviewee, 'the PM had a view that he wants to be a leader—with one-sixth of the world's population and a fragile ecology, he did not want India to appear unwilling [for climate action].'[34] As another interviewee puts it, 'India is not a pushover in climate change negotiations ... the PM wanted the image of India to change without compromising on our interests.'[35]

Almost all the interviewees attributed the initial idea for the alliance to PM Modi. Several interviewees noted that PM Modi was of the belief that if oil producing countries could have a resource-based alliance with the Organization of the Petroleum Exporting Countries (OPEC), then countries endowed with solar power could come together as 'solar rich' countries.[36] Leading up to the Paris climate talks, the Indian government solicited several big ideas from organizations working in the climate policy space, who suggested different templates for achieving solar energy-based cooperation.[37] Around the same time, internal research within different ministries led to the finding that solar energy is a central element in the Official Development Assistance (ODA) provided by India to African countries.[38] According to one of the interviewees, this

---

[32] Participant 22, interview with author, 25 Jul. 2018; Participant 5, interview with author, 26 Jul. 2018; Participant 16, interview with author, 17 Jul. 2018.

[33] Participant 13, interview with author, 17 Jul. 2018; Participant 17, interview with author, 6 Aug. 2018; Participant 16, interview with author, 17 Jul. 2018.

[34] Participant 17, interview with author, 6 Aug. 2018.

[35] Participant 5, n. 30.

[36] The Working Paper on ISA prepared by the Ministry of new and Renewable Energy for the Paris COP also captured this with a quote from PM Modi: 'There are several countries blessed with high solar radiation. We are making efforts to bring these countries together for enhanced solar energy utilization through research and technology upgradation. These countries have immense strength and capabilities to find solutions for their energy needs through solar energy.' See, ISA, n. 1, 7.

[37] In particular, the Council on Energy, Environment and Water (CEEW), the Centre for Policy Research (CPR), and the Centre for Science and Environment (CSE), and The Energy and Resources Institute (TERI).

[38] Participant 14, interview with author, 8 Aug. 2019. By 2016, in order to increase availability of investment for solar energy in prospective ISA member countries in Africa, India had earmarked 15–20 per cent of the US$10 billion line of credit for solar projects in next five years. See

was a key factor signalling that an alliance conceived around solar energy could stand a chance as a multilateral effort.[39]

India's leadership role in the creation and operationalization of the ISA was reinforced by its own solar energy ambitions. Domestically, the genesis of ISA lay in two key factors: First, the conceptual underpinning of Paris had changed the game—Nationally Determined Contributions (NDCs) made climate action voluntary and across the board. Second, a change in government in mid-2014 brought the issue of climate change to the fore, in a way previous governments had not. There was a holistic thinking of domestic programmes with climate change connotations—in which solar got the most resonance with ramped up targets.[40]

Interviewees across the government, industry, and academia believed that while ISA can be viewed as an image makeover for India during climate change negotiations, it was also the first time India realized the power of its own markets. The overwhelming view was that measurable benefits in the Indian markets could be extended to other developing country markets as well. There was a certain obviousness to the idea that there needs to be something around solar energy—an abundant resource in developing countries with tremendous potential to be harnessed for addressing concerns of energy access and low-carbon growth. Several interviewees attested to the fact that solar energy markets in India looked primed to achieve economies of scale and contribute to domestic goals of energy access, job creation, and increased incomes—and it was this template that PM Modi wanted to extend to countries that had a potential but not the means to harness solar energy. The then Environment Secretary recalls that the world business community had started seeing India's ambitious renewable energy programme as a major economic opportunity

---

also Power for All, 'Multi-billion dollar Africa-India partnership aims to eradicate electricity poverty', *Medium* (13 Jun. 2017), https://medium.com/energy-access-india/multi-billion-dol lar-afro-india-partnership-aims-to-eradicate-electricity-poverty-298ec3b95525, accessed 15 Dec. 2022.

[39] Participant 13, n. 33.
[40] Some domestic programmes with climate change connotations are Skill India Mission (to provide skill-based training to 400 million people), Make in India (to encourage greater manufacturing and investment in India), Swachch Bharat Abhiyan (also known as the Clean India Mission), Smart Cities Mission (an urban renewal program to develop 100 citizen-friendly and sustainable cities across India), National Solar Mission (an initiative to promote solar power).

that could transform the solar energy sector.[41] As one interviewee observed, 'it [ISA] was the first instance where the government has talked about looking at climate change as a business opportunity.'[42]

Moreover, with solar energy becoming significantly cheaper, it appeared ready to take centre stage in global conversations around transitioning to clean energy sources. Therefore, the ISA was conceived as a 'market-making' mechanism,[43] which could drive the flow of finance and technology into 'solar-rich' countries. The organization, to which 94 countries have signed up so far, will help aggregate different solar projects into larger tenders, allowing developers to benefit from economies of scale. It will also create an industry-funded insurance scheme to encourage banks to lend to what they might otherwise see as overly risky projects. Interestingly, even those sceptical about the future of ISA acknowledged that the reason for its creation lies in the enormous market potential of solar energy:

Flow of capital into renewable energy is being driven by economics—it is not happening because of a legal regime or global arrangements. The shift is taking place despite the fact that there is no solid international legal foundation. Solar (energy) is becoming much, much cheaper.[44]

Although PM Modi is credited with envisaging India as a leader on solar cooperation through the creation of ISA, it would be hard to ignore China's role in lowering the prices of solar energy around the world due to low-priced panel exports.[45] China's solar credentials with its massive domestic capacity additions and domination of solar supply chains could present a real challenge to India's efforts to use solar energy

---

[41] A. Lavasa, 'Reaching agreement in Paris: A negotiator's perspective', in N.K. Dubash, ed., *India in a warming world: Integrating climate change and development* (New Delhi: Oxford University Press, 2019), 169–86, 178.

[42] Participant 10, interview with author, 19 Jul. 2018; Participant 1, interview with author, 31 Jul. 2018. These interviewees cited the successful example of the government scheme for distributing LED bulbs: by increasing the target size of the LED bulb market, LED manufacturing in India got a huge boost, and in turn, the economies of scale increased affordability.

[43] ISA, n. 6.

[44] Participant 19, interview with author, 18 Jul. 2018.

[45] India is now producing the world's cheapest solar power: The costs of building large-scale solar installations in India fell by 27 per cent in 2018, year-on-year, thanks to a combination of low-priced panel imports from China, abundant land and cheap labour. See, IRENA, 'Renewable power generation costs in 2018', available at: https://www.irena.org/-/media/Files/IRENA/Agency/Publication/2019/May/IRENA_Renewable-Power-Generations-Costs-in-2018.pdf [update].

for geopolitical gains.[46] Therefore, it becomes important to address the fact that China is conspicuous by its absence from the ISA. China has participated in four out of the six ISC meetings, but it is yet to sign the Framework Agreement. From the Indian perspective, however, it can be argued that there is an effort to delink India's position from that of China's during climate change negotiations, and taking leadership on the ISA appears to be a concrete step in that direction.

The bilateral relationship between India and China has been 'an uneasy relationship', and is marked by growing frictions and an ever-increasing distrust between the two countries even as they continue their global ascent.[47] India and China found some real convergence of interests at the international level and coordinated their efforts in the past, particularly on issues such as climate change, trade negotiations, energy security, and the global financial crisis.[48] However, the tensions between the two countries are now visible in all aspects of their bilateral relationship, and the selective convergence on global issues has reached a dead end.[49] India's main security concern, according to the Indian policy elites, is an increasingly aggressive China whose ambitions could reshape the contours of the global balance of power with disastrous consequences for Indian interests.[50] In a recent survey, the majority of India's strategic community views China's assertiveness as the most significant external challenge.[51]

---

[46] S. Shidore & J.W. Busby, 'One more try: The International Solar Alliance and India's search for geopolitical influence', *Energy Strategy Reviews*, 26 (2019), 100385, 5.

[47] H.V. Pant, *Indian foreign policy* (Manchester: Manchester University Press, Manchester, 2016).

[48] Ibid., 38. Under the climate change regime, this convergence was reflected during the Copenhagen climate talks when China and India together blocked the adoption an international agreement. In the lead up to the Copenhagen talks, the US wanted developing countries such as India and China to agree to control the emissions being produced by their rapidly growing economies, setting time-bound targets to this effect. However, both countries argued that such binding targets would hurt their economic growth. Ultimately, India and China, joined by Brazil and South Africa, were successful in blocking a protocol that called for more ambitious climate targets and mandatory greenhouse gas cuts from both industrialized and major emerging economies.

[49] Ibid., 43–44.

[50] Ibid.

[51] D. Jaishankar, *Survey of India's strategic community* (New Delhi: Brookings India, Mar. 2019). The major security challenges identified with respect to China are: the boundary dispute and China's relations with Pakistan (including the China–Pakistan Economic Corridor), China's role in the Indian Ocean, Chinese investments in Sri Lanka and the Maldives.

China has realized that its energy interests lie in geopolitical relations and has been aggressively securing its energy requirements by buying foreign oil and gas fields.[52] Meanwhile, Indian concerns about China's rising influence across the globe stems from the perception that it is losing out to China in the energy race and with respect to international diplomacy in the energy realm.[53] Therefore, India's efforts to be a global solar institutional leader is different from the Chinese ambition—India hopes to leverage its own domestic experience to countries around the developing world.

The ISA is perceived as a collaborative effort that is inclusive of other developing countries. According to a former US climate change negotiator, 'India's tone with the ISA is much better than that of China, which is now left alone on climate action.'[54] Moreover, several interviewees involved in ISA's early negotiations, expressed their reservations about China's active involvement stating that it could either overpower or derail the agenda. As one interviewee remarked, '[given the politics] if China comes in, then our leadership is challenged.'[55] Therefore, the ISA in its final form renews India's clean energy credentials on an international stage and marks its commitment to the multilateral order. According to one interviewee,

It [ISA] was beneficial in two ways: first, it signaled that India was serious towards contributing to a successful Paris COP, and second, it was an instance of a strong developing country initiative.[56]

From a long-term perspective, the ISA successfully raised the profile of solar energy in the world energy mix and transformed India's image as 'climate change-sensitive'.[57] Ultimately, ISA embodies India's shifting strategy to change its perceived image of being a spoiler during climate change negotiations without compromising on its core interests. As one interviewee explains, 'For India, the ISA could be viewed as a culmination

---

[52] Pant, n. 47, 43–4.
[53] Ibid.
[54] Participant 3, interview with author, 30 Jul. 2019.
[55] Participant 22, n. 32.
[56] Participant 4, interview with author, 3 Aug. 2018.
[57] Participant 17, n. 33.

of three interests: the need to increase solar goals; the need to create a clean future at Paris COP; and the need to meet electricity demand that is yet to be created.'[58] To do so, it declared an ambitious domestic programme on solar energy, steered countries to forge a global alliance on solar energy cooperation, and charted a new leadership space in global energy governance.

Bringing Allies on Board and Building the Indo–French Partnership

The government's efforts to build this new alliance intensified in the months leading up to the Paris climate conference (Figure 3.1). In the words of one interviewee, 'Paris was an opportune moment for India to announce this [ISA] on the world stage.'[59] It was important for India to garner support from other countries since the credibility of the ISA could have been seriously diminished if it was perceived to be a single-country effort. As one interviewee noted, 'for an international organization to be credible, it has to be reflective of the interests of more than one or two countries.'[60] In mid-2015, Piyush Goyal—then India's energy minister—began holding meetings with local mission heads of eligible ISA countries, letting them know about India's plans to steer such an international organization. He held three interactions leading up to the Paris climate talks, and a fourth one in the months after.[61] Before the first meeting of the ISC, preliminary proposals on the ISA's activities and governance structure had been circulated to all prospective member countries.[62] According to several interviewees within the government, these informal discussions generated a fair amount of interest among developing countries around collaborations on solar energy. One interviewee, who was closely involved in the climate change negotiations, reported that India's domestic commitment to solar energy was crucial in providing other

---

[58] Participant 1, n. 42.

[59] Participant 21, interview with author, 26 Jul. 2018.

[60] Ibid.

[61] The meetings with Resident Diplomatic Missions in New Delhi were held on 30 Jul. 2015, 5 Nov. 2015, 24 Nov. 2015 and 6 Apr. 2016.

[62] ISA, n. 6, 1.

National-level efforts	*Bilateral/Multilateral efforts*
26 May 2014 Narendra Modi sworn in as Prime Minister of India	
20 June 2014 Inter-ministerial meeting where Prime Minister Modi suggest that India take steps for working together with groups of nations with high solar potential for mutual cooperation on solar energy policies. Mandate given to MNRE, in collaboration and consultation with MEA.	
14 May 2015 Minister Piyush Goyal green-flagged the location of ISA at the National Institute of Solar Energy, Gwalpahari, Gurgaon, India.	
	30 July 2015 Meeting between Minister Piyush Goyal and Resident Diplomatic Missions of eligible ISA countries in New Delhi, India, where a non-paper on ISA detailing its aims, objective, and programme of activities was presented.
	20 August 2015 Concept of ISA presented at the 2nd Summit of the Forum of India-Pacific Island Countries in order to apprise prospective member countries.
19 September 2015 PMO requests the Foreign Secretary to coordinate the launch of ISA in Paris.	
19 October 2015 Inter-ministerial meeting PMO, MEA, MNRE, and MoEFCC on ISA.	
	28–30 October 2015 Prime minister Modi invited African countries to support and join ISA at the 3rd India-Africa Summit.
	4 November 2015 Secretary, MNRE chaired a meeting with representatives from bilateral and multilateral agencies in New Delhi, India and appraised the about ISA.
	5 November 2015 Meeting between Minister Piyush Goyal, and Resident Diplomatic Missions of eligible ISA countries in New Delhi.
8 November 2015 Inter-ministerial meeting between PMO, MEA, MNRE, and MoEFCC on ISA.	
19 November 2015 Inter-ministerial meeting between PMO, MEA, MNRE, and MoEFCC to review the preparations for the launch of the ISA.	
	24 November 2015 Meeting between Minister Piyush Goyal and Resident Diplomatic Missions of eligible ISA countries in New Delhi.
30 November 2015 ISA Launch Event in Paris	
	6 April 2016 Meeting between Minister Piyush Goyal and Resident Diplomatic Missions of eligible ISA countries in New Delhi.

Figure 3.1 Pre-Paris Chronology of the ISA
Source: Author's own analysis

developing countries with the assurance to come on board the new alliance.[63] Even though the exact form of the ISA was undefined at that

---

[63] Participant 16, n. 32.

moment, India's domestic efforts signalled a level of seriousness about wanting to create a collaborative global platform for increasing the deployment of solar energy in member countries.

In addition to bringing interested countries on board, India also fostered a partnership with France to announce this new alliance. According to several interviewees within the government, this partnership emerged as a result of French outreach before the Paris COP. France was conducting extensive outreach with the Indian government prior to the Paris climate talks and it was immediately attracted to the ISA idea. By mid-2015, there were intensive negotiations at the Ambassadorial level between India and France.[64] One of the sticking points during these early talks was to bring the French on board the idea of developing ISA as a treaty-based international organization. There was a lot of back and forth between the Indian and French negotiators on the issue of treaty form—the Indians wanted clarity on the issue before the Paris COP, while the French were keen on keeping it as an informal alliance without legal character. The French were primarily interested in convincing India to sign the Paris Agreement, whereas India wanted an assurance that the ISA could become a treaty-based international organization in the future. As one interviewee noted, 'the brief from the PMO was clear that we're in the game [to sign onto a Paris Agreement] if we get a treaty-based organization ... we had the clarity that it [ISA] could turn into something bigger.'[65]

Interestingly, the French solar industry was one of the main stakeholders driving the process in France. Solairedirect, a French renewable energy company, was the main producer of solar power in France and has international operations in the US, Chile, India, and South Africa. In July 2015, Engie, the French utility company, acquired Solairedirect for 200 million Euros in a bid to double renewable power capacity in Europe and expand in high-growth countries such as India and Chile.[66] Representatives from Engie had met with officials at the Indian Embassy even before the French government got involved with the ISA.[67] They

---

[64] Participant 8, interview with author, 9 Aug. 2020.

[65] Ibid.

[66] T. Patel & S. Nicola, 'Engie buys Solairedirect for $222 million in renewables push', *Bloomberg* (1 Jul. 2015), https://www.bloomberg.com/news/articles/2015-07-01/engie-buys-solairedirect-for-222-million-in-renewables-push, accessed on 15 Dec. 2022.

[67] Participant 8, n. 64.

acted as interlocutors between the two governments, and were at the fore-front of efforts to make solar energy more affordable around the world. They played a crucial role in bringing the two governments together and converge on the idea of ISA.[68]

The insistence on the part of the Indians for a treaty-based inter-national organization was reinforced by three factors: first, the French in-dustry was very interested in the idea of ISA; second, membership based on the tropics would initially bring 120 countries into the fold of the new international organization; and third, France could have leverage with the francophone countries to help bring them on board to sign the treaty.[69] Moreover, from the Indian government's perspective, support from a P5[70] country could prove to be 'a big advantage' in furthering India's ef-forts at building a new international organization.[71] As the host country, France's decision to work with India to organize the launch event could set the stage for a successful COP. Even though the French remained sceptical about the future of ISA as a treaty-based international organ-ization, they eventually agreed with the idea in principle and a middle ground was reached between the two sides by terming it an 'alliance'.[72] As one interviewee put it:

> The French viewed it as a win-win where launching the ISA along with India—one of the major players during the climate talks—could either be a considered a minor success if the main negotiations [on the Paris Agreement] were to fail, or a major one for setting a positive tone for a successful agreement at Paris.[73]

The partnership with France can be better understood against the back-drop of the increased defence and security relationship between the two countries. India's relationship with France goes back over three decades and is best described as a 'bilateral security partnership' for furthering

---

[68] Participant 9, interview with author, 14 Sep. 2020.
[69] Participant 8, n. 64.
[70] P5 refers to the Permanent Members of the United Nations Security Council, i.e. China, France, Russia, the United Kingdom, and the United States of America.
[71] Participant 10, n. 42.
[72] Participant 8, n. 64.
[73] Interview with Participant 21, n. 59.

its strategic interests in the Indo-Pacific region.[74] The Modi government brought a renewed push into the Indo-Pacific, which further strengthened the bilateral and trilateral cooperation with France.[75] The latest efforts include setting up a new bilateral dialogue on East Asia and agreeing on a Reciprocal Logistics Support agreement that would enable mutual use of each other's military facilities in the Indo-Pacific.[76] According to another interviewee, France's interest in partnering on the ISA could also be viewed from a defence perspective. The French government was keen on the completion of the multi-billion-dollar defence deal for the sale of Rafale fighter aircrafts to the Government of India. The ongoing diplomatic process played a big part in bringing France on board as partners for the ISA, as according to this interviewee, 'France's only concern (at the time) was the Rafale deal and they would've agreed to anything as long as it got them that (Rafale) deal.'[77] In addition, the public opinion around nuclear energy in France had shifted post-Fukushima and their move towards strengthening ties on the basis of solar energy cooperation marked a clear shift in the Indian bilateral relations.[78] According to one of the diplomats, 'the important pillars of India's relationship with France has been a troika—defense, nuclear and space—and with the ISA, solar has become the fourth pillar of that relationship.'[79]

Once the decision to announce the ISA during the Paris climate talks was on track, the MEA (India's foreign ministry) did the legwork of organizing the launch event. This included major diplomatic efforts and outreach activities to bring other countries on board. Invitation letters were jointly sent from PM Modi and French President Francois Hollande. The launch was a high-profile event attended by more than 70 countries, including 33 heads of state and prominent figures such as the UN Secretary General, Ban Ki-moon, and US Secretary of State, John Kerry.[80] Maintaining the momentum of the successful launch, the first

[74] D. Scott, 'India and the Indo-Pacific discourse', in H.V. Pant, ed., *New directions in India's foreign policy: Theory and praxis* (Cambridge: Cambridge University Press, 2019), 195–214, 196. Other countries that India has shaped key strategic partnerships with in the Indo-Pacific region are Singapore, Indonesia, Vietnam, Australia, Japan, and the United States.

[75] Ibid., 202.

[76] Ibid.

[77] Participant 7, interview with author, 27 Jul. 2018.

[78] Participant 8, n. 64.

[79] Ibid.

[80] ISA, n. 6, 1.

meeting of the ISC was held the very next day and attended by representatives from 21 prospective ISA member countries. Although France was the co-sponsor of the ISA, its administrative role beyond the launch event was nominal. The operational responsibilities were mainly carried out by the Indian government.[81] This division in labour between the two governments was evident during subsequent ISC meetings in which the Indian Co-Chair led the meetings, expressing 'deep gratitude' to France for its continued cooperation and support,[82] while the French Co-Chair stressed the importance of the ISA for the implementation of the Paris Agreement.[83] France's financial contributions to the ISA, however, have come at regular intervals and mark their deep commitment to the institution. The French Development Agency announced contributions in support of the ISA's mission: 300 million Euros in 2015[84], 700 million Euros in 2018[85], and 500 million Euros in March 2019.[86]

---

[81] Participant 16, n. 32: 'The French counterparts were involved but were not a part of the decision-making. As co-sponsors they lent support and were a part of the discussions, but all the agenda-setting, meetings etc. were orchestrated by the Government [of India], primarily the Prime Minister's Office'.

[82] See, remarks of the Chair during the various meetings of the ISC: ISA, 'Report of the second meeting of the International Steering Committee', *Steering Committees* (Abu Dhabi, 18 Jan. 2016), https://isolaralliance.org/about/steering-committees, accessed 15 Dec. 2022: 'thanked the Government of France for their continued support and cooperation'; ISA, 'Report of the third meeting of the International Steering Committee', *Steering Committees* (New York, 21 Apr. 2016), https://isolaralliance.org/about/steering-committees, accessed 15 Dec. 2022: 'expressed its deep appreciation of France's support and collaboration in developing the initial ideas for ISA programmes'; ISA, 'Report of the fifth meeting of the International Steering Committee', *Steering Committees* (New Delhi, 27 Sep. 2017), https://isolaralliance.org/about/steering-com mittees, accessed 15 Dec. 2022: 'thanked France for their continuous engagement in structuring the ISA process'; ISA, 'Report of the sixth meeting of the International Steering Committee', *Steering Committees* (New Delhi, 20 Feb. 2018), https://isolaralliance.org/about/steering-com mittees, accessed 15 Dec. 2022: 'put on record his deep appreciation to Government of France for continued and profound support in shaping ISA vision'.

[83] ISA, *Second ISC meeting*, n. 82, 4. See also ISA, *Third ISC meeting*, n. 82: The French Co-Chair noted that the Alliance should be the driver of the 'change of scale' which is indispensable for deploying solar energy in line with needs and with the effective implementation of the Paris Agreement on Climate Change. See also ISA, *Fifth ISC meeting*, n. 82: The French Co-chair praised the leadership of India, and stated that 'the ISA is one of the most important initiatives and a central piece for the implementation of the Paris Climate Agreement'.

[84] Express News Service, 'India, France warm up to solar alliance', *The Indian Express* (26 Jan. 2016), https://indianexpress.com/article/india/india-news-india/india-france-warm-up-to-solar-alliance/, accessed on 15 Dec. 2022

[85] Times News Network, 'Macron announces extra €700m for green energy, hails 'solar mamas'', *The Economic Times* (12 Mar. 2018), https://energy.economictimes.indiatimes.com/news/renewable/macron-announces-extra-700m-for-green-energy-hails-solar-mamas/63262 680, accessed on 15 Dec. 2022

[86] IANS, 'France pledges 500 million Euros more to ISA', *Business Standard* (14 Mar. 2019), https://www.business-standard.com/article/news-ians/france-pledges-500-million-euros-more-to-isa-119031401268_1.html, accessed on 15 Dec. 2022

Post-Paris: Period of Operationalization

Once an idea is launched, the skeleton needs to be worked out.[87]

It was following the widely positive reception to the launch that India decided to up the ante on operationalizing the newly announced alliance as an international organization. According to a senior diplomat, the 'persuasion came after Paris.'[88] It was only after the Paris climate talks that India argued for the ISA to become a treaty-based international organization, and the MEA was tasked with figuring out the nuts and bolts of setting up a new international organization. Meanwhile, the MNRE was responsible for the day-to-day operationalization of the ISA (Figure 3.2).

The location of the ISA appears to have been uncontested, largely because India engineered the process of situating the headquarters in Gwal Pahari before the launch event in Paris.[89] The government had set aside land and money for the operations of ISA.[90] The formal offer to host the ISA's secretariat came from the Government of India in the first meeting of the ISC, whereby it was suggested that an initial cell would be set up in the MNRE to coordinate ISA's activities and programmes until the Founding Conference.[91] In January 2016, following the launch event in Paris, President Hollande was also invited as a guest at India's Republic Day parade—a trip that coincided with the foundation stone of the headquarters being laid down.

In terms of ISA's operations and scope of work, two key decisions to emerge from the first ISC meeting were that the ISA would position itself as 'a credible organization with no duplication of work'[92], and that it

---

[87] Participant 10, n. 42.

[88] Participant 17, n. 34.

[89] The Government of India had green-flagged the location of ISA at the National Institute of Solar Energy (NISE) in Gwal Pahari as early as 14 May 2015. On 22 Dec. 2015, weeks after the Paris COP, the Cabinet approved the establishment of ISA headquarters in India.

[90] PIB, *International Solar Alliance will be the first international and inter-governmental organisation of 121 countries to have headquarters in India with United Nations as Strategic Partner* [media release] (25 Jan. 2016), https://pib.gov.in/newsite/printrelease.aspx?relid=135794, accessed 15 Dec. 2022.

[91] ISA, n. 6, 1.

[92] Several countries such as Australia, Chile, France, Ethiopia, Netherlands and the UAE called for the ISA to undertake tangible, action-oriented projects and avoid duplication of efforts with other organizations working in the renewable energy sector. See ISA, n. 6, 2–4.

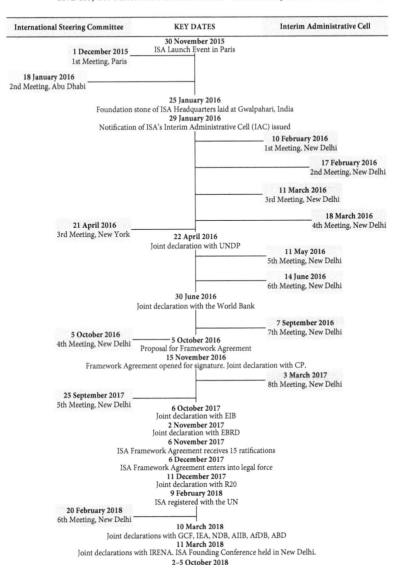

International Steering Committee	KEY DATES	Interim Administrative Cell
	30 November 2015 ISA Launch Event in Paris	
1 December 2015 1st Meeting, Paris		
18 January 2016 2nd Meeting, Abu Dhabi		
	25 January 2016 Foundation stone of ISA Headquarters laid at Gwalpahari, India **29 January 2016** Notification of ISA's Interim Administrative Cell (IAC) issued	
		10 February 2016 1st Meeting, New Delhi
		17 February 2016 2nd Meeting, New Delhi
		11 March 2016 3rd Meeting, New Delhi
		18 March 2016 4th Meeting, New Delhi
21 April 2016 3rd Meeting, New York	**22 April 2016** Joint declaration with UNDP	
		11 May 2016 5th Meeting, New Delhi
		14 June 2016 6th Meeting, New Delhi
	30 June 2016 Joint declaration with the World Bank	
		7 September 2016 7th Meeting, New Delhi
5 October 2016 4th Meeting, New Delhi	**5 October 2016** Proposal for Framework Agreement **15 November 2016** Framework Agreement opened for signature. Joint declaration with CP.	
		3 March 2017 8th Meeting, New Delhi
25 September 2017 5th Meeting, New Delhi		
	6 October 2017 Joint declaration with EIB **2 November 2017** Joint declaration with EBRD **6 November 2017** ISA Framework Agreement receives 15 ratifications **6 December 2017** ISA Framework Agreement enters into legal force **11 December 2017** Joint declaration with R20 **9 February 2018** ISA registered with the UN	
20 February 2018 6th Meeting, New Delhi		
	10 March 2018 Joint declarations with GCF, IEA, NDB, AIIB, AfDB, ABD **11 March 2018** Joint declarations with IRENA. ISA Founding Conference held in New Delhi. **2–5 October 2018** First Assembly of the ISA	

Figure 3.2   Post-Paris Chronology of the ISA

Source: Author's own analysis

would plan to 'suitably accommodate corporate sector and non-Member countries.'[93]

Avoiding Duplication

According to the interviewees within the foreign ministry, the most important consideration in setting up a new international organization was ensuring cooperation from other countries and avoiding duplication of existing institutions. First, it was important for India to garner support from other countries since the credibility of ISA could have been seriously diminished if it was perceived to be a single-country effort. As one interview noted, 'for an international organization to be credible, it has to be reflective of the interests of more than one or two countries.'[94] Therefore, the ISA gained momentum as a multi-country idea with India stepping up its efforts to pursue a multilateral route and bringing interested countries together. Second, there was a clear need to demonstrate that there would be no parallels or competing interests with other organizations. For instance, the French were initially hesitant about the ISA being registered as a treaty-based organization since they believed that it would duplicate the mandate of the International Renewable Energy Agency (IRENA) and that there was no need for a new organization working on renewable energy. As one interviewee recalled, 'France had helped in the creation of the IRENA, which could explain their initial reluctance about the ISA being a treaty-based organization.'[95]

Establishing and maintaining an identity outside the UNFCCC process was crucial for the ISA, as was differentiation from other similarly situated organizations in the clean energy landscape, particularly IRENA and the International Energy Agency (IEA). While there has been little systematic comparison of IRENA, the IEA, or other international energy organizations, several scholars have noted that the IEA responded negatively to IRENA's creation as the IEA itself was keen to capitalize

---

[93] Many countries, such as Australia, France, Maldives, and the Netherlands, emphasized the need to leverage and promote private sector participation. See ISA, n. 6.

[94] Participant 21, n. 56.

[95] Participant 8, n. 61.

on the growing global interest in renewables.[96] Therefore, the ISA made conscious efforts to differentiate itself from these two organizations by focusing squarely on solar energy and emphasizing its action-oriented profile. This is a particularly important distinction from IRENA, which has a research-oriented profile and produces statistics on the state of renewable energy around the world. According to an interviewee closely involved in the early ISA negotiations, assuring both of these organizations that ISA did not overlap with their objectives was a strategic manoeuvre.[97]

India's diplomatic efforts included outreach to representatives of both IRENA and the IEA in order to keep them abreast of ISA developments. Their support was crucial to kick-start ISA's activities and is evidenced by their participation as observers in the very first ISC meeting.[98] The ISA maintains a clear stance that it will not duplicate or replicate the efforts of other organizations,[99] but will instead establish networks and develop synergies with them and supplement their efforts in a sustainable and focused manner.[100] For instance, India has continued to engage with the IRENA over the years, including as a member of the IRENA Council. In April 2015, India was designated to chair the 9th Meeting of the IRENA Council,[101] which is accountable to the assembly and facilitates consultations and cooperation among Members and considers the draft work programme, draft budget and annual report. IRENA has also been closely involved with the MNRE in providing policy guidance for scaling up India's renewable energy targets to 175 GW.[102]

---

[96] Overland & G. Reischl, 'A place in the sun? IRENA's position in the global energy governance landscape', *International Environmental Agreements*, 18 (2018), 335–50; J. Urpelainen & T. Van de Graaf, 'The International Renewable Energy Agency: a success story in institutional innovation?', *International Environmental Agreements: Politics, Law and Economics*, 15/2 (2015), 159–77.

[97] Participant 21, n. 59.

[98] ISA, n. 6, 5.

[99] Particularly institutions working in the renewable energy sector, such as IEA, IRENA, Renewable Energy and Energy Efficiency Partnership (REEEP), Renewable Energy Policy Network for the 21st Century (REN21), United Nations bodies, bilateral organizations etc.

[100] ISA, *Background*, https://isolaralliance.org/about/background, accessed 15 Dec. 2022.

[101] PIB, *India designated as chair to the ninth meeting of the International Renewable Energy Agency (IRENA)* [media release] (10 Apr. 2015), https://pib.gov.in/newsite/PrintRelease.aspx?relid=118146, accessed on 15 Dec. 2022. India subsequently chaired the 10th Meeting (23–24 Nov. 2015) and 11th Meeting (24–25 May 2016) of the IRENA Council.

[102] MNRE (Government of India), 'Annual Report 2016–17', https://mnre.gov.in/img/documents/uploads/file_f-1608050046985.pdf, accessed 15 Dec. 2022

Participation by Non-State Actors

The ambitions of the International Solar Alliance seem perfectly achievable and respond to a strong expectation from the market. Indeed, resources from solar are well-known, technology is available, capital is abundant. Everything is ready to make this momentum concrete, as soon as the regulatory framework is there. What we need is a solar common market. The private sector is willing, with great impatience, to enter now at full speed into the energy transition and design economic strategies to bring large scale solutions to the world, be it technology providers, financiers or energy companies like ENGIE.[103]

Early on, starting from the first ISC meeting, the French Co-Chair stressed that countries should start work on a collaborative framework within the ISA, along with the private sector, which would lead to 'delivering solutions, accelerating action'.[104] The Terrawatt Initiative (TWI), was launched by Gérard Mestrallet, Chairman and CEO of ENGIE, in parallel with the ISA in Paris on 30 November 2015. TWI was incorporated as a non-profit organization to continue and strengthen a multi-stakeholder cooperation on delivering very low-cost solar power, and to support the International Solar Alliance.[105] TWI's mission is to work together with ISA and its member states in establishing the proper regulatory conditions for a massive deployment of competitive solar generation.[106] TWI supported the creation of the ISA on the initiative of the Indian and French governments, and until the ISA became fully operational in 2018, TWI provided regular ideas and knowledge to help the Indo-French leadership.[107]

---

[103] Statement by Gérard Mestrallet, Chairman and CEO of ENGIE. See, Engie, *Launch of the Terrawatt Initiative aimed at meeting the International Solar Alliance's objective of 1TW of additional solar capacity by 2030* [media release] (1 Dec. 2015), https://www.engie.com/en/journali sts/press-releases/terrawatt-initiative-international-solar-alliances-objective-2030, accessed 15 Dec. 2022.

[104] ISA, n. 6, 2.

[105] A. Legrain & J. Pham-Ba, *Well below two cents* (Paris: Terrawatt Initiative, 2020), 6.

[106] Engie, n. 103.

[107] Legrain & Pham-Ba, n. 105, 23.

Figure 3.3 ISC Meeting-Wise Participant Data
Source: Author's own analysis

A close look at the participant data from the meetings of the ISC (Figure 3.3) and IAC (Figure 3.4) also reveals that non-state actors and private-sector entities were a part of the deliberations about ISA from

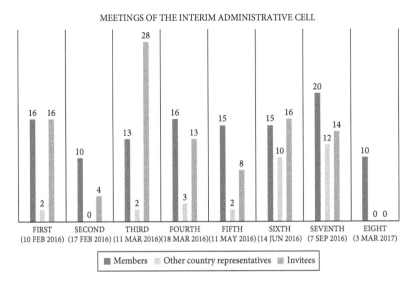

Figure 3.4 IAC Meeting-Wise Participant Data
Source: Author's own analysis

the onset. In the course of its operationalization, ISA partnered with several organizations that could help ISA achieve its objectives.[108] So far, the ISA has 31 Partner Organizations (Table 3.2) and 17 Corporate Partners (Table 3.3), which include several non-state actors such as multilateral and regional developments banks, intergovernmental organizations, financial institutions, and private actors.[109]

The main objective of the IAC meetings was to 'quick-start ISA activities'.[110] In order to facilitate investment for the solar energy projects and programmes in prospective ISA member countries, the IAC established early contacts with non-state actors and private sector entities, such as the New Development Bank, Soft Bank, and ENGIE.[111] The second ISC meeting featured presentations by the UN, the World Bank, Exim Bank of India, New Development Bank, YES Bank, SoftBank and the Asian and Pacific Centre for Transfer of Technology (APCTT)[112] on different aspects of cooperation for achieving ISA objectives.[113] By the third ISC meeting, four months after the launch event, the ISA had laid the foundation stone of the ISA Headquarters and entered into engagement with professional bodies, think tanks, and the corporate sector for developing its programme of activities.[114]

In May 2017, the governments of 18 ISA member states commissioned an international task force to structure a common mechanism aimed at de-risking investments in solar. The task force consisted of the Council on Energy, Environment and Water (CEEW)[115], the Currency Exchange

---

[108]   Article VIII, Framework Agreement.

[109]   ISA, 'Partner Organizations', *Partners and Collaborations*, https://isolaralliance.org/partners/organisations, accessed 15 Dec. 2022.

[110]   ISA, 'Report of the third meeting of the Interim Administrative Cell of the International Solar Alliance', *Steering Committees* (New Delhi, 11 Mar. 2016), https://isolaralliance.org/about/steering-committees, accessed 15 Dec. 2022.

[111]   ENGIE is a French multinational electric utility company, which operates in the fields of energy transition, electricity generation and distribution, natural gas, nuclear, renewable energy and petroleum.

[112]   APCTT is a Regional Institute of the United Nations Economic and Social Commission for Asia and the Pacific (UNESCAP) with a geographic focus of the entire Asia-Pacific region. The mandate of APCTT is to assist the members and associate members of UNESCAP through strengthening their capabilities to develop and manage national innovation systems; develop, transfer, adapt, and apply technology; improve the terms of transfer of technology; and identify and promote the development and transfer of technologies relevant to the region.

[113]   ISA, *Second ISC meeting*, n. 82, 2–3.

[114]   ISA, *Third ISC meeting*, n. 82, 1.

[115]   CEEW is an India-based not-for-profit policy research institution.

Table 3.2 ISA's Partner Organizations

Technical Expertise	Financing Capacity	Bilateral & Multilateral Initiatives	Global Networks & Associations
• International Energy Agency (IEA) • International Renewable Energy Agency (IRENA) • United Nations Convention to Combat Desertification (UNCCD) • United Nations Development Programme (UNDP) • United Nations Economic and Social Commission for Asia and the Pacific (UNESCAP) • United Nations Environment Programme (UNEP) • United Nations Industrial Development Organization (UNIDO) • World Resources Institute (WRI)	• African Development Bank (AfDB) • Asian Development Bank (ADB) • Asian Infrastructure Investment Bank (AIIB) • CAF Development Bank of Latin America • Department for International Development (DFID) • European Bank for Reconstruction and Development (EBRD) • European Investment Bank (EIB) • Green Climate Fund (GCF) • New Development Bank • World Bank	• Commonwealth Secretariat • European Union • Sustainable Energy for All (SE4ALL) • East African Centre for Excellence for Renewable Energy and Efficiency (EACREEE) • ECOWAS Centre for Renewable Energy and Energy Efficiency (ECREEE) • Global Green Growth Institute (GGGI) • Indian Ocean Rim Association (IORA) • Scheinder Electric Foundation	• Climate Parliament • Global Off-Grid Lighting Association (GOGLA) • Global Solar Council • R20—Regions of Climate Action • World Association of Investment Promotion Agencies (WAIPA)

Source: Author's own analysis

Table 3.3 ISA's Corporate Partners

Conventional Energy	Non-conventional Energy	Financial Institution	Foreign Investor
• Bharat Petroleum Corporation Limited (BPCL) • Coal India Limited • Hindustan Petroleum Corporation Limited (HPCL) • Neyveli Lignite Corporation Limited • NTPC Limited • Powergrid Corporation of India	• Gas Authority of India Limited (GAIL) • Indian Renewable Energy Development Agency (IREDA) • National Hydroelectric Power Corporation • Satluj Jal Vidyut Nigam Limited • Solar Energy Corporation of India (SECI)	• India Trade Promotion Organisation (ITPO) • Power Finance Corporation (PFC) • Rural Electrification Corporation (REC) • State Bank of India (SBI)	• China Light and Power Company Limited (CLP) • SoftBank

Source: Author's own analysis

Fund (TCX)[116], the Terrawatt Initiative (TWI)[117], and the Confederation of Indian Industry (CII).[118] At the fourth ISC meeting, an international expert group with representatives from the World Bank, TWI, CEEW, CII, and the TCX led deliberations on a future roadmap for an instrument for de-risking and reducing the financial cost of solar projects in the ISA member countries.[119] They designed an innovative instrument to address uncertainties in solar financing in ISA countries: the Common Risk Mitigation Mechanism (CRMM). Their report was published on the sidelines of the UN climate talks in Bonn in 2017, and was later selected as one of 30 projects, from more than 240, by the Green Climate Fund in 2018.[120] By 2019, the CRMM was officially taken over

[116] TCX is designed to mitigate currency and interest rate risks in order to attract and lock in long-term private equity and private debt in local currency. Through these risk mitigation instruments, the TCX intends to enable and scale climate change mitigation investments.

[117] TWI is a global non-profit organization designed to work together with ISA and its member states in establishing the proper regulatory conditions for a massive deployment of competitive solar generation.

[118] CII is an industry association in India.

[119] ISA, *Fifth ISC meeting*, n. 82, 11.

[120] Legrain & Pham-Ba, n. 105, 24.

by the World Bank to mobilize US$500 million of concessional finance to unlock the potential of renewables in developing countries by 2025. The Solar Risk Mitigation Initiative led by the World Bank Energy Sector Management Assistance Program, in partnership with Agence Française de Développement, IRENA, and ISA, aims to support countries in developing sustainable solar programmes that will attract private investments and so reduce reliance on public finances.[121]

TWI was a key private player at this stage of the negotiations and brought to the table a demonstration for countries that solar could be affordable with common rules, common practices, and common markets, and that all three forces together would bring prices down. In the words of Upendra Tripathy, the first Director General of the ISA, 'the early history of the Alliance is closely linked to that of Terrawatt Initiative.'[122] Following the Paris COP, TWI also worked closely with the International Solar Alliance to ensure the success of the Paris Declaration. It advised the ISA leadership to adopt concrete work programmes to bring together stakeholders, governments, businesses, and investors around specific projects. On 22 April 2016 in New York City, the second ISC meeting adopted two work programmes which shaped the initial ISA roadmap: Scaling Solar Applications for Agricultural Use, and Affordable Finance at Scale. TWI was involved in the drafting the Affordable Finance at Scale programme.[123] TWI, along with CEEW, said that the ISA needed to be attractive by bringing people around concrete ideas. The first effort on the Programme for Affordable Finance in April 2016.[124]

The work programmes under the ISA, such as scaling solar applications for agricultural use, have been designed to transplant the Indian experience of lowering costs by offering a large aggregated market to manufacturers. For instance, following the success of solar-based irrigation in India, the ISA intends to aggregate demand for solar pumps in

---

[121] World Bank, *Solar risk mitigation initiative*, https://www.worldbank.org/en/topic/energy/brief/srmi, accessed 15 Dec. 2022.
[122] Legrain & Pham-Ba, n. 105, 191. The TWI came to a close in June 2020, with the publication of its seminal report titled 'Well below two cents'.
[123] Ibid., 138.
[124] Participant 9, n. 68.

member countries in order to yield significant cost benefits to the end users.[125]

Before entering into legal force on 6 December 2017, ISA had already launched three work programmes in consultation with member countries and partner organizations.[126] By the time the ISA held its Founding Conference in March 2018, it had introduced a total of five work programmes.[127] As an interviewee noted: 'There was work going on without any formal legal structure. Different stages of work were being presented at the International Steering Committee meetings. All this demonstrates a gradual building of trust and overcoming initial skepticism around [the ISA].'[128]

ISA's efforts to engage and work with a multitude of non-states actors are captured in the statement of the Director General, wherein he states that '[w]ith this multidimensional approach, ISA becomes an enabler for the deployment of appropriate benchmarks, facilitator of resources and their assessments, supporter of research and development in solar sector, eventually playing a vital role in encouraging innovative and affordable applications of solar technologies world over.'[129] The ISA's joint collaborations with Partner Organizations are with a view to leverage their technical and financial expertise, as well as tap into the wide global networks and associations, for achieving its long-term objectives of bringing solar power to the developing world.

According to an interviewee, unless a government's underlying policy framework supports renewable energy deployment, there are limits on what corporations and the private sector can contribute.[130] In that

[125] K. Chawla, 'The International Solar Alliance: From promise to action', *India Global Business*, 15 Nov. 2018, https://www.indiaglobalbusiness.com/igb-archive/the-international-solar-alliance-from-promise-to-action-india-global-business, accessed 15 Dec. 2022.

[126] Two programmes, 'Scaling solar applications for agricultural use' and 'Affordable finance at scale', were launched on 22 Apr. 2016 on the margins of the signing of the Paris Agreement in the United Nations in New York. A third programme, 'Scaling solar mini grids', was launched on the 52nd Annual Meeting of the African Development Bank Group on 24 May 2017 in Gandhinagar, Gujarat (India).

[127] The fourth and fifth work programmes, 'Scaling Rooftop solar' and 'Scaling solar e-mobility and storage', were launched on the sidelines of the ISA Founding Conference in March 2018.

[128] Participant 4, n. 56.

[129] M. Oza, 'Interview with Upendra Tripathy, Director General, International Solar Alliance', *Energetica India* (1 Apr. 2019), https://www.energetica-india.net/powerful-thoughts/online/upendra-tripathy, accessed 15 Dec. 2022.

[130] Participant 11, interview with author, 29 Jul. 2019.

regard, India's renewable energy ambitions and accompanying leadership on ISA was an attractive proposition for investors in the solar energy sector. Foreign investors, such as the Japanese multinational conglomerate, SoftBank Group, became closely involved in ISA's activities. SB Energy,[131] has been extremely bullish on India's solar potential with plans to invest $60–100 billion towards solar power generation.[132] Masayoshi Son's enthusiastic support for the ISA was evident when he promised to supply free electricity to ISA member-countries, including India, once SB Energy's power purchase agreements come to an end. He said:

I chose India as the big first country that I would like to support because India has great sunshine, a big wasteland and also supportive government …it is important to have no dependency of energy source. To serve over a billion people, you have to have security and independence of the energy source by itself.[133]

On 6 March 2018, the ISA constituted a Global Leadership Task Force of Corporates on Innovation, to put forth recommendations to promote innovation in the areas of solar finance, solar technologies, solar applications, R&D and capacity building. Members of this task force include GE (United States), Total SE (France), LG Chem (South Korea), GCL-Poly (China), SMA Solar Technology (Germany), and State Bank of India (India).[134] The Chair of the Task Force and chief executive of Softbank, Masayoshi Son said, '[the Task Force] will be a key driver initiating large scale solar transformation in all member countries … [the] aim is to expand the footprint of ISA to include many more corporates, and to facilitate this transformative action globally.'[135]

---

[131] SB Energy, a subsidiary of the SoftBank Group in India for building solar power projects.

[132] S. Jai, 'CEO Masayoshi Son offers free power from Softbank's solar plants in India', *Business Standard* (4 Oct. 2018), https://www.business-standard.com/article/companies/ceo-masayoshi-son-offers-free-power-from-softbank-s-solar-plants-in-india-118100400071_1.html, accessed 15 Dec. 2022.

[133] R. Laha, 'SoftBank chief Masayoshi Son to offer free solar power to India', *Fortune India* (4 Oct. 2018), https://www.fortuneindia.com/macro/softbank-chief-masayoshi-son-to-offer-free-solar-power-to-india/102542, accessed 15 Dec. 2022.

[134] FICCI, *ISA constituted Global Leadership Task Force of Corporates on Innovation meets in Delhi* [media release] (29 Apr. 2018), http://www.ficci.in/pressrelease-page.asp?nid=3101, accessed 15 Dec. 2022.

[135] Ibid.

Universalizing Membership

The initial membership of ISA was limited to countries lying between the two tropics—Tropic of Cancer and Tropic of Capricorn. The logic behind this was that countries between the tropics received maximum sunshine and had the best potential to harness solar energy. This classification meant that countries such as Germany—a world leader in renewable energy—was left out of the list of potential members. According to an interviewee, 'the Germans were clearly unhappy at being left out [of the ISA], especially since they have been the leader on renewables in Europe.'[136]

However, another interviewee noted that, 'the purpose of the tropics was not to exclude but to draw attention—almost shine a light—on where the potential for maximum deployment was based on solar radiation. This means that a country like Germany would not benefit from the ISA bringing solar technologies to the country, but rather their investors or companies could profit by taking these technologies to underserved markets with a high potential for solar deployment, such as those in Africa.'[137] The next section discusses how the interests of the private sector and non-state actors were woven into the ISA's legal form, so that their expertise could help drive the goals of the ISA.

Over the months, the initial eligibility criteria was softened and several western countries qualified to attend ISA meetings as prospective members by virtue of their island territories that fell within the two tropics.[138] In the final ISC meeting, a number of countries that do not lie between the tropics, namely Nepal, Germany, Republic of Korea, Tunisia, and Italy, had expressed their interest for becoming a fully fledged member country of ISA.[139] Based on this it was decided that the membership could be opened to all countries that are UN members, which will make ISA a global initiative.[140]

At the first assembly, India made a proposal for an amendment to the Framework Agreement to expand the scope of membership of the ISA

[136] Participant 28, interview with author, 12 Dec. 2016.
[137] Participant 4, n. 56.
[138] For example, the United States, the United Kingdom, France, the Kingdom of Netherlands.
[139] ISA, *Sixth ISC meeting*, n. 82, 7.
[140] Ibid.

to all countries that are members of United Nations. The first general assembly of the ISA, held on 3 October 2018, adopted the amendment of the Framework Agreement on the establishment of the International Solar Alliance, to expand the scope of Membership of the ISA to all Member States of the United Nations. After the necessary ratifications/ approvals/ acceptances were obtained from the requisite number of ISA Member countries as mandated by the Framework Agreement of the ISA, the said amendment has entered into force on 15 July 2020. The coming into force of the amendment of the ISA Framework Agreement will now allow all the Member States of the United Nations to join the International Solar Alliance, including those beyond the tropics.[141]

Legal Form

Issues of legal form emerged only in the months after the Paris climate talks and were critical to the future of the ISA as a long-term institution. Following the positive response of developing countries at the ISA's launch event, PM Modi insisted on the ISA acquiring legal form so that it would be 'difficult to wipe away the success'.[142] Although creating a treaty-based organization required a more tortuous process, the decision to take this route was cemented by the Indian government's view that this legal form would ensure a long-term commitment by sovereign governments. Moreover, the threshold for treaty ratification was kept very low—15 countries—and several interviewees within the foreign ministry believed that this would be a very realistic goal. Another crucial determinant for the ISA's legal form appears to be the fact that IRENA is also a treaty-based organization.

The decision on treaty form and the drafting of the treaty text were marked by difficult diplomatic negotiations within the ISC and IAC. An early draft of the Framework Agreement of the ISA was circulated at the first ISC meeting in December 2015 and placed before the IAC for input

[141] MEA (Government of India), *Universalization of the membership of the International Solar Alliance (ISA)* [media release] (31 Jul. 2020), https://www.mea.gov.in/press-releases.htm?dtl/32866/Universalization_of_the_Membership_of_the_International_Solar_Alliance_ISA, accessed 15 Dec. 2022.

[142] Participant 5, n. 32.

from prospective ISA member countries.[143] In March 2016, by the fourth IAC meeting, Piyush Goyal, India's energy minister, urged members to 'speed up the activities' in order to 'develop the shape and form of ISA in a legally established manner'.[144] Minister Goyal also held consultative discussions with resident diplomatic missions of 73 prospective ISA member countries in New Delhi on 6 April 2016, in which he sought further input on the Framework Agreement.[145] Based on the several ISC and IAC meetings, as well as the feedback received from prospective member countries, it was decided that the Framework Agreement would: (1) outsource the ISA's finance and administrative functions to the UN or its organs, in order to maintain the ISA's agility and action-orientation; and (2) rely on non-mandatory, voluntary contributions from ISA members.[146] This appears to reflect the major concerns raised by developed countries during the negotiations for a treaty text. For instance, Guy-Cedric Werlings, ISA Focal Point from France, remarked that 'the core principle of ISA is to create a buyer's market by creating bigger volumes and a participatory approach'.[147] The US called for the ISA to be 'a nimble organization, based on voluntary membership, in which projects and activities are more valued than dues and voting rights'.[148]

Ultimately, the first draft of the Framework Agreement was prepared jointly by India and France based on the input received in previous ISC meetings.[149] On 5 October 2016, during the fourth ISC meeting, the draft Framework Agreement was presented. It was decided that it would be circulated to prospective ISA member countries for comment, after which the revised draft would be opened for signature.[150] Feedback was sought through the network of ISA National Focal Points, French and Indian Missions in prospective member countries, and also through Missions

---

[143] ISA, n. 9, 3.

[144] ISA, 'Report of the fourth meeting of the Interim Administrative Cell of the International Solar Alliance', *Steering Committees* (New Delhi, 18 Mar. 2016), https://isolaralliance.org/about/steering-committees, accessed 15 Dec. 2022.

[145] ISA, n. 110, 2.

[146] ISA, n. 11.

[147] ISA, n. 110, 1.

[148] Remarks of George N. Sibley, Minister Counsellor, US Embassy. See, ISA, n. 11, 2.

[149] ISA, 'Report of the fourth meeting of the International Steering Committee', *Steering Committees* (New Delhi, 5 Oct. 2016), https://isolaralliance.org/about/steering-committees, accessed 15 Dec. 2022.

[150] Ibid, 7.

of prospective countries in New Delhi and Paris.[151] The IAC produced a revised version of the Framework Agreement, which was circulated to all members for comment on 26 October 2016. The final draft of the Framework Agreement was presented for signature on 15 November 2016 at COP22 in Marrakesh. On 6 November 2017, the minimum threshold of 15 countries ratified the Framework Agreement and on 6 December 2017 the ISA entered into force. According to several interviewees, the biggest achievement of the ISA was to gain legal force in a short period of time, and to consistently signal ongoing work throughout this process of signature and ratification.

Some interviewees argue that there was no deep thinking behind the decision to make the ISA a treaty-based organization. Others noted that countries viewed the organizational question through different lenses: France sought private-sector involvement,[152] and the US did not want a treaty-based structure.[153] Yet other interviewees pointed out that India insisted on a formal legal structure and, in so doing, wished to make a political statement. The final choice of form appears to have been driven by concerns of legitimacy, especially as regards bringing predominantly poor and developing countries on board. As a result, the treaty text reads more like 'a political document that is easy on language and low on legalese',[154] while the 'obligations were not kept onerous in order to encourage more countries to join'.[155] A standardized legal treaty-based organization was preferable so that these governments understood exactly what the organization does, what their benefits and liability would be, and most importantly, ensure a long-term value of the organization and its activities.[156]

A core interest for India all along was to ensure the legally binding nature of the institution, which explains the design of the ISA: first, the 'hard' legal form of a treaty and, second, the 'soft' legal terms with opt-in and non-legally binding obligations. This choice of form, which I describe

---

[151] Ibid.
[152] ISA, n. 110.
[153] ISA, n. 11.
[154] Participant 10, n. 42
[155] Participant 17, n. 34.
[156] Participant 5, n. 32: 'treaty-based organization is assured of longevity'; Participant 16, n. 32: 'treaty-based organization has long-term value'; Participant 17, n. 34: 'treaty form makes more serious otherwise it [the organization] could remain unstructured'.

as 'soft law in a hard shell', is motivated by twin concerns of ensuring legitimacy through legal form and flexibility by way of the legal terms.

Interestingly, even as the ISA brought states together through the ratification process, it associated itself early with non-state actors. Some have argued that the ISA might exert limited geopolitical influence because of India's limited capacity to provide financial support, and its low levels of technological prowess in solar energy.[157] However, the primary force behind the implementation of ISA's mission may ultimately derive from multilateral organizations, financial institutions, and subnational actors and networks. As a consequence, India's perceived weaknesses on financial and technological power could be overcome by the host of allies working alongside the ISA. As a former Indian diplomat puts it, the ISA exemplifies a kind of 'flexible multilateralism'.[158] According to another interviewee, 'we wanted a lean organization that works fast and doesn't have too much bureaucracy'.[159] Therefore, the ISA relies on the faculties and capabilities of its partner organizations, which are the primary research and technical partners leading the charge on operationalizing the ISA through both programmatic support and capacity building. According to an interviewee,

> A full multilateral system was not being envisioned. ISA works like an opt-in or club-like alliance that doesn't require everyone to sign up. Striking that balance between giving it the flavor of something that has a clear statist hook, but also providing the flexibility of a docking station where countries could plug in based on their specific solar interests was why this legal form was chosen.[160]

As another interviewee noted, existing multilateral institutions joined in to lead the charge on implementation since '[the ISA] is an organization of the future ... being pushed by developing countries. They cannot afford to not be a part of this, especially if it takes off in a big way'.[161]

---

[157] Shidore & Busby, n. 46.
[158] Participant 21, n. 59.
[159] Participant 10, n. 42.
[160] Participant 4, n. 56.
[161] Participant 1, n. 42.

The final design of the Framework Agreement was chosen to avoid the pitfalls of both a top-down arrangement (where it would be hard to forge consensus across countries) and a bottom-up model (which could degenerate into a coalition of leading solar countries neglecting the majority of nations). Instead, the ISA was envisaged as a platform for attracting both finance and technology related to solar energy deployment in the developing world. Formalizing the institution brought a degree of seriousness that would make its dealings with other institutions more structured and predictable, allowing finance and technology to flow into projects more easily.[162] Going forward, as one interviewee notes, 'the value [of ISA] would be to demonstrate replicable financial models or technologies for increasing the uptake of solar energy across member countries.'[163] The defining feature of the ISA is its blend of top-down and bottom-up approaches, as reflected in the contrast between its statist approach to ratification and its reliance on non-state actors during operationalization.

The goal of this chapter was to explore the process behind the creation of the ISA and uncover the reasons for the resulting choice of a treaty-based organization. In doing so, this chapter outlines the political economy factors behind the treaty-making process and finds that the degree of formality of the ISA, which I describe as 'soft law in a hard shell', is explained by three motivations. First, India's lead role in the treaty-making process, viewed against the backdrop of its global rule-making ambitions, ensured the 'hard' treaty form of the new organization. The permanence of the institution is a clear indication of India's desire to leave a mark in the international arena. Second, none of the member states that ratified the Framework Agreement wanted a new international organization with a large bureaucracy. Therefore, the focus was on creating 'soft', non-binding, flexible treaty terms which could rely on other non-state actors, such as multilateral development banks, financial institutions, and other regional or subnational entities. Third, the preference of developing countries for a 'hard' legal form, but one without onerous obligations, cemented the treaty-based structure of the ISA and its use of 'soft' treaty terms to involve participating organizations in its implementation. Next, Chapter 4 on 'Politics' provides a detailed background on India's

---

[162] Participant 19, n. 41.
[163] Participant 16, n. 32.

domestic politics on climate change and makes the case for how it led India to take on a lead role in the creation of a new international organization. Later, Chapter 5 on 'Players' illustrates the main actors responsible for operationalizing the vison for a new, India-led solar alliance and the motivations for the choice of legal form of ISA.

4

Politics

India's Political Leadership and Climate Change

> *The vast majority of humanity is blessed with generous sunlight*
> *round the year. Yet, many are also without any source of power.*
> *This is why this alliance is so important.*
> —Prime Minister Narendra Modi (Modi, 'PM's remarks at
> launch of the International Solar Alliance at CoP-21, Paris', 30
> Nov. 2015)

Domestic politics has typically not been a powerful driver of India's global stance, and domestic climate policy is mostly shaped by international pressure before key multilateral events. This chapter focuses on the spoken word of two Prime Ministers of India—Dr Manmohan Singh and Narendra Modi—to highlight the role of political leadership in bringing about a change in the direction of domestic climate policy and India's external engagement on the issue of climate change. An analysis of the Prime Ministers' speeches, over two significant periods of climate policymaking in India, suggests a clear shift in the narrative around solar energy. In particular, this chapter illustrates that Prime Minister Modi's speeches had a stronger emphasis on solar energy and exhibited his personal ambition to lead on the issue of climate change, both in the country and abroad. Ultimately, this chapter argues that Prime Minister Modi's leadership marks the first instance of India's domestic politics shaping its position in multilateral climate negotiations. His vision for a new, India-led global effort on solar energy was the primary driver behind the creation of the ISA, and underscores the importance of the political leadership in empowering an international rule-making stance.

The Making of the International Solar Alliance. Vyoma Jha, Oxford University Press. © Vyoma Jha 2023.
DOI: 10.1093/oso/9780198884705.003.0004

From Singh to Modi: Shifting Discourse on Solar Energy

In a recent book, Anandita Bajpai has looked at the discourse of 'India Emerging' through the spoken words of different Indian Prime Ministers. In doing so, she traces the shifting discourse of 'India, the economy/democracy in crisis' to 'India, the emerging power' through the speeches of four Prime Ministers of India. She draws a distinction between speeches for the outside world ('external' audience), and for Indians in and outside India ('internal' audience).[1] According to her, speeches serve two inter-related purposes: first, they are the tools to voice the official vision of the state; and second, they leave a space for the public to have a dialogic engagement with those visions.[2] Through their spoken word, prime ministers can be viewed as the 'sense-making' or 'meaning-lending' actors that translate ongoing politico-economic changes to wider audiences.[3]

In India, as in other parts of the world, politicians speak in light of their particular tradtions of orality. The Prime Minister's Office (PMO) and the tradition of public speeches have had a distinct legacy since Jawaharlal Nehru—the first prime minister of independent India.[4] A prime minister's address—one of the most popular modes of communicating statist visions in India—formulates the vision of the leader both nationally and internationally. In India, they are often judged in terms of their oratorical talent, their rhetorical victories, and most importantly, the frequency of their speeches.[5] Another tradition is the ritualistic annual address delivered to the nation on the commemoration celebrations of Independence Day.[6] By presenting the long-standing history of orality and aurality in India, she calls for more scholarly attention on the spoken word of the politician—an unexplored arena of shifting tropes, styles, strategies, and tactics.[7]

---

[1] A. Bajpai, *Speaking the nation: the oratorical making of secular, neoliberal India* (New Delhi: Oxford University Press, 2018), 2–3.

[2] Ibid., 22.

[3] Ibid., 31.

[4] Ibid., 49.

[5] Ibid., 37.

[6] Ibid., 69–70.

[7] Ibid., 37.

Historically, climate change has been a non-issue in organized Indian politics as captured in the words of a former Environment Minister: 'climate change as an issue is not a constituency mover.'[8] It is for this reason that tracing the spoken word of two prime ministers, across two significant periods of climate policymaking in India, became an important part of this research.[9] Several interviewees, in the course of this research, attributed India's central role in the creation of the International Solar Alliance (ISA) to Prime Minister Modi's leadership on issues relating to solar energy and climate change. Therefore, a goal of this research is to present an empirical analysis on whether changing political systems in the country affected climate policies and outcomes—in this case, both at the national level and in the international sphere. Did the change in national leadership—from the INC-led government to the BJP-led government—significantly impact the politics of climate change in India? Was there a shift in the political discourse on climate change between the governments of Dr Manmohan Singh and Narendra Modi? (See Table 4.1)

In context of environmental discourse analysis, Hajer defines discourse as 'a specific ensemble of ideas, concepts, and categorizations that is produced, reproduced, and transformed in a particular set of practices and through which meaning is given to physical and social realities.'[10] The focus of discourse analysis is not merely on what is said, rather who is saying something, where, in which context, and what practices and expectations structure the spoken word.[11] Discourse analysis can also be understood as a tool to examine how an issue is constituted as a policy problem and how that affects the approach to the policy problem.[12]

Relying on discourse analysis to examine how a policy problem is defined could also reveal the underlying rationale of actors' policy positions. This could either make explicit political conflicts that may hinder ambitious policy action, or increase the understanding of the common ground

---

[8] N.K. Dubash, 'The politics of climate change in India: narratives of equity and cobenefits', *WIREs Climate Change*, 4/3 (2013), 191–201, 194.

[9] See 'Research design and methods' in Chapter 1, Introduction.

[10] M. A. Hajer, *The politics of environmental discourse: ecological modernization and the policy process* (New York: Oxford University Press, 1995), 44.

[11] P. Späth. 'Understanding the social dynamics of energy regions—the importance of discourse analysis', *Sustainability*, 4 (2012), 1256–73.

[12] M. Jernnäs & B. Linnér. 'A discursive cartography of nationally determined contributions to the Paris climate agreement', *Global Environmental Change*, 55 (2019), 73–83, 75.

Table 4.1 Key Dates in the Political Discourse Analysis

Date	Milestone
30 Jun. 2008	Launch of National Action Plan on Climate Change
1–12 Dec. 2008	COP14 Poznan, Poland
16 Apr.–13 May 2009	General Elections to the 15th Lok Sabha
22 May 2009	Manmohan Singh sworn in as Prime Minister (second term)
7–18 Dec. 2009	COP15 Copenhagen, Denmark
11 Jan. 2010	Launch of National Solar Mission (NSM)
29 Nov.–10 Dec. 2010	COP16 Cancun, Mexico
7 Apr.–12 May 2014	General Elections to the 16th Lok Sabha
26 May 2014	Narendra Modi sworn in as Prime Minister
1–12 Dec. 2014	COP20 Lima, Peru
1–2 Oct. 2015	India announces its Nationally Determined Contribution
30 Nov.–12 Dec. 2015	COP21 Paris, France
7–18 Nov. 2016	COP22 Marrakesh, Morocco

Source: Author's own analysis

where cooperation is possible.[13] Discourse analysis can aid our understanding of where divisions lie and highlight the reasons for negotiation difficulties in the post-Paris landscape of international cooperation on climate governance.[14] For instance, in a recent paper, Jernnäs and Linnér argue that discourses inform the focus and direction of climate governance. Using the Nationally Determined Contributions (NDC) submitted by countries to the UNFCCC as the starting point of the discourse analysis, they develop different storylines that provide insights into parties' representations of climate change as a political problem and the steps they outline for climate action.[15]

Several scholars have written about the climate change discourse in India, but almost all of these works look at the Indian position during the

[13] Ibid.
[14] Ibid., 82.
[15] Ibid.

multilateral negotiations and argue that the climate change discourse is limited to a small of elite actors and foreign policy experts.[16] Some others have tried to identify the drivers of shifting discourses of climate change in India, and argue that the primary shift in discourse has been from a frame that externalized the climate change problem towards a 'co-benefits' approach.[17] Saran and Jones's work uncovers the underlying identities in Indian climate discourse. They reveal six distinct groups in order to explain India's climate change identity. First, the rural identity, which is a critical component of India's self-identification and covers issues of rural poverty and energy access. Second, the energy security identity, which manifests from India being a resource-scare country with wide inequities in energy demand and supply. Third, the industrial identity, which is an important feature of India's rapidly growing economy and energy needs. Fourth, the entrepreneurial identity, which can be seen through the impressive growth of the renewable energy sector. Fifth, the developing country identity, which is a function of India's positioning during international climate negotiations. Sixth, the emerging country identity, which stems from India's alliance with the fast emerging economies of the world, such as the BASIC and BRICS countries.[18]

There are important political takeaways and insights from what a leader says, and this particular focus on the 'spoken word' is missing in the exciting literature on Indian climate change discourses. Therefore, this chapter relies on the Prime Minister's official speeches to provide the empirical evidence for the shifting discourses of climate change since 2014, as well as give an account of Modi's positive leadership on solar energy. It attempts to allay concerns that the announcement of the ISA was merely an image-building exercise by India at the international climate negotiations. Rather I argue that the creation of the new institution reflects the

[16] S. Jasanoff, 'India at the crossroads in global environmental policy', *Global Environmental Change*, 3/1 (1993), 32–52; M. Kandlikar & A. Sagar, 'Climate change research and analysis in India: an integrated assessment of a south–north divide', *Global Environmental Change*, 9/2 (1999), 119–38; S. Jakobsen, *India's position on climate change from Rio to Kyoto: a policy analysis* (Copenhagen: Centre for Development Research, Jan. 1998); L. Rajamani, 'India and climate change: what India wants, needs, and needs to do', *India Review*, 8/3 (2009) 340–74; M.G. Rajan, *Global environmental politics: India and the north–south politics of global environmental issues* (New Delhi: Oxford University Press, 1997); Dubash, n. 8.

[17] J. Thaker & A. Leiserowitz, 'Shifting discourses of climate change in India', *Climatic Change*, 123/2 (2014), 107–19.

[18] S. Saran & A. Jones, *India's climate change identity: between reality and perception* (New Delhi: Springer, 2016).

changing politics of climate change in India, which was leveraged at the international level in great part by Modi's leadership and India's foreign diplomacy. It illustrates how Modi actively sought to shape the climate discourse, particularly on solar energy, in the country and abroad.

Climate policy has moved ahead of climate politics in India, facilitated in part by two narrative shifts: first, a growing awareness of climate-related damage and the resulting focus on climate adaptation; and second, a clearer understanding on the merits of the 'co-benefits' approach to climate policy, that is measures that promote development objectives while also yielding benefits of addressing climate change effectively.[19] This discrepancy between climate policy and climate politics in India is explained, in part, by the tendency for climate policy to be driven by international pressure before key multilateral events, such as the COP15 (Copenhagen) or COP21 (Paris) climate talks.[20] It is suggested that Indian domestic climate politics has not been a powerful driver of its global stance.[21] However, I argue that this case study illustrates how domestic politics has, for the first time, shifted India's position in multilateral climate negotiations. Through the empirical evidence presented in this chapter, I show how the creation of the ISA was driven by the vision and leadership of Modi, which was leveraged at the international stage by an empowered Indian diplomacy looking to cement its role as a global leader.

An overall analysis[22] of the two sets of speeches, via their representative word clouds, reveals an interesting contrast in how the two leaders project India before their audiences. Modi's speeches have a much stronger emphasis on India and its place in the world (Figure 4.1). While both Prime Ministers' speeches mention energy, it appears to be slightly more prominent in Modi's speeches. Modi also has a strong emphasis on solar energy in his speeches.[23]

---

[19] N.K. Dubash & L. Rajamani, 'Multilateral diplomacy on climate change', in D.M. Malone, C.R. Mohan, & S. Raghavan, eds, *The Oxford handbook of Indian foreign policy* (Oxford: Oxford University Press, 2015), 663–77, 668–9; Dubash, n. 8.

[20] Dubash & Rajamani, n. 19.

[21] Ibid.

[22] When I began collecting the speeches of the Prime Ministers, the initial search yielded 336 speeches by Dr Manmohan Singh and 405 by Narendra Modi during the specified time frame. After two rounds of coding to check their relevance for the discourse analysis, I ended with a sample size of 109 speeches by Dr Manmohan Singh and eighty speeches by Narendra Modi.

[23] Although it is more qualitative than quantitative, and can be seen in how 'solar' finds a spot in his representative word cloud.

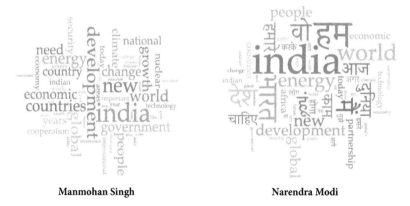

Manmohan Singh   Narendra Modi

Figure 4.1 Word Clouds of the Prime Ministers' Speeches
Source: Author's own analysis via voyant-tools.org

Another interesting aspect of their speeches is that Singh speaks of Africa in the context of development and energy cooperation, whereas Modi emphasizes India's role in the world and its global identity, and speaks of a direct relationship with Africa (Figure 4.2).

Overall Singh's speeches strike a fairly diplomatic tone on the issue of climate change. There are two main trends in the narrative: first, recognizing the problem and framing it as a challenge to India's developmental goals; and second, providing information on India's efforts at climate

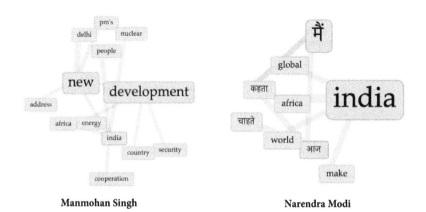

Manmohan Singh   Narendra Modi

Figure 4.2 Key Links Within the Prime Ministers' Speeches
Source: Author's own analysis via voyant-tools.org

action, particularly the NAPCC. Across the speeches, Singh acknow-
ledges the seriousness of climate change by using phrases such as 'global
concern over climate change'[24], 'problem of climate change'[25], 'challenge
of climate change', or 'threat of climate change'. In several speeches, Singh
states climate change as one of many global challenges along with food
and energy security, the financial crisis, global security and terrorism,
nuclear disarmament, and pandemics.

The mentions of 'solar' or 'solar energy' in Singh's speeches are limited
to being informative about the government's efforts at launching the NSM
and making solar energy one of the components of India's energy strategy.
Singh's speeches strike an objective tone on issues of 'solar' and 'solar energy' informing the audience about the government's efforts at launching
the NSM and making solar energy one of the components of India's energy
strategy.

On the other hand, Modi's speeches on the issue of climate change
have a more confident and ambitious tone than Singh's. The three central
trends in the narrative are: first, an action-oriented approach, particularly relating to solar energy; second, a focus on building new or consoli-
dating existing partnerships by highlighting shared interests; and third,
a new assertiveness about India's leadership on the global stage with the
creation of the ISA. Modi's speeches also outline a new vision on climate
action through solar energy in a bid to energize domestic constituencies
such as the energy sector[26] and state-level environment ministers[27] to

[24] Singh, 'PM's address at the 95th Indian Science Congress', 3 Jan. 2008; Singh, 'PM's
Independence Day Speech', 15 Aug. 2009

[25] Singh, 'PM's address at the CII Annual General Meeting', 29 Apr. 2008; Singh, 'PM's remarks
on the release of the Report of the Commission on AIDS in Asia', 30 Jun. 2008; Singh, 'PM's state-
ment at the XV Summit of the Non Aligned Movement', 15 Jul. 2009; Singh, 'PM's Independence
Day Speech', 15 Aug. 2009; Singh, 'PM's address at the Conference of Speakers and Presiding
Officers of Commonwealth Countries', 5 Jan. 2010; Singh, 'PM's Independence Day Speech', 15
Aug. 2010; Singh, 'PM's Inaugural address at Petrotech-2010', 1 Nov. 2010.

[26] 'The color of energy is—saffron. So when I talk of a saffron revolution, I talk about an energy revolution. We are the beneficiaries of solar radiation. How do we promote solar energy?
How do we promote renewable energy? How do we move the energy sector towards a gas-based
economy? How do we come up with an overall solution for the energy sector? in the gas page
economy, how do we do an overall solution in the energy sector? We should move forward on
that.' Modi, 'Text of PM's address at the dedication to the Nation of Unit-II of ONGC Tripura
Company Ltd Power Plant', 1 Dec. 2014.

[27] 'This [climate change] is a subject which is our inheritance, it's in our DNA. Our ancestors
have done a great service to mankind. We should lead the world on the issue of climate. We can
show the whole world that this is our subject. This is our tradition.' Modi, Text of PM's address at
the inauguration of the Conference of State Environment and Forest Ministers', 6 Apr. 2015.

come up with practicable solutions (I describe this increased focus on solar energy in the sections below).

Notably, while talking about climate change in the context of poor and developing countries, Singh does not move away from the status quo stance of equity and the principle of common but differentiated responsibilities. Even when speaking before developing country allies, his tone is rather passive as he talks about the impact of climate change on these countries: 'they are the least responsible for climate change and yet the most vulnerable to its impact';[28] or 'climate change action must not perpetuate the poverty of developing countries'[29]. Modi's rhetoric, on the other hand, rests on treating climate change as an opportunity instead of a problem.[30] One of the actionable items in his speeches is the potential for skill development among in the solar energy sector.[31] He also spoke of increasing ambition around the use of solar energy and micro grids so that it could provide clean power to villages not just in India, but across the developing world.[32]

Modi's emphasis on interest-based alliances—in this case on the issue of climate change and solar energy—can be seen in his speeches while visiting foreign countries. For instance, in his address to the Fiji Parliament, Modi said:

We also share many common challenges. For you, climate change is not a matter of debate, but a basic question of existence. India, too, is a nation of a long coastline and more than 1000 islands, a nation that is nurtured by monsoon rain and the Himalayan glaciers. We, too, are facing the searing impact of climate change … In India, we have a comprehensive national plan and strategy to both mitigate and adapt to climate change. And, I have a deep personal commitment to it. And, we look forward to working with Fiji in areas such wind and solar energy … India has stood shoulder to shoulder with Fiji and the Small Islands Developing States is seeking a fair and urgent response from the

[28] Singh, 'Intervention by PM on Climate Change—CHOGM Summit 2009', 27 Nov. 2009.
[29] Singh, 'PM's statement at the XV Summit of the Non Aligned Movement', 15 Jul. 2009
[30] 'My government is treating the challenge of adapting to climate change as an opportunity rather than a problem'. Modi, 'PM's address during the International Conference on Rule of Law for supporting 2030 Development Agenda', 4 Mar. 2016.
[31] Modi, 'Text of the PM's keynote address at the "Invest Madhya Pradesh: Global Investor Summit 2014"', 9 Oct. 2014; Modi, 'Text of PM's address at inauguration ceremony of "Urja Sangam-2015"', 27 Mar. 2015.
[32] Modi, 'PM's speech at the SAARC Summit', 26 Nov. 2014.

international community for a sustainable future. Fiji is a leader in the region and a strong voice in the developing world. Together, we can also work for a future in the region, in which there is an equal place for all nations—big and small, developed and developing—and a climate of peace and tranquility.[33]

Modi used a similar tone while addressing a gather in Seychelles while delivering the message that India's solar ambitions would protect the interests of small island countries:

Our inspiration is not just lighting a lamp in any house in India. Our inspiration comes from people who spend their lives on small islands ... our resolve is to protect the lives of those in these small countries. And that's why even if solar power is in India, we hope it will provide a direct benefit to the future generations in Seychelles—that's the dream that we are working towards.[34]

While he continued emphasizing India's shared interests with Pacific Island nations[35] and African nations[36], he also drew similarities with South Korea[37] and Bangladesh.[38]

---

[33] Modi, 'PM's address to the Fiji Parliament', 19 Nov. 2014.

[34] Modi, 'Text of PM's address at the Civic Reception in Seychelles', 11 Mar. 2015

[35] 'Our global challenges are similar. Climate change is an existential threat to the Pacific Islands. It is also taking a toll on the teaming millions on India's shoreline of 7500 kilometers and its nearly 1300 islands.' Modi, 'Text of PM's opening remarks at Forum for India Pacific Island Countries (FIPIC) Summit, Jaipur', 21 Aug. 2015

[36] 'I think both India and Africa have had a tradition and it is in their culture not to pollute or not to damage the environment, and we have perhaps sinned the less and contributed the minimum to this big problem to the world. I think this also is a common factor between India and Africa. As we now look to the future, we will continue to work with Africa in these areas, but also address emerging challenges: climate resilient agriculture and adaptation to climate change. India–Africa economic partnership is not transactional. It rests in the belief of our shared destiny and the power of South–South cooperation in transforming the lives of our people. India will always work in accordance with the requirements and priorities of our friends in Africa.' Modi, 'PM's interaction with African journalists at the Editors Forum for 3rd India–Africa Forum Summit' 23 Oct. 2015.

[37] 'Reverence for nature is part of our shared heritage ... combating climate change is in our enlightened self-interest.' Modi, 'Text of PM's remarks at the Asian Leadership forum at Seoul', 19 May 2015.

[38] 'Both our countries are fortunate in a way and have the blessing of the hot sun, which until now was a cause of trouble. But the same sun has now become the cause of power, solar energy can be our great wealth.' Modi, 'Text of PM's address at Bangabandhu Convention Centre', 7 Jun. 2015.

Overall, Modi's confident tone on India's leadership role at the global level can be seen across speeches, both before domestic and international audiences.[39]

A closer analysis of the two samples reveals that the incidence of words 'climate change' and 'solar energy' were the highest in and around the weeks of the UNFCCC Conference of Parties, that is, COP15 at Copenhagen for Singh and COP21 at Paris for PM Modi (Figure 4.3).

Another similarity in both the samples is that the focus on these issues was highest in the weeks and months leading up to the multilateral climate negotiations. However, the findings from the discourse analysis reveal significant shifts in the discourse on climate change, particularly on solar energy, from Singh to Modi. The findings from the discourse analysis are characterized under four broad themes: energy diplomacy, personal ambition, symbolism, and innovation and climate justice.

Energy Security to Energy Diplomacy

The foreign policy position during Singh's tenure can be understood in terms of securing an external environment that could work for India's economic development. For instance, in an address to the nation on the first anniversary of the UPA government's second term, Singh said: 'In foreign policy, our core objective is to secure for India an external environment that is conducive to our long-term economic development and to peace and stability in our region. We hope to consolidate our relations with neighbors and all major powers in the years ahead.'[40]

Previously, he had similarly stated that:

---

[39] For example: 'India launched the International Solar Alliance to forge a partnership between solar-rich countries'. Modi, 'Text of PM's inaugural address at 103rd session of Indian Science Congress', 3 Jan. 2016; 'The ISA's headquarters is in India, but it is a global institution'. Modi, 'Text of PM's address on the inauguration ceremony of International Solar Alliance Headquarters in Gurgaon', 25 Jan 2016; 'We formed the International Solar Alliance to counter climate change', Modi, 'PM's statement to the media, in the joint media briefing with President of Mozambique', 7 Jul. 2016; 'India has led the efforts to form an International Solar Alliance'. Modi, 'PM's press statement during his visit to Tanzania', 10 Jul. 2016; 'As a responsible global citizen, India is committed to combatting climate change'. Modi, 'PM's address at the inaugural session of PETROTECH—2016 exhibition', 5 Dec. 2016.
[40] Singh, 'PM's opening remarks at the First Anniversary of UPA-II Government', 1 Jun. 2010.

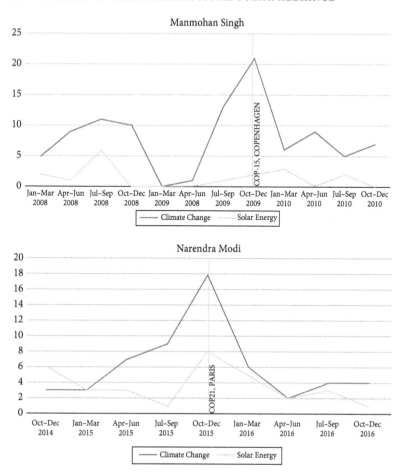

Figure 4.3 Timeline of the Prime Ministers' Speeches
Source: Author's own analysis

India's domestic and foreign policy priorities are closely linked. The primary task of our foreign policy is to create an external environment that is conducive for our rapid development. Our policy seeks to widen our development choices and give us strategic autonomy in the world. The independence of our foreign policy enables us to pursue mutually beneficial cooperation with all major countries of the world.[41]

---

[41] Singh, 'PM's address at the Chinese Academy of Social Sciences', 15 Jan. 2008.

Therefore, under Singh's tenure, India's energy foreign policy rested the concept of energy security rested on the need to find new and alternative sources of energy for India's domestic needs.[42] At the time, the core focus of India's energy security concerns was on nuclear power, and solar energy was one among the various other sources of clean energy. As a former member of India's Planning Commission put it: 'Given the limited hydrocarbon resources of the country, even if there was no threat to climate change, it would be imperative that we develop solar technology for power.'[43] The initial objective for entering into decentralized power generation through solar and renewable energy was to help India meet its energy access problem.[44]

In the lead-up to the Copenhagen talks, there was a weaving of climate change concerns in India's energy security argument and a growing emphasis on renewable energy, and not merely nuclear power.[45] With the launch of the NSM in January 2010, solar power assumed a central role in

---

[42] 'We have to diversify our sources of energy supply. ... What is the nuclear agreement about? It is all about widening our development options, promoting energy security in a manner which will not hurt our precious environment and which will not contribute to pollution and global warming'. Singh, 'PM's reply to the debate on the Motion of Confidence in the Lok Sabha', 22 Jul. 2008; 'India is registering rapid economic growth and has combined it with declining energy intensity. However, our total demand will keep increasing and we are actively looking for all possible sources of clean energy. The opening of international civil nuclear cooperation with India will have a positive impact on global energy security and on efforts to combat climate change.' Singh, 'Statement by Prime Minister of India at the General Debate of the 63rd UN General Assembly', 27 Sep. 2008; 'We must apply modern science and technology to find long term solutions to our energy problem. Our crude oil and gas reserves are limited. We must find alternative energy sources. I would like our scientists and engineers to find ways in which we can make better use of solar energy, wind energy, bio-gas and other sources of energy. ... All over the world, there is growing realization of the importance of atomic energy to meet the challenge of energy security and climate change. It is a clean, environmental friendly and renewable source of energy.' Singh, 'PM's Independence Day Speech, 2008', 15 Aug. 2008; 'Our energy needs will continue to rise in the foreseeable future. We do not have the luxury of limiting our options of energy sources. We therefore wish to create an international environment in which nuclear technology is used not for destructive purposes but for helping us meet our national development goals and our energy security.' Singh, 'PM Inaugurates International Conference on "Towards a World Free of Nuclear Weapons"', 9 Jun. 2008; 'We must widen our energy basket to ensure energy security. In recent years we have expanded the use of natural gas as a new source of energy. ... At the same time, we must also further develop our nuclear energy potential. Our Government is committed to further development of nuclear energy both as an environment-friendly source of power and as a means of widening the energy basket available to us.' Singh, 'PM Lays Foundation Stone of Bawana Power Project', 24 Mar. 2008.
[43] K. Parikh, 'It's time for India to turn to the sun', *Hindustan Times* (30 Dec. 2010), https://www.hindustantimes.com/delhi/it-s-time-for-india-to-turn-to-the-sun/story-A5SoH6aPSC5VwPlhnpryrO.html, accessed 15 Jan. 2022.
[44] MOEFCC, n. 60, 22.
[45] For example: 'A rational energy policy, with appropriate policies for renewable and non-conventional energy sources, is also important for climate change. We need to dovetail our

addressing India's twin challenges of energy security and climate action. In Singh's words:

> The Sun has long been recognized as a primal source of all energy on earth. In an ancient civilization like India, the Sun has been worshipped as the God who bestows life and sustains it. The bounty of the Sun is truly inexhaustible, renewable and free. It is to this source of energy that humankind must turn to meet the twin challenge of energy security and climate change.[46]

The emphasis on interweaving climate change and energy security concerns is evident in Singh's speeches, which contain a higher number of mentions of the terms 'climate change' and 'energy security' (Figure 4.4). In contrast, only five of Modi's speeches within the sample size included the term 'energy security'. However, Modi's speeches contain a higher number of references to solar energy than Singh's.

Under Modi's leadership, there is an insertion of energy diplomacy in India's foreign policy. Modi himself highlights this new energy diplomacy in several speeches: in a 2015 address, he noted that energy diplomacy is the need of the hour in global relations, especially as Indian companies become more multinational;[47] in another 2016 speech, he noted that 'our proactive foreign policy and energy diplomacy is helping us to strengthen our ties with our neighboring countries.'[48]

---

strategy for energy with our national action plan for climate change'. Singh, 'PM's concluding remarks at Full Planning Commission meeting', 1 Sep. 2009; 'As far as energy is concerned, renewable and clean energy supplies will need to pay a much bigger role than what they do currently. Nuclear and solar energy supplies will need to increase considerably'. Singh, 'PM Inaugurates 97th Indian Science Congress', 3 Jan. 2010; 'Increased use of solar energy is a central component of our strategy to bring about a strategic shift from our current reliance on fossil fuels to a pattern of sustainable growth based on renewable and clean sources of energy'. Singh, 'PM launches Jawaharlal Nehru National Solar Mission—Solar India', 11 Jan. 2010; We have formulated an ambitious National Action Plan on Climate Change that is intimately linked to our energy security .... I believe that it is vital for any country to keep its development options open. That is why we worked so hard on a civil nuclear initiative that has opened the doors for India to develop the option of clean nuclear energy as an important plank of our energy security'. Singh, 'PM's address at Khazanah Global Lecture Series 2010', 27 Oct. 2010.

[46] Singh, 'PM launches Jawaharlal Nehru National Solar Mission—Solar India', 11 Jan. 2010.
[47] Modi, 'Text of PM's address at inauguration ceremony of "Urja Sangam-2015"', 27 Mar. 2015.
[48] Modi, 'PM's address at the inaugural session of PETROTECH—2016 exhibition', 5 Dec. 2016.

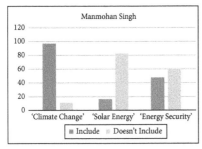
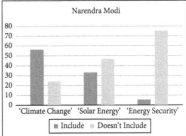

Figure 4.4 Counting 'Climate Change', 'Solar Energy', and 'Energy Security' Within the Sample
Source: Author's own analysis

This shift in discourse from energy security to energy diplomacy from Singh to Modi can also be ascertained from where the speeches were given. A much higher percentage of Modi's speeches raising issues of climate change and solar energy were outside India as compared to Singh (Figures 4.5 and 4.6). In fact, more than half of Modi's speeches raising these issues were outside India, either at multilateral forums or during bilateral visits and meetings.

One of the clear themes in Modi's early speeches is the effort to establish new partnerships through solar energy. He focused on building energy partnerships across different regional groups such as ASEAN,[49] SAARC,[50] and the East Asia Summit.[51]

Interestingly the idea to bring South Asian countries together in efforts to tap renewable energy sources was first signalled by Prime Minister Singh in 2008: 'We should also pool our resources to tap renewable sources such as solar energy, hydropower and wind energy, all of which

---

[49] 'Let us think of a major ASEAN India Solar Project for research, manufacturing and deployment.' Modi, 'PM's remarks at the 12th India–ASEAN Summit, Nay Pyi Taw, Myanmar', 12 Nov. 2014.
[50] 'We should also think with ambition to use solar energy and micro grids to quickly provide clean power to villages across the region.' Modi, 'PM's speech at the SAARC Summit', 26 Nov. 2014.
[51] 'We should also start major initiatives on energy partnership, for example, in the area of solar energy, with the objective of bringing affordable clean energy within the reach of all.' Modi, 'English rendering of PM's remarks at the East Asia Summit, Nay Pyi Taw', 13 Nov. 2014.

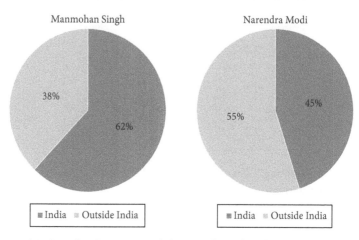

Figure 4.5 Speeches Mentioning 'Climate Change' in the Sample
Source: Author's own analysis

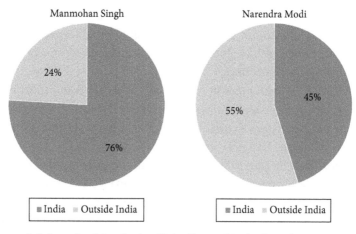

Figure 4.6 Speeches Mentioning 'Solar Energy' in the Sample
Source: Author's own analysis

South Asia has in abundance.'[52] However, there is no subsequent mention of this idea or any related plans in Singh's speeches. The momentum

---

[52] Singh, 'Statement by the Prime Minister of India Dr Manmohan Singh at the Inaugural Session of the 15th SAARC Summit', 2 Aug. 2008.

around creating new energy partnerships through solar energy clearly gained steam under Modi's leadership. In addition to highlighting the need to coalesce efforts around solar energy in different regional forums, the Modi government also partnered with countries in other ways, such as setting up solar projects in Mozambique[53] and extending a line for credit for renewable energy development to Fiji.[54]

The first concrete suggestion about a new grouping of countries based on solar energy cooperation was outlined in Modi's interaction with African journalists before the Third India–Africa Forum Summit held in October 2015. He noted:

> I think between India and Africa there is another aspect that links us with many countries in Africa and that is solar power from which many African countries are benefiting. I think this is going to become a very strong community of nations and in the times to come the problem of climate change that the world is trying to counter and fight, we are going to be playing a very major role in mitigation and lessening the effects of climate change.[55]

He further added that the 'India–Africa economic partnership is not transactional' and 'rests in the belief of our shared destiny and the power of South–South cooperation in transforming the lives of our people.'[56] In his plenary address, he invited the fifty-four participating African countries to join the yet-to-be launched alliance of solar-rich countries, saying:

> When the sun sets, tens of millions of homes in India and Africa become dark. We want to light up lives of our people and power their future.... No one has done less to contribute to global warming than India and Africa. No one can be more conscious of climate change than Indians and Africans ... But, it is also true that the excess of few cannot become the burden of many. So, when the world meets in Paris in December, we

---

[53] Modi, 'Text of PM's statement at the media briefing with President Filipe Nyusi of Mozambique', 5 Aug. 2015.
[54] Modi, 'PM's address to the Fiji Parliament', 19 Nov. 2014.
[55] Modi, 'PM's interaction with African journalists at the Editors Forum for 3rd India–Africa Forum Summit', 23 Oct. 2015.
[56] Ibid.

look to see a comprehensive and concrete outcome that is based on the well-established principles in the UN Convention on Climate Change. We will all do our part for it. But, we also want to see a genuine global public partnership that makes clean energy affordable; provides finance and technology to developing countries to access it; and the means to adapt to the impact of climate change. I also invite you to join an alliance of solar-rich countries that I have proposed to launch in Paris on November 30 at the time of COP-21 meeting. Our goal is to make solar energy an integral part of our life and reach it to the most unconnected villages and communities.[57]

Modi continued his focus on the renewed India–Africa energy partnership by highlighting two aspects: the need for energy access and abundance of solar energy in the two regions. At the launch of the ISA, Modi said:

We want to bring solar energy into our lives and homes, by making it cheaper, more reliable and easier to connect to grid.... There is already a revolution in solar energy. Technology is evolving, costs are coming down and grid connectivity is improving. It is making the dream of universal access to clean energy become more real.[58]

While Manmohan Singh's speeches focused on poverty alleviation as an overriding priority for the country,[59] the issue of energy access only found mention in one speech at the launch of the National Solar Mission. He stated:

The importance of this Mission is not just limited to providing large-scale grid connected power. It has the potential to provide significant multipliers in our efforts for transformation of India's rural economy.

---

[57] Modi, 'Text of PM's statement at the Inaugural Ceremony of the Third India-Africa Forum Summit', 29 Oct. 2015.

[58] Modi, 'PM's remarks at launch of the International Solar Alliance at CoP-21, Paris', 30 Nov. 2015.

[59] Singh, 'Statement by Prime Minister of India at the General Debate of the 63rd UN General Assembly', 27 Sep. 2008; Singh, 'Intervention at Major Economies Meeting on Climate Change', 9 Jul. 2008.

Already, in its decentralized and distributed applications, solar energy is beginning to light the lives of tens of millions of India's energy-poor citizens. The rapid spread of solar lighting systems, solar water pumps and other solar power-based rural applications can change the face of India's rural economy.[60]

It is this thinking that appears to have been actualized by Narendra Modi, who has sought to leverage India's domestic experience with solar energy and take it to other parts of the world facing similar problems of energy access through the creation of the ISA. Within India's foreign policy framework, the move from energy security towards energy diplomacy can be also seen through the annual reports of the foreign ministry.[61] Until 2015, issues of energy were handled by the Energy Security Division in the MEA and developments were captured in a chapter titled 'Energy Security'. Following the launch of the ISA, all issues relating to energy and the ISA are being handled by the Economic Diplomacy Division within the MEA.

Modi's outlook on multilateralism and global institutions can also provide some insights into why the ISA was created as a multilateral institution. He has said:

the global order, its institutions and our mindsets continue to reflect the circumstances that existed at the end of the last World War. These institutions have served us well, but they must be reformed in order to remain effective and relevant in the new era. If global institutions and systems do not adapt, they will risk irrelevance. We might have a more fragmented world and our collective ability to deal with the challenges and changes of our era will also be weakened.[62]

And that 'India has always had great faith in multilateralism. We believe that as the world becomes more complex, the role of multilateral institutions will increase.'[63] Therefore, the ISA is a definite step towards

---

[60] Singh, 'PM launches Jawaharlal Nehru National Solar Mission—Solar India', 11 Jan. 2010.

[61] MEA (Government of India), *Annual Reports*, https://meacms.mea.gov.in/annual-reports.htm?57/Annual_Reports, accessed 15 Jan. 2022.

[62] Modi, n. 155.

[63] Modi, 'Text of PM's Address at the MOF-IMF Conference on "Advancing Asia: Investing for the Future"', 12 Mar. 2016.

capturing a new coalition of solar-rich actors and presenting a set of issues that are not captured in any other existing multilateral institution.

Modi's Personal Ambition

Modi's interest in issues of climate change and his strong push for renewable energy began during his stint as Chief Minister of Gujarat. When he came to power as the Prime Minister in 2014, one of his first moves was to rename the Ministry of Environment and Forests (MOEF) as the Ministry of Environment, Forests and Climate Change (MOEFCC).[64] The insertion of 'climate change' in India's environment ministry, followed by his announcement to ramp up India's clean energy targets, were very early examples of his seriousness to tackle the issue of climate change.

The shifting political discourse also reveals Modi's personal ambition to lead the charge internationally on issues of climate change, particularly solar energy. This is evident from several speeches before the Paris climate talks in December 2015. During President Obama's visit to India in January 2015, Modi expressed hope for a successful Paris Conference and emphasized how 'clean and renewable energy is a *personal* and national priority' for both Obama and him.[65] He reiterated his personal commitment while elucidating India's latest efforts on clean energy measures during his visit to the United States in September 2015:

> *President and I share an uncompromising commitment on climate change,* without affecting our ability to meet the development aspirations of humanity. *We have both set ambitious national agendas.* In India, our measures include not just a plan to add 175 GW of renewable energy by 2022, but a development strategy that will enable us to transition to a more sustainable energy mix. This is an exercise we are undertaking in

---

[64] ET Bureau, 'Ministry of environment and forests undergoes a nomenclature change; government serious to tackle climate change', *The Economic Times* (28 May 2014), https://econom ictimes.indiatimes.com/news/economy/policy/ministry-of-environment-and-forests-underg oes-a-nomenclature-change-government-serious-to-tackle-climate-change/articleshow/35651 292.cms, accessed 15 Jan. 2022.

[65] Modi, 'Text of Prime Minister's Media Statement during Joint Press Interaction with President of United States of America', 25 Jan. 2015 (emphasis added).

the spirit of our culture and tradition, but also because of our commitment to the future of this planet.[66]

Modi's vision for the ISA took shape as early as November 2014 at the
SAARC Summit in Kathmandu, Nepal where he spoke of building a regional partnership that could harness solar energy for providing clean
power. He said:

> I also believe that if we can light up each other's towns and villages, we
> can build a brighter tomorrow for our region. Or, face a future when
> someone looks down at us from Space, and says that this is world's
> darkest corner. Let us treat electricity as a commodity like any other that
> we invest and trade in. India will fully support these initiatives in the re-
> gion. We should also think with ambition to use solar energy and micro
> grids to quickly provide clean power to villages across the region.[67]

At the launch of the ISA, too, Modi underscored his contribution in conceptualizing the ISA and thanked President Hollande for extending support to the endeavour. He said:

> To my long cherished dream of an international alliance of solar-rich
> countries, President Hollande responded with keen interest and imme-
> diate and full offer of support. This is the inaugural day of a defining
> global conference on climate change. For his support at every step, and
> his decision to co-chair the launch, I am deeply grateful.[68]

Earlier in the day, too, Modi noted that President Hollande would be
joining him as co-chair at the 'launch of *my* long cherished dream of
an international solar alliance to promote greater use of solar energy in
the 121 solar-rich Nations.'[69] The stress on his own role in steering the
ISA was also visible when he invited other countries to participate in the

---

[66] Modi, 'Text of PM's statement to the media in the Joint Press Briefing with US President
Barack Obama', 28 Sep. 2015 (emphases added).

[67] Modi, n. 150.

[68] Modi, n. 158.

[69] Modi, 'PM's address at the inauguration of the Indian Pavilion at CoP-21, Paris', 30 Nov.
2015 (emphasis added).

launch event at Paris: 'I have also proposed an international solar alliance of 122 solar-rich countries, which French President Hollande and I will launch in Paris on November 30. We look forward to your participation in the launch and the alliance.'[70]

New Symbolism Around the Sun

India's solar policy—National Solar Mission—was launched under Dr Manmohan Singh and was the government's flagship programme on climate action. However, the mentions of 'solar' relative to 'climate change' or 'energy' in PM Singh's speeches was less frequent than in Modi's (see Figures 4.7 and 4.8). In fact, the highest mention of 'solar' in Singh's speeches happened at the launch of the NSM; whereas Modi's speeches illustrate his sustained focus on solar both before the launch of the ISA and afterwards as he tried to bring more countries on board the new organization.

A notable feature in Modi's speeches is the new symbolism around solar energy. He uses the colours of the Indian flag—saffron, white, green, and blue—to talk about creating a revolution in different fields: energy, dairy, organic farming, and maritime security respectively.[71] Very early into his term as the prime minister, Modi equated the colour of saffron with energy, specifically solar energy. Modi's address was at an event to dedicate the Oil and Natural Gas Company's (ONGC) first thermal power plant to the country. He spoke about creating a 'saffron revolution' or an 'energy revolution', where India should give impetus to solar energy owing to the fact that it is blessed with high solar radiation.[72] He continued this emphasis on the 'saffron revolution' across different events, such as a meeting with the environment ministers of different Indian states,[73] an address to

---

[70] Modi, 'Text of PM's opening statement at the ASEAN-India Summit', 21 Nov. 2015.
[71] Modi, 'Text of PM's address at the dedication to the Nation of Unit-II of ONGC Tripura Company Ltd Power Plant', 1 Dec. 2014.
[72] Ibid.
[73] Modi, 'Text of PM's address at the inauguration of the Conference of State Environment and Forest Ministers', 6 Apr. 2015.

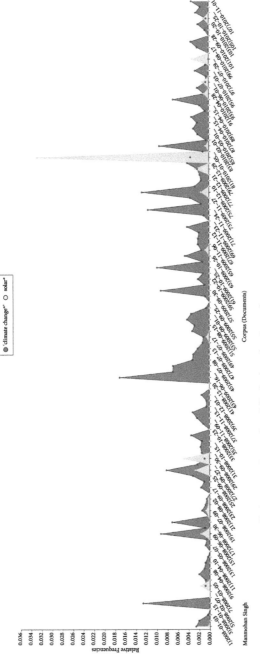

Manmohan Singh

Figure 4.7 Frequency of 'Climate Change' and 'Solar' in the Sample

Source: Author's own analysis via voyant-tools.org

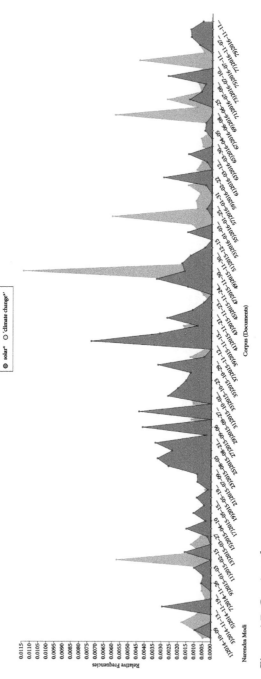

Figure 4.7 Continued

the Indian diaspora in Canada,[74] or a speech at an education institute in the state of Odisha.[75]

Hall has identified a new, albeit thin, normative agenda in Modi's treatment of climate change and the global environment.[76] He argues that Modi has seemingly departed from the liberal normative agenda and made the case for Hindu thought and practices providing lessons that can help the world tackle climate change.[77] Modi relied on the promise of ancient Hindu Vedas that 'contain a whole spectrum of knowledge' relevant to the issue of climate change. He has repeatedly called for lifestyle-focused solutions for climate change, drawn from Hindu beliefs and practices.[78] Narlikar, similarly, illustrates Modi's use of Indian traditions to claim and reshape the climate agenda. For instance, in April 2015 on his visit to Germany, Modi said that treating nature well 'comes naturally' to Indians.[79] Modi's embrace of the conservation agenda—rooting it in India's own traditions—was an important shift in India's willingness to take on climate action. Until then, negotiators have almost always pitted the conservation agenda against the development agenda. But Modi has argued that solutions to global warming lie in India's traditions and customs and that India has no reason to be defensive about it.[80] Modi's commitment to environmental ethics and sustainability is also evident in India's NDC, which contains references to national literary and religious traditions as it advanced the case for India's commitment to climate-change mitigation.[81] Therefore, there is a clear attempt by PM Modi to advance India's climate ambitions at the international level by rooting it in Indian traditions and customs. During his visit to the UK in November 2015, while addressing a gathering of the Indian diaspora, he stated India's ambitions to 'lead' an alliance of countries that get a lot of

[74] Modi, 'Text of PM's address at the Indian Diaspora Event, at Ricoh Coliseum, in Toronto, Canada', 15 Apr. 2015.
[75] Modi, 'Text of PM's speech at National Institute of Science Education and Research in Odisha', 7 Feb. 2016.
[76] I. Hall, 'Narendra Modi and India's normative power', *International Affairs*, 93/1 (2017), 113–31, 128–30.
[77] Ibid.
[78] Ibid.
[79] Narlikar, n. 92, 102–15.
[80] Ibid.
[81] Ibid.

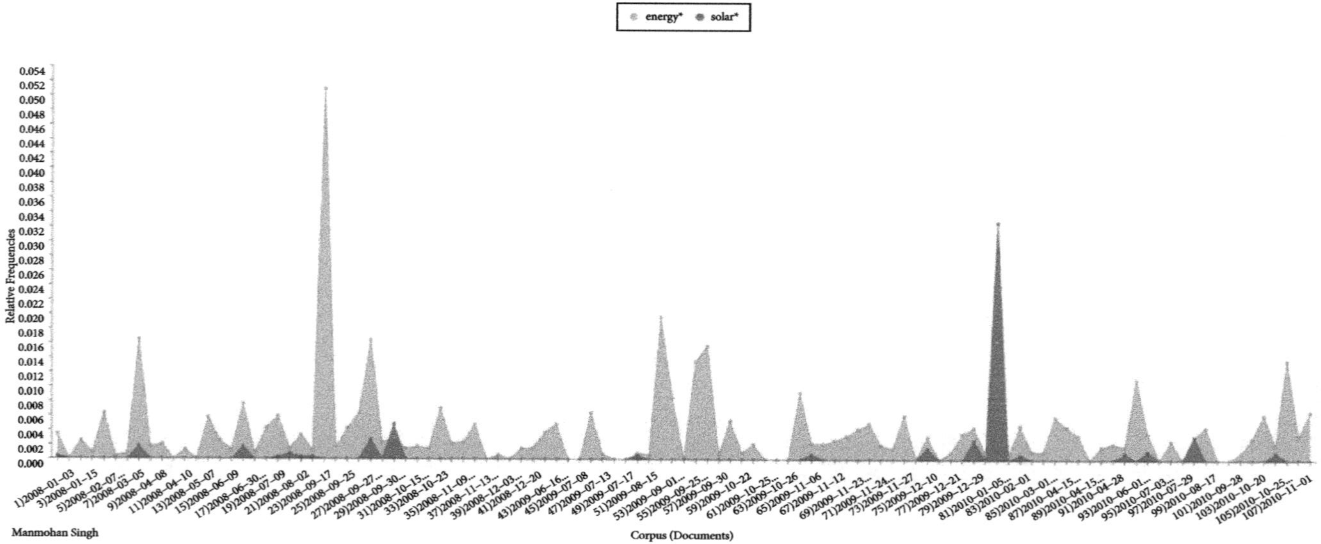

Figure 4.8 Frequency of 'Energy' and 'Solar' in the Sample

Source: Author's own analysis via voyant-tools.org

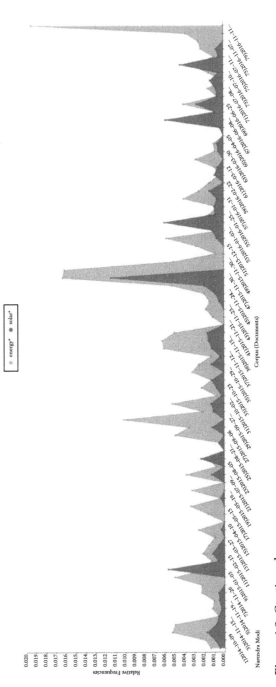

Figure 4.8 Continued

sunlight and should come together to act on climate change. He termed these countries *suryaputra*, or sons of the sun.[82]

Innovation and Climate Justice

Another noticeable shift can be seen in India's position on finance and technology transfer under the multilateral climate talks. Under Manmohan Singh, it was clear that any climate action by India would be based on the principle of common but differentiated responsibilities and contingent on financial support and technology transfers from the developed countries. This was reiterated by Prime Minister Singh at different forums, where he said that India 'can do even more if a supportive global climate change regime is put in place',[83] and 'the full incremental cost of any mitigation by them (developing countries, emphasis added) must be fully compensated by transfers of financial and technological resources from developed countries'.[84]

Under Modi's leadership, the Indian government has maintained its stance on the principle of common but differentiated responsibilities, including the emphasis on facilitating climate finance and technology transfers to developing countries. For example: '[i]n the area of climate change, G20s priorities should include facilitating climate finance and technology transfer to developing countries';[85] '[t]he world had agreed on a beautiful balance of collective action—common but differentiated responsibilities. That should form the basis of continued action. This also means that the developed countries must fulfil their commitments for funding and technology transfer';[86] '[we] underlined the need for an effective climate change accord in Paris later this year, which also provides the means and technology to developing countries to transition to clean

---

[82] Modi, 'Text of PM's address at community reception at Wembley Stadium, London', 13 Nov. 2015.

[83] Singh, 'PM's remarks at the Informal Plenary of HOS/Gs at the 15th COP at Copenhagen', 18 Dec. 2009.

[84] Singh, 'PM's statement in Lok Sabha on the debate on the PM's recent visits abroad', 29 Jul. 2009.

[85] Modi, 'Lead intervention by PM at G20 working lunch on development and climate change', 15 Nov. 2015.

[86] Modi, n. 133.

energy sources';[87] '[a]s much as we speak of goals and emission reductions, we should focus equally on access to affordable technology and adequate finance that makes transition to clean energy natural and easy'.[88]

However, after the Paris talks the Indian government appears to have nuanced this position on financial support and technology transfer by adding the innovation argument to the mix. At the annual address to the Indian Science Congress, Modi stated:

We succeeded in bringing innovation and technology to the heart of the climate change discourse. We were consistent in our message that it is not enough to speak of targets and restraints. It is essential to find solutions that help us transition easily to a future of clean energy. I also said in Paris that innovation is important not just for combating climate change, but also for climate justice. For, the developed world must leave enough of the little carbon space left for developing countries to grow. For this, we need research and innovation to make clean energy technology available, accessible and affordable for all. At Paris, President Hollande, President Obama and I joined a number of global leaders for an Innovation Summit. We pledged to double national investments in innovation; and, build a global partnership that combines the responsibility of governments with the innovative capacity of the private sector. I also suggested an international network of 30–40 universities and labs focusing for next ten years on transforming the way we produce, distribute and consume energy. We will also pursue this in G20. We need innovation to make renewable energy much cheaper; more reliable; and, easier to connect to transmission grids. This is especially critical for India to achieve our target of adding 175 GW of renewable generation by 2022.[89]

After the Paris climate talks concluded, Modi highlighted India's role in both the ISA and Mission Innovation as markers of success in its clean

---

[87] Modi, n. 153.

[88] Modi, 'Text of PM's closing remarks at Forum for India Pacific Island Countries (FIPIC) Summit, Jaipur', 21 Aug. 2015.

[89] Modi, 'Text of PM's inaugural address at 103rd session of Indian Science Congress', 3 Jan. 2016.

energy efforts. He spoke about being part of Mission Innovation and its focus on innovation in order to make renewable energy and solar energy cheaper and more affordable around the world.[90] However, by weaving in the element of climate justice in the innovation argument, India appeared to signal that will not rest its clean energy ambitions entirely on developed country financial support and technology transfers. Rather there is a suggestion that it hopes to leverage its own innovation and research landscape, as well as the enormous market potential, with the help of both global partnerships and the private sector in order to meet its ambitious clean energy goals.

This chapter provided evidence of the shifting discourse on solar energy under Modi's political leadership. It finds that the initial idea for a new, India-led global alliance based on solar energy came from Modi himself and further raises the question of how India's domestic politics affected its global stance on climate change. I argue that Modi's political leadership marked a key shift in India's foreign policy, wherein climate change became a point of consideration to further India's strategic interests. The next chapter traces India's negotiating history and character during multilateral climate negotiations, in order to explain how the creation of ISA reveals a new kind of Indian economic diplomacy that leveraged the vision of the political leadership and underexplored strategic partnerships.

[90] Ibid.; Modi, 'Text of PM's address on the inauguration ceremony of International Solar Alliance Headquarters in Gurgaon', 25 Jan. 2016; Modi 'PM's address at Centenary Year Convocation of Banaras Hindu University, Varanasi', 22 Feb. 2016.

5

Players

The Role of India's Foreign Policy in Shaping a New Global Identity

ISA is a way to find a global aggregation and convergence towards a global target for solar. India has domestic targets but we hope to extend it into the international arena.
—Former Indian climate negotiator (Participant 32, interview with author, 14 Dec. 2016)

The previous chapter presented empirical evidence to highlight the Modi government's increasing thrust on solar energy. Against the backdrop of India's engagement with multilateral climate negotiations, this chapter investigates the main players behind operationalizing Modi's vision for a new, India-led solar alliance. This chapter presents India's negotiating strategy and legal culture, in order to explain the shift in its foreign policy to capture the political and economic leadership on solar energy. It finds that the dominance of diplomats in India's negotiating teams, often without legal advisers or international lawyers, is responsible for shaping India's external climate strategies. Diplomacy sits at the core of India's international rule-making identity and the process itself is not legalized. Therefore, the broader politico-legal culture of the diplomatic community—a multipolar worldview combined with a long-standing wariness of negotiators to sign onto legally binding provisions—played a determinative role in the choice of legal form of the ISA. Most importantly, the creation of the ISA marks a new kind of economic diplomacy, making it the first deliberate instrument of India's foreign policy on climate change and energy.

The Making of the International Solar Alliance. Vyoma Jha, Oxford University Press. © Vyoma Jha 2023.
DOI: 10.1093/oso/9780198884705.003.0005

A number of scholars have written on how India's negotiating position during multilateral talks derives its basis from the country's foreign policy.[1] Almost all the studies on India during international climate negotiation focus on this issue of 'position'. Sengupta examines India's role in international climate negotiations since the start of the United Nations Framework Convention on Climate Change (UNFCCC).[2] Dubash and Rajamani argue that India's negotiating position is largely defined within a foreign policy frame,[3] with relatively little evolution in domestic politics around climate change since the start of multilateral climate negotiations.[4] Mohan traces the evolution of India's climate policy through the perspective of its broader foreign policy strategy, and argues that India's engagement with international climate politics is best understood by locating its climate policy as a subset of its foreign policy agenda.[5] Vihma makes the case for how the domestic climate policy dialogue in India has been influenced by international negotiations and is shifting toward a more 'internationalist' and proactive approach,[6] while some others describe personality politics as playing a key role in shaping India's climate diplomacy.[7] Dubash also criticizes India's small negotiating team during climate talks,[8] especially the approach where climate change was understood strictly as foreign policy issue that could be managed by a few skilled diplomats backed by a small number of specialists.[9] Within this wide-ranging commentary on India's evolving position in multilateral

[1] N.K. Dubash & L. Rajamani, 'Multilateral Diplomacy on Climate Change', in D.M. Malone, C.R. Mohan, & S. Raghavan, eds, *The Oxford handbook of Indian foreign policy* (Oxford: Oxford University Press, 2015), 663–77; N.K. Dubash, 'Of maps and compasses: India in multilateral climate negotiations', in W.P.S. Sidhu, P.B. Mehta, & B. Jones, eds, *Shaping the emerging world: India and the multilateral order* (Washington, DC: Brookings Institution Press, 2013), 261–79; P.S. Mehta & B. Chatterjee, India in the 'International trading system', in D.M. Malone, C.R. Mohan, & S. Raghavan, eds, *The Oxford handbook of Indian foreign policy* (Oxford: Oxford University Press, 2015), 636–49. https://academic.oup.com/edited-volume/28082/chapter-abstract/212147514?redirectedFrom=fulltext
[2] S. Sengupta, 'International climate negotiations and India's role', in N.K. Dubash, ed., *Handbook of climate change and India: development, politics and governance* (New Delhi: Oxford University Press, 2012), 101–17.
[3] Dubash & Rajamani, n. 1.
[4] Ibid.
[5] A. Mohan, 'From Rio to Paris: India in global climate politics', *Rising Powers Quarterly*, 2/3 (2017), 39–61.
[6] A. Vihma, 'India and the global climate governance: between principles and pragmatism', *The Journal of Environment & Development*, 20/1 (2011), 69–94.
[7] Dubash, n. 1; Dubash & Rajamani, n. 1; see also K. Michaelowa & A. Michaelowa, 'India as an emerging power in international climate negotiations', *Climate Policy*, 12 (2012), 575–90.
[8] Dubash, n. 1.
[9] Ibid., 273.

climate negotiations, Dubash and Rajamani raise an intriguing question for future research: will the emergent framework for climate policy in India create domestic constituencies that shift India's foreign policy stance on climate change?[10]

In this chapter, I build on the argument that Modi's climate leadership, particularly on solar energy, is the first instance of an Indian Prime Minister actively shaping India's position in multilateral climate negotiations. In keeping with Modi's broader vision for a new alliance, India's foreign policy embraced shifting geopolitical realities and used strategic partnerships for climate change gains. The creation of the ISA marks an important shift in India's foreign policy, wherein climate change became a point of consideration to further India's strategic interests: one, to take a leadership role in a climate-adjacent space—solar energy—and reinforce its seriousness about climate action; and two, to assert its global power by creating a new international organization. Against the backdrop of how India engages with international law and multilateral climate negotiations, I attempt to explain how India's foreign policy was at the centre of forging a political and economic leadership on solar energy. Ultimately, as I explained in Chapter 4, ISA's treaty-making process was a function of the key players, in this case Indian diplomats, and how they brought different parties to the table.

Institutional Arrangements for Multilateral Climate Negotiations

In India, the task of foreign policymaking is that of the Ministry of External Affairs (MEA) and falls primarily under the guidance of the Prime Minister's Office (PMO) and Cabinet. The MEA is the political head and the Foreign Secretary is the administrative head of the foreign ministry.[11] The PMO, headed by the Prime Minister, is aided by a number of secretaries, additional secretaries and joint secretaries from different line ministries.[12] Since 1998, India also has a National Security Advisor,

---

[10] Dubash & Rajamani, n. 1, 669.
[11] M. Chatterjee Miller, 'The un-argumentative Indian?: ideas about the rise of India and their interaction with domestic structures', *India Review*, 13/1 (2014), 1–14, 6.
[12] Ibid.

who reports directly to the Prime Minister on domestic and international security issues.[13] The common link between these key departments is the officers of the Indian Foreign Service (IFS), who comprise the dominant foreign policy decision-making elite in India.[14]

India treated climate change as a diplomatic problem from the early years of the international climate negotiations until 2007.[15] Climate policy was synonymous with foreign policy and the main emphasis was on preparing diplomatically for negotiations; India played a leading role in the creation of the UNFCCC and in articulating the concept of 'differentiated responsibility' to ensure that primary responsibility for mitigation rested with the developed countries.[16] At this time, climate policy was handled collaboratively by the MEA and the Ministry of Environment and Forests (MOEF), with a very small number of experienced officials.[17] An influential force in the delegation was the MEA's Ambassador Chandrashekhar Dasgupta, who 'dominated the scene' in India's foreign policy on climate change and is credited with negotiating India's position under the UNFCCC.[18] In fact, he continued to be part of Indian delegations even after his retirement from the government in the year 2000. He remained a part of the official delegations until COP15 in Copenhagen in 2009 and is said have been 'holding the fort together.'[19]

During this time, there was little engagement with or oversight by Parliament, the Cabinet or the PMO.[20] Different line ministries would provide technical inputs on specific issues, such as Ministry of Power or the Department of Science and Technology. Two environmental research

[13] Ibid.
[14] Ibid.
[15] N.K. Dubash & N.B. Joseph, 'Evolution of institutions for climate policy in India', *Economic & Political Weekly*, 51/3 (2016), 45–54.
[16] C. Dasgupta, 'Present at the creation: the making of the framework convention on climate change', in N.K. Dubash, ed., *India in a warming world: integrating climate change and development* (New Delhi: Oxford University Press, 2019), 142–56; S. Sengupta, 'India's engagement in global climate negotiations from Rio to Paris', in N.K. Dubash, ed., *India in a warming world: integrating climate change and development* (New Delhi: Oxford University Press, 2019), 114–41.
[17] S. Jakobsen, *India's position on climate change from Rio to Kyoto: a policy analysis* (Copenhagen: Centre for Development Research, Jan. 1998); N.K. Dubash & S. Ghosh, 'National climate policies and institutions', in N.K. Dubash, ed., *India in a warming world: integrating climate change and development* (New Delhi: Oxford University Press, 2019), 329–48; Dubash & Joseph, n. 15.
[18] Vihma, n. 6, 82.
[19] Ibid.
[20] Jakobsen, n. 17; Dubash & Joseph, n. 15.

organizations, namely The Energy and Resources Institute (TERI) and the Centre for Science and Environment (CSE), had some informal links with the two key ministries. In fact, TERI and CSE played a crucial role in shaping the Indian position on 'common but differentiated responsibilities'.[21] Both organizations worked to advise the MEA and MOEF on global warming issues prior to and during the UNFCCC negotiations. While the MEA officials had grasped the division of responsibilities between developed and developing countries vis-à-vis climate change, these organizations were responsible for drilling down the importance of adopting a political stance that emphasized equity and not collective action. As a result, they were the earliest interest group in sensitizing Indian officials to the risks accompanying acceptance of emissions reduction pledges.[22] Overall, however, there was limited institutionalization of climate policymaking in this period, and a limited number of individuals formulated India's negotiating position.[23]

In 2007, in a significant move, then Prime Minister, Dr Manmohan Singh, established the Prime Minister's Council on Climate Change.[24] Following this, climate policymaking was in the hands of an inter-ministerial group led by the Prime Minister, and India's negotiating position was no longer formed by only a couple of top-level bureaucrats.[25] This period marked an increase in public deliberation on international climate politics, with more political commentators and journalists covering the issue.[26] The Prime Minister's Special Envoy on Climate Change, Ambassador Shyam Saran, played an important coordinating role in the formulation of the National Action Plan on Climate Change (NAPCC)—the main policy document on climate change—and was one of the key negotiators at Copenhagen. However, in March 2010, due to growing inter-institutional tensions, the Office of the Special Envoy was

---

[21] K. Nachiappan, *Does India negotiate?* (New Delhi: Oxford University Press, 2019), 63–70

[22] Ibid., 195.

[23] Dubash & Joseph, n. 15, 46.

[24] PIB, *PM's Council on Climate Change constituted* [media release] (5 Jun. 2007), https://archivepmo.nic.in/drmanmohansingh/press-details.php?nodeid=575, accessed 15 Jan. 2022.

[25] Vihma, n. 6, 82–3.

[26] A. Jogesh, 'A change in climate? Trends in climate change reportage in the Indian print media', in N.K. Dubash, ed., *Handbook of climate change and India: development, politics and governance* (New Delhi: Oxford University Press, 2012) 266–86; A. Jogesh, 'Looking out, looking in: the shifting discourse on climate change in the Indian print media', in N.K. Dubash, ed., *India in a warming world: integrating climate change and development* (New Delhi: Oxford University Press, 2019), 301–25; Vihma, n. 6.

closed and the task of coordination of climate policy across the government went to the MOEF. Then Environment Minister, Jairam Ramesh, took a personal interest in coordination across ministries, but inter-ministerial power equations came in the way of effective coordination on domestic actions on climate change. To overcome this problem of coordination, a new Executive Committee on Climate Change was constituted in 2013, which was chaired by the principal secretary to the PM and comprised Secretaries of all relevant ministries.[27] Therefore, from mid-2010 to 2014, it was the MOEF that took the lead on all matters of domestic climate policy and international negotiations.

In 2014, soon after the Modi government came to power, the MOEF was renamed as the Ministry of Environment, Forest and Climate Change (MOEFCC)—with an added emphasis on climate change. However, scholars have noted that despite signalling an intent to take climate change more seriously, there has not been any significant growth in climate institutions or enhancement of the government's capacity to consider climate issues.[28] At the moment, the Climate Change Division in the MOEFCC has a core team of seven persons working on climate issues, which is assisted by consultants from time to time.[29] One of the key processes of domestic climate policymaking in this period was formulation of the Nationally Determined Contributions (NDC) in the lead up to COP21 in Paris in 2015.[30] The MOEFCC initiated intensive consultations in various ministries, departments, and state governments, and inter-ministerial committees were constituted to develop sector-specific background material for India's submissions. In addition, the environment ministry also reached out to think tanks and research organizations for inputs on modelling studies.[31] Crucially, during this period, Modi and the PMO played a direct role in making the 'political judgment calls, trade-offs and compromises' during the climate negotiations.[32]

---

[27] PIB, *Executive Committee on Climate Change constituted* [media release] (31 Jan. 2013), https://archivepmo.nic.in/drmanmohansingh/press-details.php?nodeid=1568, accessed 15 Jan. 2022.

[28] Dubash & Ghosh, n. 17, 340–2.

[29] MOEFCC, *Climate Change Division*, http://moef.gov.in/dy-contact-details/?id=15718

[30] Dubash & Ghosh, n. 17, 335–6.

[31] Ibid.

[32] Sengupta, n. 16, 134.

India's Climate Negotiating Teams

Mapping the Indian delegation to the COP over two decades (Table 5.1), reveals that the negotiating teams typically comprise bureaucrats from the MOEFCC, MEA, and sometimes other line ministries such as the MNRE or Ministry of Power. Between 1997 and 2007, the size of Indian delegation size ranged from eight to twenty-six persons, with an average delegation size of about ten to twelve persons. Between 2008 and 2015 (not including the Copenhagen and Paris conferences), the average delegation size increased to about thirty persons. The two most significant, and high-profile years for climate negotiations—Copenhagen (2009) and Paris (2015)—saw dramatically larger Indian delegations. India sent seventy-seven delegates to COP15 in Copenhagen, and 185 delegates to COP21 in Paris.[33]

Significantly, in most years, almost half the delegation size comprises the diplomats or embassy staff in the host country of the climate conference. Although, legal advisers in international law are located in the Legal and Treaties (L&T) Division in India's foreign ministry, that is, MEA, they have not regularly been a part of the climate negotiations. Only two conferences—Copenhagen (2009) and Paris (2015)—had legal officers from the L&T Division. The only other instance of legal expertise on the negotiating team was when a legal consultant was hired by the MOEFCC in the run-up to the Paris climate talks.

In light of the fact that India aspires to move from a 'rule-taker' to a 'rule-maker', or at least a 'rule-shaper' in the multilateral realm, Madan has written extensively about India's state capacity for multilateralism.[34] She criticizes India's capacity to deal with its external commitments, from the relatively small size of the IFS to capacity issues related to other parts of officialdom.[35] Several accounts from retired foreign policy officials also suggest that Indian bureaucrats and diplomats have insufficient

---

[33] Interestingly, these numbers remain very small in comparison to the Chinese delegation of three hundred persons in Copenhagen and nearly four hundred persons in Paris.

[34] T. Madan, 'What in the world is India able to do? India's state capacity for multilateralism', in W.P.S. Sidhu, P.B. Mehta, & B. Jones, eds, *Shaping the emerging world: India and the multilateral order* (Brookings Institution Press, Washington DC, 2013) 96–114.

[35] T. Madan, 'What in the world is India able to do? India's state capacity for multilateralism', in W.P.S. Sidhu, P.B. Mehta, & B. Jones, eds, *Shaping the emerging world: India and the multilateral order* (Washington, DC: Brookings Institution Press, 2013) 96–114.

Table 5.1 Composition of the Indian Delegation at the UNFCCC Conference of Parties (1997–2015)*

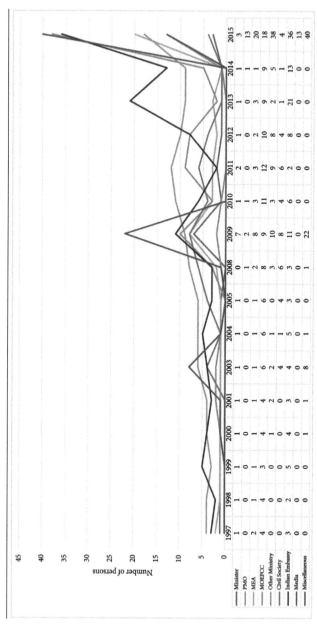

	1997	1998	1999	2000	2001	2003	2004	2005	2008	2009	2010	2011	2012	2013	2014	2015
Minister	1	1	0	0	1	1	1	0	0	7	1	2	1	1	1	3
PMO	0	0	0	0	0	0	0	0	1	2	1	0	0	0	1	13
MEA	2	1	1	1	1	0	1	1	2	8	3	3	2	3	1	20
MOEFCC	4	4	3	4	4	6	6	6	8	9	11	12	10	9	9	18
Other Ministry	0	0	0	0	2	2	1	0	3	10	3	9	8	2	5	38
Civil Society	0	0	0	0	0	4	1	4	6	8	4	6	4	1	1	4
Indian Embassy	3	2	5	4	3	4	5	3	3	11	6	2	8	21	13	36
Media	0	0	0	0	0	0	0	0	0	0	0	0	0	0	0	13
Miscellaneous	0	0	0	1	1	8	1	0	1	22	0	0	0	0	0	40

Number of persons

Source: Author's own analysis based on the Conference of the Parties (COP) participation data available on https://unfccc.int/

* The participation data for the years 2002, 2006, and 2007 was not available on the official website of the UNFCCC. For the purposes of this research, however, the missing data does not detract from the broader trends that can be observed in the Indian delegation over the years.

respect for professional inputs and believe that they are 'infallible'.[36] Most of the accounts on India's state capacity for foreign policy lack a focus on legal actors and legal capacity.[37]

India has instituted a formal role for legal advisers within the Legal and Treaties (L&T) Division within the MEA. Created in 1957, this division is the 'nodal point' to deal with all aspects of international law advice to the Government of India and serves as the sole source of legal advice for the MEA. However, there is little evidence to determine this division's impact on Indian foreign policymaking. McCosker finds that legal advisers are treated as 'diplomat-lawyers' with more emphasis on their diplomatic functions.[38] Specialized areas of international law are now spread out across various ministries. For instance, the MOEFCC handles all matters relating to climate change, Ministry of Commerce and Industry (MOCI) handles international trade, and MNRE is responsible for solar energy. However, the L&T Division in MEA remains the only source of legal advice for these Ministries on all matters of international law; any legal advice to non-MEA ministries is based on 'ad hocism'.[39] India's relatively small negotiating team, with limited legal capacity, has been a frequent point of criticism in analysis of India's engagement with global climate governance.[40] Key stakeholders involved closely with climate negotiations have highlighted the need for creating institutional memory, as well as the need for legal capacity during climate negotiations.[41]

As a long-time Indian climate negotiator explains:

---

[36] E. Gonsalves, 'India in a future world: reflections of an Indian diplomat', *India Quarterly*, 71/4 (2015), 287–99.

[37] B.N. Patel, *State practice of India and the development of international law: dynamic interplay between foreign policy and jurisprudence* (Leiden: Brill, 2016); K.S. Rana, *Asian diplomacy: the foreign ministries of China, India, Japan, Singapore and Thailand* (Washington DC: Woodrow Wilson Center Press, 2009).

[38] S. McCosker, 'The intersecting professions of the international law adviser and diplomat in rising Asia: Australia, India and Malaysia', in A. Zidar & J. Gauci, eds, *The Role of Legal Advisers in International Law* (Leiden: Brill, 2017), 96–127.

[39] Ibid.

[40] N.K. Dubash, 'The politics of climate change in India: narratives of equity and cobenefits', *WIREs Climate Change*, 4/3 (2013), 191–201; L. Rajamani, 'India's approach to international law in the climate change regime', *Indian Journal of International Law*, 57/2 (2017), 1–23.

[41] V. Jha, 'Sunny skies ahead? Political economy of climate, trade and solar energy in India', *Trade, Law and Development*, 9/2 (2017), 255–304.

The Indian delegation was always much smaller than the requirement or even compared to delegations of other similar countries. Briefs for climate change meetings were prepared jointly by the Ministry of Environment, Forests and Climate Change (MOEFCC) and the Ministry of External Affairs (MEA). Political negotiations had MEA officials in the lead with MOEFCC and other ministries playing this role during particular substantive negotiations but it was a team effort. While the Prime Minister's Office was always in the loop given the importance of climate change negotiations, right from the time of finalizing the delegation; post 2014 it was the PM I believe who took a more direct role.[42]

Even as India is being touted as a 'rule-maker' in the global realm, it continues to have little to no legal capacity within its core negotiating teams during multilateral talks. Who, then, are key actors shaping India's negotiating positions and helping draft international rules? If not legal expertise, then what is it about India's negotiating teams that is turning them into 'rule-makers'?

Understanding India's Negotiating Character

India's role in multilateral institutions is that of an emerging global power acutely aware of its rising global influence, and it has used different international institutions to advance specific Indian ideas and norms.[43] An Indian diplomat, when asked once what India does best internationally, replied without a moment's hesitation saying 'multilateral diplomacy.'[44] India has long showcased her intentions to gain a permanent seat in the United Nations (UN) Security Council and has held a non-permanent seat in the UN Security Council for seven terms,[45] with the eighth and

[42] Mohan, n. 5, 54.
[43] A. Michael, 'India and multilateralism: concepts, new trajectories and theorizing', in H.V. Pant, ed., New directions in India's foreign policy: theory and praxis (Cambridge: Cambridge University Press, 2019), 149–71, 156.
[44] R. Mukherjee & D.M. Malone, 'From high ground to high table: the evolution of Indian multilateralism', Global Governance, 17 (2011), 311–29, 323.
[45] 1950–2, 1965–7, 1970–2 1976–8, 1983–5, 1990–2 and 2011–13.

most recent term beginning in 2021.[46] A recent milestone in India's soft power outreach via global multilateralism came with the successful campaign at the UN for the introduction of an International Day of Yoga.[47] For India, a strong focus underlying its efforts to create the ISA as a treaty-based organization was to have a greater say in the international arena. One interviewee adds, 'the ISA offered an opportunity for India to be a serious player [at the multilateral climate negotiations] and get into the club of the decisionmakers.'[48]

Negotiation strategies can either be the strict distributive, or value-claiming, strategy; or the integrative, or value-creating, strategy.[49] The distributive strategy involves tactics that are useful only for claiming value from others and defending against such claiming, when one party's goals are in conflict with those of others'. For instance, very high opening demands, refusing to make any concessions, and holding the other's issues hostage. The integrative strategy, meanwhile, includes actions that are aimed at expanding rather than splitting the pie.[50] Indian negotiators have used the strict distributive strategy with continued aplomb, both over time and across issue areas.[51]

India's domestic political culture supports grandstanding abroad, and has over the years reinforced a worldview that supports distributive strategies.[52] The costs of India's defensive, nay-saying strategy (referred to by negotiation analysts as the 'strict distributive strategy') have ranged from impasse, unrealized gains from the failed negotiations, penalties from negotiating partners, as well as being labelled a disruptive influence and a trouble-maker.[53] However, Indian negotiators and diplomats have shown remarkable consistency in their willingness to say 'no'.[54] This willingness to bear the costs of using a distributive strategy is captured in the following

---

[46] PTI, 'India elected non-permanent member of UN Security Council for 2-year term', *Business Standard* (18 Jun. 2020), https://www.business-standard.com/article/current-affairs/india-elected-non-permanent-member-of-un-security-council-for-2021-22-term-120061800081_1.html, accessed 15 Jan. 2022.

[47] Michael, n. 43, 153–4.

[48] Participant 9, interview with author, 14 Sep. 2020.

[49] A. Narlikar, 'Peculiar chauvinism or strategic calculation? Explaining the negotiating strategy of a rising India', *International Affairs*, 82/1 (2006), 59–76, 61–2.

[50] Ibid.

[51] Ibid.

[52] Ibid., 61.

[53] Ibid., 60.

[54] Ibid.

statement by an Indian negotiator: 'It is easier for our minister to come back home empty-handed as a wounded hero, rather than to come back with something after having had to make a compromise.'[55] Echoing the distributive strategy, one interviewee noted that 'India will not negotiate if it's not forced into it.'[56] Former Indian Foreign Secretary and Prime Minister's Special Envoy on Climate Change, Shyam Saran, also notes that 'in multilateral negotiations India has adopted a mostly defensive stance instead of leading international opinion towards an alternative solution.'[57]

From the perspective of the Indian negotiator saying no is the safer option, particularly in the context of international institutions whose rules are binding, and whose decision-making structures are seen by the negotiator to privilege the developed countries.[58] While the distributive negotiation strategy is dominant in its bargaining with the established powers, Indian negotiators are willing to adopt a mixed distributive strategy with other rising powers and an integrative strategy with smaller powers.[59] As a result, India's coalitions and framing tactics map out quite closely and consistently with its negotiation strategy. It has a tendency to create and strengthen coalitions with other developing countries, both rising powers and smaller developing countries, in order to balance against the established powers.[60] Most of these coalitions are 'issue-based' and usually comprise developing countries (rather than a mix of developed and developing).[61] Within the climate change regime, India has tactically forged alliances to adapt to shifting circumstances.[62]

Historically, India has been among the leaders of the G77—the developing countries. In recent years, however, India had begun to alienate many traditional allies within this negotiating bloc with whom it shares much in common, such as the Least Developed Countries (LDC), the Alliance of Small Island States (AOSIS), and the Africa Group.[63] Some

---

[55] Ibid., 72.

[56] Participant 7, interview with author, 6 Dec. 2016

[57] S. Saran, *How India sees the world: Kautilya to the 21st century* (New Delhi: Juggernaut, 2017), 191.

[58] Narlikar, n. 49, 73.

[59] A. Narlikar, 'India rising: responsible to whom?', *International Affairs*, 89/3 (2013), 595–614, 610.

[60] Ibid.

[61] Ibid.

[62] Dubash & Rajamani, n. 1, 671–3.

[63] Ibid.

experts are extremely critical of India's negotiating strategy, saying that it's 'virtually non-existent.'[64] Others described India's negotiating tactic during climate change negotiations as maintaining a 'heroic victim' discourse at the global level.[65] As one interview puts it:

> The Chinese head of delegation [in the climate change negotiations] is the same for 20 years. In India, a diplomat's travel plans are dependent on approval from the Finance Ministry, which comes a day or two before the conference—where is the headspace for negotiations? Where is the institutional memory? There is a major need for administrative reforms as the MEA has no expertise on niche negotiations ... Indian climate change negotiators have been stuck on the principle of equity, but need to think harder on how to advance a more nuanced position on equity to reflect a changing world.[66]

India's External Climate Strategy

India's external positions on climate change have been influenced and shaped by a number of institutional factors. A core group of serving and retired MOEF and MEA officials have held a near monopoly in terms of determining what India's interest on this issue were and what its negotiating position should be.[67] India's early behaviour in climate change negotiations stemmed from an interest-based understanding of the climate regime, and India's desire to secure enough policy space and carbon space within it to ensure its future development.[68] The tenor of India's approach at UNFCCC negotiations has been more political than

---

[64] Participant 7, n. 168.
[65] J. Plagemann & M. Prys-Hansen, ' "Responsibility", change, and rising powers' role conceptions: comparing Indian foreign policy roles in global climate change negotiations and maritime security', *International Relations of the Asia-Pacific* 20/2 (2020), 275–305.
[66] Participant 7, n. 168.
[67] S. Sengupta, 'Deciphering India's foreign policy on climate change: role of interests, institutions and ideas', in J. Plagemann, S. Destradi, & A. Narlikar, eds, *India rising: a multilayered analysis of ideas, interests and institutions* (New Delhi: Oxford University Press, 2020) 166–94, 183.
[68] Ibid., 181.

environmental mostly due to the MEA officials overseeing these negotiations. Negotiations were seen as a constraint and not as an opportunity, which in turn affected the approach of MEA officials.[69]

The main reason for the long continuity in India's foreign policy on climate was a strong belief among these officials that their reasoning and positions were right and required no changing.[70] This belief grew stronger in the face of the global North's unwillingness to abide by their prior promises under the UNFCCC and Kyoto Protocol.[71] Internal capacity constraints have also led to a continuity in India's foreign policy on climate as the natural tendency of India's climate negotiators was to stick to existing and agreed defendable positions, rather than propose or consider any new concepts or approaches.[72]

Over time, however, there have been some important changes in India's negotiating position that can be attributed to a few factors: first, the emergence of powerful new voices within India's policymaking bodies on climate change, particularly the internal shift in the balance of power between the political and bureaucratic leadership;[73] second, the growing international and peer pressure (from new alliances) on India to undertake climate action;[74] and third, the broader geopolitical implications of India emerging as a powerful economic and political actor on the global stage.[75]

India's understanding of its domestic interests has evolved over time. For instance, it was first seen on the Clean Development Mechanism (CDM), where India moved its position in the late 1990s from opposition to support. This resulted from a revised understanding among key policymakers, aided in great part by domestic industry groups and research think tanks, that participating in the CDM could yield grater material benefits and advantages for India.[76] Over the years, India's foreign policy on climate has evolved a greater appreciation of the risks that climate

---

[69] Nachiappan, n. 21, 193.

[70] Sengupta, n. 67, 183; Sengupta, n. 16, 133; Vihma, n. 6, 82–3.

[71] Sengupta, n. 67.

[72] Ibid.

[73] A. Atteridge et al., 'Climate policy in India: what shapes international, national and state policy?', Ambio, 41/1 (2012), 68–77.

[74] Sengupta, n. 16, 134.

[75] Ibid., 136–7.

[76] Sengupta, n. 67, 181; Jakobsen, n. 17.

change—and global inaction—pose to India's future welfare and security. More recently, there is a growing understanding that taking action on climate change can yield other material co-benefits for the country, such as improving local health by tackling household, vehicular, and industrial emissions or enhancing the country's energy security by lowering its dependence on fossil fuel imports.[77]

Regional-level factors, however, have not been salient in influencing India's interests on climate change. India's South Asian neighbours don't have similar interests or preferences because of their smaller size, different international positions and ambitions, and a unique set of vulnerabilities of their own. Even though SAARC countries a part of the larger developing country bloc—G77—many belong to different coalitions within the international climate negotiations. For instance, Nepal and Bangladesh are part of the LDC group, while Maldives is a member of the AOSIS.[78]

Legal Form and Legal Bindingness

Since the beginning of climate talks, the ideas of securing equity and justice have been central in framing India's external policies on climate change.[79] India's negotiators sought to operationalize these principally through the ideas of 'historical responsibility', 'per capita convergence' and 'equitable carbon space'.[80] India's resistance to any legally binding emissions reduction commitments has been driven by a strong desire to protect India from constraints that could curtail India's development trajectory. This long-standing leadership on the principle of common but differentiated responsibility is an important precursor to understanding the shift it India's negotiating strategy before the Paris climate talks.

As Rajamani notes, architecture, legal form and differentiation are the three central, intertwined issues in the international climate change regime, and 'the stronger the legal character of the obligation, the less

---

[77] Sengupta, n. 67.
[78] Ibid.
[79] Ibid.
[80] Ibid.

autonomy states have, and thus greater the differentiation sought by developing countries.'[81]

The key legal instruments to emerge from the international climate change regime have had different architecture and legal form over the years. The 1997 Kyoto Protocol (KP), representing the 'top-down' architecture, had legally binding targets and timetables for developed countries (categorized as Annex I countries in the UNFCCC and Annex B countries in the KP). These targets were based on commonly agreed rules, with a strong system for measurement, reporting, and verification (MRV), and a stringent compliance mechanism.[82] For developing countries the Kyoto Protocol signified developed country leadership, even as several developed countries were unhappy with the final agreement and refused to be party to it.[83] Most significantly, the United States did not ratify the Kyoto Protocol and did not become a party to the agreement. The second commitment period of the Kyoto Protocol was even less popular, with countries such as Russia and Japan withdrawing form the agreement.[84]

The 2009 Copenhagen Accord, reflecting a complete departure from the Kyoto-like architecture, was a political agreement with no legal force and that provided for parties to submit self-selected national actions and commitments.[85] This 'bottom-up' approach was followed in the 2010 Cancun Agreements, which deferred to national autonomy in arriving at commitments in the face of diverse national circumstances and constraints.[86]

In the build-up to the Paris climate talks, the 2013 Warsaw Decision had firmly cemented the 'bottom-up' approach to climate action by inviting parties to initiate/intensify domestic preparations for NDCs.[87] Further, the 2014 Lima Call to Climate Action laid out a blueprint for the information countries were supposed to provide in their NDCs.[88]

---

[81] L. Rajamani, 'Understanding the 2015 Paris Agreement', in N.K. Dubash, ed., *India in a warming world: integrating climate change and development* (New Delhi: Oxford University Press, 2019) 205–21, 206.

[82] Ibid.

[83] Ibid.

[84] Ibid.

[85] D. Bodansky & L. Rajamani, 'Issues that never die', *Carbon and Climate Law Review*, 12/3 (2018), 184–90, 184.

[86] Rajamani, n. 81, 207.

[87] L. Rajamani, 'The Warsaw Climate Negotiations: emerging understandings and battle lines on the road to the 2015 Climate Agreement', *International and Comparative Law Quarterly*, 63/3 (2014), 721–40.

[88] Rajamani, n. 81, 207–8.

Therefore, the climate change negotiations at Paris sought to design a 'hybrid' instrument with bottom-up substance to promote participation (contained in parties' contributions) and a top-down process to promote ambition and accountability.[89]

In 2015, after almost two decades of negotiations, the Paris Agreement in 2015 reached a compromise between the legal form of the instrument as a whole and the legal character of the provisions.[90] In other words, the Paris Agreement is a legal instrument, or 'treaty' under international law but its provisions have varying degrees of normative force.[91] The Agreement creates some procedural obligations on parties with respect to the preparation and communication of NDCs, but it does not make the content of these NDCs legally binding on parties.[92]

An important distinction is made between the legal form of an agreement and the legal character of provisions within the agreement.[93] A treaty—a legally binding instrument requiring state consent[94]—could contain a range of provisions with differing legal character.[95] The legal character of a provision rests on three considerations: (1) the extent to which the provision creates rights and obligations for parties; (2) whether it sets standards for state behaviour; and (3) whether it lends itself to assessments of compliance/non-compliance and the resulting visitation of consequences.[96]

While the Paris Agreement has 'treaty' form in international law, it contains provisions that are spread across the spectrum of the legal character—from 'hard law' provisions that create the central obligation

---

[89] Ibid.

[90] D. Bodansky, 'The legal character of the Paris Agreement', *Review of European, Comparative and International Environmental Law*, 25(2) (2016), 142–50.

[91] L. Rajamani, 'The 2015 Paris Agreement: interplay between hard, soft, and non-obligations', *Journal of Environmental Law*, 28/2 (2016), 337–58; Bodansky, n. 90.

[92] Bodansky & Rajamani, n. 85.

[93] L. Rajamani, 'Ambition and differentiation in the 2015 Paris Agreement: interpretative possibilities and underlying politics', *International and Comparative Law Quarterly*, 65/2 (2016), 493–514.

[94] Vienna Convention 1969, Article 11.

[95] Rajamani, n. 81, 208.

[96] Ibid. The legal character of a provision depends on a range of factors, including location (where the provision occurs), subjects (whom the provision addresses), normative content (what requirements, obligations, or standards the provision contains), language (whether the provision uses mandatory or recommendatory language), precision (whether the provision uses contextual, qualifying, or discretionary clauses), and oversight (what institutional mechanisms exist for transparency, accountability, and compliance).

on countries to submit NDCs, to 'soft law' provisions that set standards with qualifying and discretionary elements and in recommendatory terms.[97] The Paris Agreement even contains, what is described as 'non-law' provisions, which capture understandings between parties, provide context or offer a narrative in the operational part of the legally binding instrument, but lack in normative content.[98] This dynamic interplay between the hard, soft, and non-law elements is a unique feature of the Paris Agreement, wherein each provision reflects the demands of the relevant issue area and the particular politics that drove its negotiation.[99]

The question of legal bindingness, or the degree to which the legal regime should impost legally binding obligations on countries, has been the longest-standing issues for India under the international climate change regime.[100] A negotiated legal instrument is considered to be 'legally binding' when it renders a particular state conduct mandatory, and judicially enforceable.[101] Under the international climate change regime, India has consistently rejected legally binding mitigation commitments in light of its significant development, energy, and poverty challenges.[102] In relation to the UNFCCC and Kyoto Protocol, India agreed to the legally binding nature of the agreements at the outset since they explicitly contained differentiated commitments for developed and developing countries.[103]

Some commentators have noted that although India was very successful in shaping the original climate regime and defending it in the early years, it found international climate negotiations harder to navigate in subsequent years.[104] As climate negotiations moved towards extending the mitigation commitments to developing countries in the 2000s, India grew wary of the legal form of the negotiated instrument.[105] One of the reasons for this wariness has been ascribed to a concern that the

[97] Rajamani, n. 93.

[98] Ibid. For example, Article 6(8), stating that 'parties recognize the importance of integrated, holistic and balanced non-market approaches being available to Parties'.

[99] Rajamani, n. 81, 215.

[100] Bodansky & Rajamani, n. 85.

[101] Rajamani, n. 40, 2; J. Brunnee, 'COPing with consent: law-making under multilateral environmental agreements', Leiden Journal of International Law, 15/1 (2002), 1–52, 32.

[102] Rajamani, n. 40, 7.

[103] Ibid., 16.

[104] Sengupta, n. 16, 136–7.

[105] Rajamani, n. 40, 17.

fundamental premises and practices of international law are hegemonic, which limits the ability of countries like India to influence international instruments.[106] Another reason for the reluctance to negotiate a legally binding agreement could be traced to serious capacity constraints, particularly international legal capacity.[107]

One of the major instances of India's reluctance to agree to a legally binding instrument came at the Durban climate talks. The BASIC countries had initially opposed a legally binding instrument owing to concerns about their development space, but backed the idea of a legally binding instrument by the 2011 Durban climate talks. In the final hours of the Durban climate negotiations, India was the only country firmly opposed to a legally binding instrument—describing it as a red line it could not cross.[108] About thirty hours after the scheduled end of the Durban conference, the term 'agreed outcome with legal force' emerged as a result of a high-profile 'huddle' with the EU and India, brokered by the US, the UK, and the South African hosts.[109] Ultimately, the Durban Platform launched a new phase of negotiations towards a 'protocol, another legal instrument or agreed outcome with legal force'—this wording kept a range of possibilities open regarding the legal form of the agreement.[110] With this formulation India appeared to have retained the option of negotiating an agreement that was not internationally legally binding.[111] Then Environment Minister, Jayanthi Natarajan, in her statement to the Indian Parliament on her return stated that the Durban decision 'allows India necessary flexibility over the choice of appropriate legal form to be decided in the future.'[112]

It is suggested that India remained sceptical of a legally binding instrument primarily due to a lack of confidence that it could play a determinative role in shaping the legally binding instrument that would emerge.[113] Rajamani argues that 'a sophisticated understanding of the relationship

[106] Ibid., 17–19.
[107] Ibid., 19–21.
[108] Ibid., 10–11.
[109] Ibid., 11.
[110] L. Rajamani, 'The Durban Platform for Enhanced Action and the Future of the Climate Regime', *International and Comparative Law Quarterly*, 61/2 (2012), 501–18.
[111] Rajamani, n. 40, 11.
[112] Ibid., 12.
[113] Rajamani, n. 81, 209.

between legal form and character ... could have enabled India to support a legally binding treaty, while still calibrating the legal bindingness of particular provisions within the treaty to address their concerns and deliver the substantive provisions that were in their interest.'[114]

By the Paris climate talks, the negotiations had gathered traction on the notion of NDCs and India too had softened its stance on the legal form of the agreement.[115] There was an increasing recognition and acceptance by states of the distinction between the legal form of the instrument and the legal character of NDCs—in that by respecting national circumstances and allowing self-differentiation, it would significantly reduce the sovereignty costs of a legally binding instrument.[116] Therefore, under the Paris Agreement, the main obligation on states in relation to mitigation is merely to submit NDCs, not necessarily to achieve them.[117] The Paris Agreement marks an innovative approach to global climate change regulation, by combining elements of both the 'top-down' and 'bottom-up' architecture to ensure widespread participation.[118] In an attempt to 'balance the breadth of coverage with depth of commitments', the Paris Agreement combines ambitious long-term goals captured in NDCs, with binding obligations of conduct and a rigorous oversight system.[119] The widespread commitment at Paris came at the cost of less stringent commitments, even as the future operationalization of the Paris Rulebook will determine whether the action of states, non-state, and sub-states actors will indeed meet the goals of the Paris Agreement.[120]

India's New Economic Diplomacy

India's negotiating strategy has provided insights into how a rising India approaches the question of international responsibility. Narlikar argues

---

[114] Ibid.
[115] Ibid., 209–10.
[116] Ibid.
[117] Ibid., 214.
[118] Ibid., 216.
[119] Ibid.
[120] Ibid., 218.

that India shows considerable reluctance to share the burden of the provision of global public goods, as seen by the persistent use of the distributive strategy towards the established powers, private actors, and international organizations. Although, India shows a readiness to provide 'club goods' for smaller groups of countries, especially when it involves smaller developing countries.[121] Narlikar offers two explanations for this reluctance to provide global public goods: first, their nay-saying stems from the belief that they cannot be expected to provide public goods that they had no role or choice in identifying in the first instance; second, India cannot be expected to provide public goods at this stage in its development, when such a large part of its own populations lives in abject poverty.[122] Therefore, these two issues—willingness and ability—have acted as significant deterrents to India taking on a bigger role in global burden-sharing.[123] She argues that 'if India is to make the transition from a rising power to a Great Power, it will have to go beyond its commitment to the provision of club goods and accept some responsibilities for the provision of public goods.'[124] Miller-Chatterjee, meanwhile, has argued that 'India can be convinced to play an international role in areas where its narrow interests are at stake, but it will not respond positively to abstract calls for it to assume more global responsibility.'[125]

The traditional hardline position of Indian negotiators was on development and that the historical absence of India's emissions means that it has the developmental space and right to grow. However, the Paris climate talks saw a marked shift in India's negotiating strategy. An American commentator on India's global affairs, Ayres, notes that in the context of global climate change, India has moved from its earlier oppositional position to present itself as offering an alternative pathway and global leadership on clean energy.[126] She writes, 'in less than a decade, India has moved from a 'playing defense' approach on climate change to a new and different

[121] Narlikar, n. 59, 611.
[122] A. Narlikar, 'India's role in global governance: a Modification?', International Affairs, 93/1 (2017), 93–111, 98.
[123] Ibid., 99.
[124] Narlikar, n. 59, 610. Narlikar, n. 122, 99.
[125] M. Chatterjee-Miller, 'India's feeble foreign policy: a would-be great power resists its own rise', Foreign Affairs, 92/3 (2013), 14–19.
[126] A. Ayres, Our time has come: how India is making its place in the world (New Delhi: Oxford University Press, 2018), 164.

leadership role in setting the global agenda in a manner consistent with India's priorities and concerns.'[127] A French interviewee noted that earlier Indian governments sent envoys who would emphasize on India's reliance on coal for development, but there was a shift in the thinking of the Indian delegation before Paris.[128] A former American climate negotiator also observed: 'I noticed clear shifts in the negotiators pre-2014 and post-2014. There was a marked uptick in India's engagement [on issues of climate change] with the beginning of the Modi government. There weren't any signs of this in the earlier Congress government.'[129]

Under Modi, the PMO played a more direct role in formulating India's foreign policy on climate. Unlike the past, in the lead-up to COP21, the final shot was not called by the officials at the MEA or MOEFCC.[130] There was an emergence of two kinds of Indian negotiators in Paris: one, those who were firmly attached to the traditional position; and two, those who were pragmatic and empowered by the PMO to make deals on the Paris Agreement. In the words of an interviewee the Indian delegation at Paris was an 'enhanced Indian negotiating team' that was much more progressive than earlier Indian negotiating teams. According to him: 'Modi was far more invested in getting a new deal in Paris [than previous Indian leaders] … Modi's decisions to ramp up the targets on solar and renewable energy set a clear expectation that these domestic targets should have an international response in terms on finance and technology.'[131]

India's climate policy had operated within its overall foreign policy framework for over two decades, with the MEA playing a critical role in driving India's position and defining negotiating red-lines. Under the Modi government, too, the foreign ministry led the charge during the climate negotiations at Paris. This time, however, India's negotiating team at Paris led by S. Jaishankar—India's then foreign secretary—had a 'forward leaning' approach on climate change.[132] The primary focus was the creation of a new global institution—ISA—which I argue became a deliberate instrument of India's foreign policy on climate change and energy.

[127] Ibid., 166.
[128] Participant 9, n. 160.
[129] Participant 3, interview with author, 30 Jul. 2019.
[130] Sengupta, n. 67, 184.
[131] Ibid.
[132] Ibid.

From a negotiating perspective, this marks an integrative approach by India, as she was not only proactive in securing the final deal at Paris, but also helped create a new institution to channelize finance and technology into solar deployment in the developing world. A move that ties back to into its historic stance of 'common but differentiated responsibility', and climate action in the developing world hinging on adequate funding and technology transfer.

It should be noted that the US and China, the world's top two emitters of greenhouse gases, had announced a bilateral climate accord in the run up to the Paris conference.[133] The pressure on India, the third-largest emitter, to announce a similar deal with the US was mounting. However, as one former US negotiator noted: 'they [India] were much more invested in pursuing their own announcement—and rightly so!' Within the broader context of climate change negotiations and India's negotiating culture, the creation of ISA as an international organization indicates India's motivation to take on a bigger role in global governance, independently of the United States and China.

The motivation for the ISA was to bring developing countries together around new issue areas and recalibrate global rules of engagement.[134] This was reinforced by the strong economic potential for solar deployment in the member countries of the new organization. An interviewee noted that the ISA was a 'true illustration of economics and diplomacy being closely linked.'[135] One of the main instruments of India's development cooperation include Lines of Credit (LOCs) in India's neighbourhood, Africa, and increasingly to Southeast Asia, East and Central Asia, the Caribbean, Latin America, Pacific Island Countries, etc. The development partnership is a pillar of South–South cooperation, and the LOC mechanism is a major part of the initiative through which India assists developing countries by providing them with low-interest soft loans.[136] A significant portion of GOI LOCs were in the solar energy sector (see

[133] M. Landler, 'U.S. and China reach climate accord after months of talks', *The New York Times* (11 Nov. 2014), https://www.nytimes.com/2014/11/12/world/asia/china-us-xi-obama-apec.html, accessed 15 Jan. 2022.
[134] Participant 34, interview with author, 8 Dec. 2016. Participant 16, interview with author, 14 Dec. 2016.
[135] Participant 27, interview with author, 16 Dec. 2016.
[136] MEA (Government of India), 'Rajya Sabha unstarred question no. 460 development cooperation with foreign countries: answer by Gen. (Dr.) V.K. Singh, Minister of State in the

Table 5.2), and the ISA presented an opportunity to turn the provision of 'club goods' into 'public goods'.

By creating a new international organization for solar energy, the Indian government aimed to move this issue beyond South–South co-operation. Further, by highlighting the market potential for solar deployment in ISA's 'solar-rich' countries, the effort was to coalesce global finance and technologies in areas that need it the most and have tremendous potential for market growth. At the ISA's Founding Conference, the Government of India announced nearly US$1.4 billion worth of line of credit for solar energy projects (see Table 5.3). Further, by highlighting the market potential for solar deployment in ISA's 'solar-rich' countries, the effort was to coalesce global finance and technologies in areas that need it the most and have tremendous potential for market growth.

India's diplomats showcased a new kind of economic diplomacy at Paris: first, by creating a new global institution by leveraging its domestic renewable energy ambitions at an international level; and second, by reaching out to 'solar-rich' developing countries with shared interests, as well as developed countries and other non-state actors with keen financial interests in these untapped 'solar-rich' markets. The strategic interests and the politico-legal culture of India's diplomats help explain the legal form of the ISA. As an interviewee noted, the legal form of the ISA indicates the 'diplomatic culture of the state'.[137] Given the weak legal capacity within India's specialized negotiating teams over the last two decades, India's foreign policy positions on climate change have been framed by its diplomats and very recently, by its political leadership. The dominance of the Indian Administrative and Foreign Services officers in representing India internationally, creates a 'sticky' political culture where they appear unwilling to let go of a strong legacy of shaping the country's policy positions domestically and internationally. I argue that the limited international law skills within these elite professional bureaucracies is responsible for shaping the ideas, attitudes and expertise around international law.

Ministry of External Affairs' (7 Feb. 2019), https://www.mea.gov.in/rajya-sabha.htm?dtl/31007/question+no460+development+cooperation+with+foreign+countries, accessed 15 Jan. 2022.

[137] Participant 9, n. 160.

Table 5.2 Solar Projects Under Implementation Under GOI LOCs

S.No.	Country	Goods to be covered	Amount (US$)	Date of Approval	Status
1.	Mauritius	Design, supply, installation, testing, and commissioning of an 8 MW Solar PV farm at Henrietta (Phase II), Mauritius	10,000,000	25 May 2017	Under implementation
2.	Mozambique	Turnkey project for setting-up of solar photo voltaic modules manufacturing plant of 5 MW/year capacity on turnkey basis in Mozambique	12,995,000	8 May 2012	Completed
3.	Niger	Project management consultancy for construction of solar thermal plant of 5 MW in Malabaza and electrification of 30 villages through solar system in Niger	1,899,700	27 Mar. 2015	Under implementation
4.	Niger	Design, engineering, procurement and supply, erection, testing, and commissioning of electrification works of 50 villages by crystalline solar photovoltaic system (micro power plant and individual stand-alone solar kits)	9,273,000	2 Nov. 2016	Under implementation

(continued)

Table 5.2 Continued

S.No.	Country	Goods to be covered	Amount (US$)	Date of Approval	Status
5.	Niger	Design, engineering, procurement & supply, erection, testing, and commissioning of Solar PV 7 MW power plant in Malbaza, Niger	15,670,000	2 Nov. 2016	Under implementation
6.	Niger	Solar electrification of 50 villages in Niger	10,000,000	N.A.	Under Implementation
7.	Nigeria	Solar mini grid electrification and solar street lighting project in the Kaduna State	27,598,825	29 Jun. 2017	Completed
8.	Sierra Leone	Supply and installation of solar street lighting	20,000,000	10 Jul. 2012	Completed
9.	Sudan	Solar photovoltaic module manufacturing plant	576,900	29 Jun. 2004	Completed
10.	Sudan	Supply of equipment for solar electrification	5,000,000	25 Apr. 2007	Completed
11.	Sudan	Solar photovoltaic modules	1,000,000	10 Jul. 2007	Completed
12.	Suriname	Hf communication equipment, solar lanterns	1,500,000	24 Mar. 2005	Completed
13.	Senegal	Supply, transportation, and installation of equipment for electrical network in different regions of Senegal	27,499,970	13 Dec. 2016	Under implementation

Source: MEA (Government of India), 'Solar projects under implementation under GOI LOCs', ISA Founding Conference (11 Mar. 2018), https://meacms.mea.gov.in/ISAFoundingConference.htm

Table 5.3 List of Solar Projects Under GOI LOCs Announced at ISA's Founding Conference

S. No.	Country	Proposed solar project	Estimated cost (US$ million)
1.	Bangladesh	Establishment of solar-based base stations in hard-to-reach areas for strengthening tele-talk network coverage	30
2.	Bangladesh	Setting-up of Mollahat 100 MW Solar PV power plant	150.26
3.	Benin	Electrification by photovoltaic solar system of 550 social community infrastructures (health centres, high schools, and hand-pumped boreholes) in Benin rural areas	21
4.	Burkina Faso	Solar-powered water stations for semi-urban water supply	36.50
5.	Chad	Establishment of a Solar PV module manufacturing plant at N'djamena	27.45
6.	Democratic Republic of Congo	Building of 15 MW solar photovoltaic power plant and public electricity network at Karawa	58.94
7.	Democratic Republic of Congo	Building of 10 MW Lualaba's provincial solar photovoltaic power plant and public electricity network at Kolwezi	32.43
8.	Democratic Republic of Congo	Building of 15 MW Oriental Kasai's provincial solar photovoltaic power plant and public electricity network at Mbuji-Mayi	56.82
9.	Ghana	Solar-powered street lighting project	34.80
10.	Ghana	Solar-powered mini-grids for island and forest zone communities	6.3
11.	Guinea	Solar project for supply of electricity and drinking water for 7 public universities	14.40
12.	Guinea	Solar project for electrification and refrigeration in 200 health infrastructures in Guinea	5.82
13.	Mali	50 MW solar power plant in Fana, Mali	120

(continued)

Table 5.3 Continued

S. No.	Country	Proposed solar project	Estimated cost (US$ million)
14.	Mali	Development of 2500 hectares to be irrigated through solar power	22
15.	Mali	Construction of 2 MWc solar photovoltaic plants in Mopti	8
16.	Niger	Electrification of 250 villages through solar photovoltaic systems	38.2
17.	Nigeria	Solar PV Renewable Micro-Utility (REMU) in six political zones of Nigeria	8.36
18.	Nigeria	50 MW solar power plant in Bauchi State in Nigeria	66.60
19.	Rwanda	30 MW (2 x 15 MW) solar power project with storage capacity for supplying power to the National Grid	90
20.	Rwanda	Solar mini-grids for 50 centralized off-grid areas, 200 public institutions, and 200 business centres	32
21.	Seychelles	Solar LED street lighting project in Mahe, Praslin, and La Digue	0.60
22.	Seychelles	Solar rooftop PV project for government buildings in Seychelles	3
23.	Seychelles	2 MW (1MW x 2) solar power plant with battery storage in Praslin and La Digue	4
24.	Sri Lanka	Development of 200,000 rooftop solar units for low-income families	50
25.	Sri Lanka	Establishment of rooftop solar units in hospitals, schools, colleges, and other government establishments	50
26.	Tanzania	Development of 150 MWp Solar PV Farm at Shinyanga Region, Kishapu District.	385
27.	Togo	Electrification of 350 villages through solar photovoltaic systems	40

Source: MEA (Government of India), 'List of solar projects under GOI-LOCs for announcement at ISA Founding Conference', ISA Founding Conference (11 Mar. 2018), https://meacms.mea.gov.in/ISAFoundingConference.htm

For India, diplomacy is at its core in international relations, including international rule-making. The process of international rule-making is not very legalized. Ultimately, I identify three cultural drivers to explain India's motivations for a treaty structure for the newly created ISA: a multipolar worldview among India's diplomatic community, the wariness of Indian negotiators to sign onto legally binding provisions, and a strong motivation to preserve India's sovereignty. Ultimately, as I explain in the next chapter, the treaty-making process marked an innovation in the treaty structure of ISA, which I describe as 'soft law in a hard shell'.

6

Conclusion

India hit a moment of transformation with the changing landscape of solar energy in the country and Modi's strong desire to lead not just domestically but abroad. This paved the way for India's entrepreneurial economic diplomacy to create the International Solar Alliance (ISA). A move aimed at proving not only that India was consistent and credible in its climate action, but that it would take the lead. The ISA's creation cannot be looked at in isolation from either India's domestic political situation or the broader legal framework provided by the Paris Agreement. An interesting question arises: could any other country have created it? Why didn't they? Why did India succeed?

This case study reveals that India was successful in its efforts as it was the perfect synthesis of their interests and needs, and Paris provided the opportune moment for the birth of this new entity. India had been searching for a new opportunity to make a mark on the world stage, particularly on the issue of climate change, and with the Paris Climate Conference it found the perfect window to steer its leadership on the issue. The partnership with France, too, was a tactical move as India needed their power to bring everyone to the table. In turn, France was influential in shaping the private sector and non-state participation in ISA. India also recognized the importance of strategic partnerships and worked towards leveraging existing alliances and building new ones to ensure that the ISA did not meet an abrupt end after being announced at the Paris Climate Change Conference.

The central argument that runs through this book is that the ISA's legal form, which I describe as 'soft law in a hard shell', is best explained as a combination of three factors: India's leadership role in the treaty-making process; the early involvement of non-state actors; and the preference of developing countries for legal form. It can be argued that the treaty itself was not the goal, rather it became an instrument for India to achieve

The Making of the International Solar Alliance. Vyoma Jha, Oxford University Press. © Vyoma Jha 2023.
DOI: 10.1093/oso/9780198884705.003.0006

its interests, both domestically and internationally, as well as individually and collectively.

In each of the preceding empirical chapters, I have attempted to make the case that it is an amalgamation of the process (Chapter 3), politics (Chapter 4), and players (Chapter 5)—steered by India's confident leadership—that allowed for the creation of the ISA as a treaty-based international organization. As an international organization, the ISA is still a case in progress and its future success hinges on a multitude of geopolitical and organizational factors. This book does not concern itself with the functioning of the ISA, rather it takes an in-depth look into the process of its creation. By unpacking the creation of the ISA, we have a chance to observe the process and changes, both in form and practice, that is unfolding in global climate governance. The lessons are twofold: first, India's clear desire and intent to lead on issues of climate change; and second, a 'flexible multilateralism', where new institutions are stemming from the interests of the developing world but rest on the faculties and capabilities of non-state actors for future implementation.

Overall, this case study is also representative of India's role in contemporary international rule-making. By blending elements of political economy, treaty-making, international climate change law, and India's foreign policy, I attempt to develop an empirical account on the politics, history and legal culture behind the creation of the ISA as a treaty-based international organization. In Chapter 3 'Process', I explain how a combination of factors—most important among which was India's central role in driving the treaty-making process—shaped the legal form of the ISA. Chapter 4 'Politics' builds on the empirical findings of the treaty-making process and highlights the role of Prime Minister Modi in the creation of the new international organization. His personal ambition and desire to lead on climate change had a significant role in empowering India's diplomats to take the lead in creating the ISA. Chapter 5 'Players', in turn, illustrates the main actors behind India's proactive rule-making stance. Ultimately, this case study on the creation of the ISA marks an important shift in India's foreign policy, wherein climate change became a point of consideration to further India's strategic interests: one, to take a leadership role in a climate-adjacent space—solar energy—and reinforce its seriousness about climate action; and two, to assert its global power by creating a new international organization.

Developing countries provide many challenges and opportunities for understanding international rule-making. The goal of this contribution is to illustrate the case of the creation of the ISA in order to explain the decisions behind creating a new international organization and the choice of legal form. This case study is presented through three lenses—process, politics, and players—and each level of analysis in this project provides lessons for international rule-making.

First, the lens on process reveals the preference of developing countries for legally binding institutions as opposed to legally binding obligations. That is, a formal legal structure provides a degree of legitimacy and predictability to the institution, especially to bring predominantly poor and developing countries on board. This is a crucial factor in explaining the ISA's unique structure with a 'hard' legal form of a treaty and 'soft' legal terms with opt-in and non-legally binding obligations.

Second, the lens on politics reveals how the shifting discourses on climate change and solar energy in India was leveraged into international rule-making by a strong political leadership. It is an important example where the direction of international rule-making is from the domestic to the global level.

Third, the lens on players reveals the continued importance of multilateralism for India. Diplomacy lies at the heart of India's international rule-making identity. Moreover, legal capacity within India's negotiating teams and diplomatic corps remains low to negligible. As a result, India has not legalized the process of international rule-making in an effort to have greater buy-in from other actors and retain the 'global' character of its external actions.

This case study makes an original contribution to understanding India's rising power in global governance through the lens of international rule-making. I argue that this is the first time India used a legal tool to assert its power in the international sphere—the ISA being the first deliberate instrument of India's foreign policy on climate change. Until then, India's power was mostly seen in shaping alliances and negotiating blocs. This was the first time India asserted its power by creating a new international organization. In doing so, India demonstrated its leadership capability at the world stage by steering a new organization, bringing in ratifications and setting up the infrastructure for a new organization.

Another important takeaway from this case study is that climate change considerations became a tool for India's economic diplomacy. The ISA illustrates a diplomatic win for India in a multipolar world as it leveraged a new geography—'sunshine states'—to bring countries together on a new platform. While the idea behind it was a function of India's domestic needs and aspirations, it needed the support of both France and non-state actors to make it a reality. Indian diplomacy hit a moment of stride and a series of creative moves took advantage of both the political vision and existing partnerships to set the ball rolling on the creation of ISA. As I discuss in Chapter 3, the partnership with France and the outreach to other developing countries during the pre-Paris phase was critical to bring everyone to the table. Post-Paris, but for the active participation of non-state actors in the treaty-making process, the ISA would not have taken off at all.

This case also illustrates India's move towards an integrative negotiating strategy, as exhibited by negotiators empowered to cut deals at Paris and a clear embrace of the bottom-up architecture in climate governance. However, India's creative negotiating strategy at Paris appears to have waned as climate negotiators have fallen back to the traditional, hardline negotiating position on 'common but differentiated responsibility', and finance and technology transfer. This highlights the need for greater institutional memory and legal capacity during multilateral climate negotiations. India's role at the Paris climate talks was based on a clear understanding of how the climate negotiations had evolved and how it could use it to its advantage, that is, through the creation of the ISA. Multilateral negotiations remain siloed and India's initial success around the announcement ISA could run the risk of getting lost in future years especially as turf wars continue between MOEFCC and MNRE on the issue of solar energy. India needs to make nuanced arguments year after year that work for its own climate and development objectives. Else, India risks being sidelined at multilateral venues and losing its negotiating and diplomatic wins. As 'hybrid multilateralism'[1]—meetings that are part

---

[1] 'Modern negotiations assume ease of global movement. Gone are the days of sending a small team to negotiate a treaty in a railway car and bringing back an agreement already signed. Now, delegates gather from around the world meet in multiple rooms to work through various issues and are in constant contact with their capitals back home. Some recent meetings have used a hybrid model—part online, part in person', See IISD, 'How to make hybrid meetings work', *Earth*

online and part in-person—gains strength in a post-Covid world, Indian negotiators would be well advised to build stronger negotiating teams around specific interests that takes advantage of the virtual format. With the constraints of small teams, foreign travel and erratic schedules gone, multilateral negotiations should be approached in a focused, incremental manner where each subsequent meeting builds on the gains in the previous one. And when needed, an expert group of negotiators would travel for the in-person meetings. India need not wait to shape the conversation and secure its interests until the next landmark climate conference, when it might be 'forced on the negotiating table' once again.

This case study illustrates the first instance of India taking a global leadership role by creating a new international organization. Going forward, the question remains whether the ISA is merely indicative of India's 'soft power', or is it a first step in a more ambitious global role? India's solar story continues to move ahead at an incredible pace. In January 2020 the Economic Survey of India highlighted that India was on track to achieve its Nationally Determined Contributions (NDCs) based on the significant leap in the renewable energy sector, with almost 83 GW being achieved out of the target of 175 GW of renewable energy by 2022.[2] At the G20 Summit in November 2020, Modi reiterated that India is not only meeting Paris Agreement targets but will be exceeding them and promised 'a big step ahead by seeking to achieve 450 GW (of renewable energy) by 2030'.[3] A recent report suggests that India is the only country on track among the G20 nations to meet its climate change mitigation commitments.[4] Despite the pandemic, several industry and economic leaders in India believe that the government is on track to meet the 175 GW target

Negotiations Bulletin (22 Apr. 2021), https://enb.iisd.org/articles/how-make-hybrid-meetings-work, accessed 23 Jan. 2022.

[2] PTI, 'India on track to meet NDC goals under Paris Agreement: survey', *The Economic Times* (31 Jan. 2020), https://economictimes.indiatimes.com/news/economy/policy/india-on-track-to-meet-ndc-goals-under-paris-agreement-survey/articleshow/73809685.cms?from=mdr, accessed 15 Jan. 2022.

[3] Modi, 'Prime Minister's address at the G-20 summit side event: safeguarding the planet—the circular carbon economy approach', 22 Nov. 2020.

[4] A. Mukhopadhyay, 'India only G20 nation doing its "fair share" to meet 2 degree goal—report', *DW* (19 Nov. 2020), https://www.dw.com/en/india-only-g20-nation-doing-its-fair-share-to-meet-2-degree-goal-report/a-55657420, accessed 15 Jan. 2022.

of installed renewable capacity by 2022, and could achieve the target of 450 GW by 2030 with timely policy interventions.[5]

In September 2019, in a symbolic gesture of its commitment to sustainability and climate action, India gifted solar panels to the UN—one each for the 193 UN member states—to be installed on the roof of the UN headquarters in New York.[6] The same year, India repeated this new kind of climate leadership by announcing the Coalition for Disaster Resilient Infrastructure (CDRI) on the sidelines of the 2019 UN Climate Action Summit in New York. The CDRI is envisaged as a partnership of national governments, UN agencies, multilateral development banks, financing mechanisms, private sector, and knowledge institutions in order to promote the resilience of new and existing infrastructure systems to climate and disaster risks. Speaking at the announcement of this coalition, Modi said:

What is needed today is a comprehensive approach that covers everything including education, values to lifestyle and development philosophies. What we need is a global people's movement to bring about behavioral change; need, not greed is our guiding principal. So, therefore India is here today to present a practical approach and roadmap.... In order to make our infrastructure resilient in the face of disasters, India is launching a Coalition for Disaster Resilient Infrastructure. I invite all member states to join this Coalition.[7]

As a next step to the ISA, Modi in his 2020 Independence Day address spoke of a mega plan of 'One Sun, One World, One Grid' (OSOWOG), which is a transnational electricity grid supplying solar power across the globe. The idea was first floated by Modi in 2018 during the first

[5] N. Rana, 'India on track to meet 175 GW renewable energy targets by 2022', *The Economic Times* (16 Feb. 2021), https://economictimes.indiatimes.com/industry/energy/power/india-on-track-to-meet-175-gw-renewable-energy-targets-by-2022-etilc-members/articleshow/80976846.cms?from=mdr, accessed 15 Jan. 2022.

[6] PTI, 'India gifts solar panels to UN, one each for 193 member states', *The Economic Times* (13 Sep. 2019), https://economictimes.indiatimes.com/news/politics-and-nation/india-gifts-solar-panels-to-un-one-each-for-193-member-states/articleshow/71117091.cms, accessed 15 Apr. 2021.

[7] PIB, *Prime Minister announces Coalition for Disaster Resilient Infrastructure at UN Climate Action Summit 2019* [media release] (24 Sep. 2019), https://pib.gov.in/Pressreleaseshare.aspx?PRID=1586051, accessed 15 Jan. 2022.

assembly of the ISA. Several experts have cited this as part of India's answer to China's 'One Belt One Road' infrastructure initiative which entails investment in close to seventy countries. As per the draft plan prepared by the MNRE, OSOWOG will connect 140 countries through a common grid that will be used to transfer solar power. The plan is based on the mantra 'the sun never sets' and will be divided into three phases: the first phase will connect the Indian grid with the Middle East, South Asia, and Southeast Asian grids to share solar and other renewable energy resources; the second phase will connect the first phase nations with the African pool of renewable sources; and the third phase will be the concluding step of global interconnection.[8] In November 2021, at the COP26 summit in Glasgow, PM Modi and UK Prime Minister Boris Johnson launched the 'Green Grids Initiative— One Sun, One World, One Grid'. Given the high cost of energy storage, the initiative aims to connect energy grids across borders to drive down the need for storage and facilitate a faster transition to the use of renewable energy. A closer look at the OSOWOG target countries suggests that the ISA is a first step in India dominating the global conversation around solar energy. By bringing wide-ranging countries and non-state actors on board the ISA, and in time demonstrating the gains from massive solar energy deployment in energy poor regions of the world, India aims to expand its leadership role on the global public good—the sun.

India's climate commitments presented during COP26 at Glasgow— Modi's *panchamrit*—is an important signal to the world that it will not be addressing the problem of climate change without India on board. The PM Modi emphatically announced that India is, so far, the only big economy to have delivered on its Paris commitments in letter and spirit. He then went on to call out the hollow promises of climate finance by the developed world, insisting that the global ambition on climate finance cannot remain the same as before. Since 2015 India has become less adversarial in climate negotiations and backed its long-standing demands of finance and technology transfer with credible climate action

[8] S. Jai, 'One Sun, One World, One Grid: all you need to know about mega solar plan', *Business Standard* (15 Aug. 2020), https://www.business-standard.com/article/current-affairs/one-sun-one-world-one-grid-all-you-need-to-know-about-solar-strategy-120081500417_1.html, accessed on 15 Jan. 2022.

and ambition. It has steadily demonstrated its climate leadership by creating institutional solutions such as the ISA and CDRI, which provide new templates for low-carbon growth via solar energy and climate resilient infrastructure in the developing world. At Glasgow, both the ISA and CDRI expanded their work profiles with the announcement of the OSOWOG and the Infrastructure for the Resilient Island States (IRIS) projects respectively.

In closing, this case study opens the door to understand the value of trust as a key factor in Indian diplomacy. This case study reveals how India mended fractured relationships under the climate regime by bringing old and new allies under the 'common good' of solar energy. What explains the developing countries' trust in India? What explains their trust in a multilateral institution steered by India? India's efforts in creating the ISA, as well as the CDRI, appear to have an underlying element of doing good (either by providing energy access or making infrastructure more resilient in the developing world). It can be argued that India is driven less by economic concerns and more by geopolitical alliance-building. However, these institutions are not entirely bereft of economic concerns. India's economic diplomacy has been quite successful in bringing a wide array of developed nations and non-state actors to drive implementation under these new institutions. In the aftermath of the pandemic, India launched the 'Vaccine Maitri' (or friendship)—a major diplomatic effort to gift and supply vaccines to low-income and developing countries. It is no surprise that India's vaccine diplomacy covers the same set of countries it has brought under the ambit of the India-led climate initiatives.

Ultimately, this case study is a story of Indian diplomacy staking its claim for a leadership role at the global stage. Buoyed by the vision of the political leadership, it was India's diplomats that identified the window of opportunity and re-energized alliances in order to skilfully negotiate the creation of a new international organization. Without losing sight of India's strategic interests, they navigated the fine balance between the actors that needed this new institution and those who would drive it. Therefore, a future investigation into India's rising power should dive further into how India's economic diplomacy is using international instruments and institutions to shape the global order. This book is a first attempt to do that.

Appendix

Annex 1: Paris Declaration

Declaration on the Occasion to Launch the International Solar Alliance of Countries Dedicated to the Promotion of Solar Energy

Recognizing that sustainable development, universal energy access, and energy security are critical to the shared prosperity and future of our planet, and acknowledging that clean and renewable energy needs to be made affordable for all, we do hereby declare our intention to support India's proposal to launch an international solar alliance as a common platform for cooperation among solar resource rich countries lying fully or practically between the Tropics of Cancer and Capricorn.

United by a shared vision to bring clean, affordable and renewable energy within the reach of all, we affirm our intention to join the international solar alliance as founding members to ensure the promotion of green, clean and sustainable energy, and to draw on the beneficence of the Sun in this endeavor.

We share the collective ambition to undertake innovative and concerted efforts with a view to reducing the cost of finance and cost of technology for immediate deployment of competitive solar generation assets in all our countries and to pave the way for future solar generation, storage and good technologies adapted to our countries' individual needs.

United by our objective to significantly augment solar power generation in our countries, we intend making joint efforts through innovative policies, projects, programmes, capacity building measures and financial instruments to mobilize more than 1000 Billion US Dollars of investments that are needed by 2030 for the massive deployment of affordable solar energy. We recognize that the reduced cost of finance would enable us to undertake more ambitious solar energy programmes to bring development and prosperity for our people.

We intend working together towards the development of appropriate benchmarks, facilitating resource assessments, supporting research and development and demonstration facilities, with a view to encouraging innovative and affordable applications of solar technologies.

Desirous of establishing an international alliance of countries dedicated to the promotion of solar energy as an effective mechanism of cooperation, we agree to create an International Steering Committee, open to interested counties, to provide the necessary guidance, direction and advice to establish the international solar alliance.

Source: UNFCCC, 'International Solar Energy Alliance launched at COP21', 30 Nov. 2015, available at: http://newsroom.unfccc.int/clean-energy/international-solar-energy-alliance-launched-at-cop21/

Annex 2: Framework Agreement on the Establishment of the International Solar Alliance

We, the Parties to this Agreement,

Recalling the Paris Declaration on the International Solar Alliance of 30th November 2015 and the shared ambition to undertake joint efforts required to reduce the cost of finance and the cost of technology, mobilize more than US $1000 billion of investments needed by 2030 for massive deployment of solar energy, and pave the way for future technologies adapted to the needs,

Recognizing that solar energy provides solar resource rich countries, lying fully or partially between the Tropics of Cancer and Capricorn, with an unprecedented opportunity to bring prosperity, energy security and sustainable development to their peoples,

Acknowledging the specific and common obstacles that still stand in the way of rapid and massive scale-up of solar energy in these countries,

Affirming that these obstacles can be addressed if solar resource rich countries act in a coordinated manner, with strong political impulse and resolve, and that better harmonizing and aggregating the demand for inter alia solar finance, technologies, innovation or capacity building, across countries, will provide a strong lever to lower costs, increase quality, and bring reliable and affordable solar energy within the reach of all,

United in their desire to establish an effective mechanism of coordination and decision-making among them,

Have agreed as follows:

Article I

Objective

Parties hereby establish an International Solar Alliance (hereinafter referred to as the ISA), through which they will collectively address key common challenges to the scaling up of solar energy in line with their needs.

Article II

Guiding Principles

1. Members take coordinated actions through Programmes and activities launched on a voluntary basis, aimed at better harmonizing and aggregating demand for, inter alia, solar finance, solar technologies, innovation, research and development, and capacity building.
2. In this endeavor, Members cooperate closely and strive for establishing mutually beneficial relationships with relevant organizations, public and private stakeholders, and with non-member countries.

3. Each Member shares and updates, for those solar applications for which it seeks the benefits of collective action under the ISA, and based on a common analytical mapping of solar applications, relevant information regarding: its needs and objectives; domestic measures and initiatives taken or intended to be taken in order to achieve these objectives; obstacles along the value chain and dissemination process. The Secretariat maintains a database of these assessments in order to highlight the potential for cooperation.
4. Each Member designates a National Focal Point for the ISA. National Focal Points constitute a permanent network of correspondents of the ISA in Member countries. They inter alia interact with one another and also with relevant stakeholders to identify areas of common interest, design Programmes proposals and make recommendations to the Secretariat regarding the implementation of the objectives of the ISA.

Article III

Programmes and Other Activities

1. A Programme of the ISA consists of a set of actions, projects and activities to be taken in a coordinated manner by Members, with the assistance of the Secretariat, in furtherance of the objective and guiding principles described in article I and II. Programmes are designed in a way to ensure maximum scale effect and participation of the largest possible number of Members. They include simple, measurable, mobilizing targets.
2. Programme proposals are designed through open consultations among all National Focal Points, with the assistance of the Secretariat, and based on information shared by Members. A Programme can be proposed by any two Members or group of Members, or by the Secretariat. The Secretariat ensures coherence among all ISA Programmes.
3. Programme proposals are circulated by the Secretariat to the Assembly by digital circulation, through the network of National Focal Points. A Programme proposal is deemed open to adhesion by Members willing to join if it is supported by at least two Members and if objections are not raised by more than two countries.
4. A Programme proposal is formally endorsed by Members willing to join, through a joint declaration. All decisions regarding the implementation of the Programme are taken by Members participating in the Programme. They are carried out, with the guidance and assistance of the Secretariat, by country Representatives designated by each Member.
5. The annual work plan gives an overview of the Programmes, and other activities of the ISA. It is presented by the Secretariat to the Assembly, which ensures that all Programmes and activities of the annual work plan are within the overall objective of the ISA.

Article IV

Assembly

1. The Parties hereby establish an Assembly, on which each Member is represented, to make decisions concerning the implementation of this Agreement and coordinated actions to be taken to achieve its objective. The Assembly meets annually at the Ministerial level at the seat of the ISA. The Assembly may also meet under special circumstances.
2. Break-out sessions of the Assembly are held in order to take stock of the Programmes at Ministerial level and make decisions regarding their further implementation, in furtherance of article III.4.
3. The Assembly assesses the aggregate effect of the Programmes and other activities under the ISA, in particular in terms of deployment of solar energy, performance, reliability, as well as cost and scale of finance. Based on this assessment, Members take all necessary decisions regarding the further implementation of the objective of the ISA.
4. The Assembly makes all necessary decisions regarding the functioning of the ISA, including the selection of the Director General and approval of the operating budget.
5. Each Member has one vote in the Assembly. Observers and Partner organizations may participate without having right to vote. Decisions on questions of procedure are taken by a simple majority of the Members present and voting. Decisions on matters of substance are taken by two-third majority of the Members present and voting. Decisions regarding specific Programmes are taken by Members participating in this Programme.
6. All decisions taken by the International Steering Committee of the ISA established by the Paris Declaration on the ISA of 30th November 2015 are submitted to the Assembly for adoption at its first meeting.

Article V

Secretariat

1. Parties hereby establish a Secretariat to assist them in their collective work under this Agreement. The Secretariat comprises of a Director General, who is the Chief Executive Officer, and other staff as may be required.
2. The Director General is selected by and responsible to the Assembly, for a term of four years, renewable for one further term.
3. The Director General is responsible to the Assembly for the appointment of the staff as well as the organization and functioning of the Secretariat, and also for resource mobilization.
4. The Secretariat prepares matters for Assembly action and carries out decisions entrusted to it by the Assembly. It ensures that appropriate steps are taken to follow up Assembly decisions and to co-ordinate the actions of Members in the implementation of such decisions. The Secretariat, inter alia, shall:

a) assist the National Focal Points in preparing the Programmes proposals and recommendations submitted to the Assembly;

b) provide guidance and support to Members in the implementation of each Programme, including for the raising of funds;

c) act on behalf of the Assembly, or on behalf of a group of Members participating in a particular Programme, when so requested by them; and in particular establishes contacts with relevant stakeholders;

d) set and operate all means of communication, instruments and cross-cutting activities required for the functioning of the ISA and its Programmes, as approved by the Assembly.

Article VI

Budget and Financial Resources

1. Operating costs of the Secretariat and Assembly, and all costs related to support functions and cross-cutting activities, form the budget of the ISA. They are covered by:

   a) Voluntary contributions by its Members, Partner countries, UN & its agencies and other countries;

   b) Voluntary contributions from private sector. In case of a possible conflict of interest, the Secretariat refers the matter to the Assembly for approval of the acceptance of the contribution;

   c) Revenue to be generated from specific activities approved by the Assembly.

2. The Secretariat will make proposals before the Assembly to establish and enhance a Corpus Fund which will generate revenues for the budget of the ISA, with initial dotation of US $16 million.

3. Government of India will contribute US $27 million to the ISA for creating corpus, building infrastructure and recurring expenditure over 5 year duration from 2016–17 to 2020–21. In addition, public sector undertakings of the Government of India namely Solar Energy Corporation of India (SECI) and Indian Renewable Energy Development Agency (IREDA) have made a contribution of US $1 million each for creating the ISA corpus fund.

4. Financial resources required for the implementation of a specific Programme, other than administrative costs falling under the general budget, are assessed and mobilized by countries participating in this Programme, with the support and assistance of the Secretariat.

5. The finance and administration activities of the ISA other than Programmes may be outsourced to another organization, in accordance with a separate agreement to be approved by the Assembly.

6. The Secretariat with the approval of the Assembly may appoint an external auditor to examine the accounts of the ISA.

Article VII

Member and Partner Country Status

1. Membership is open to those solar resource rich States which lie fully or partially between the Tropic of Cancer and the Tropic of Capricorn, and which are members of the United Nations. Such States become Members of the ISA by having signed this Agreement and having deposited an instrument of ratification, acceptance or approval.
2. Partner Country status may be granted by the Assembly to the States which fall outside the Tropic of Cancer and the Tropic of Capricorn, are members of the United Nations, and are willing and able to contribute to the objectives and activities provided in this Agreement.
3. Partner Countries are eligible to participate in Programmes of the ISA, with the approval of Members participating in the Programme.

Article VIII

Partner Organization

1. Partner Organization status may be granted by the Assembly to organizations that have potential to help the ISA to achieve its objectives, including regional inter-governmental economic integration organizations constituted by sovereign States and at least one of which is a member of ISA.
2. Decisions regarding partnerships to be concluded in the context of a specific Programme are taken by countries participating in this Programme, with the approval of the Secretariat.
3. United Nations including its organs will be the Strategic Partner of the ISA.

Article IX

Observers
Observer status that may be granted by the Assembly to applicants for membership or partnership whose application is pending, or to any other organization which can further the interest and objectives of the ISA.

Article X

Status, Privileges and Immunities of the ISA

1. The ISA Secretariat shall possess juridical personality under the Host Country Agreement, the capacity to contract, to acquire and dispose of movable and immovable properties and to institute legal proceedings.

2. Under the same Host Country Agreement, the ISA Secretariat shall enjoy such privileges, applicable tax concessions and immunities as are necessary at its Headquarters for independent discharge of its functions and programmes, approved by the Assembly.
3. Under the territory of each Member, subject to its National Laws and in accordance with a separate Agreement, if necessary; the ISA Secretariat may enjoy such immunity and privileges that are necessary for the independent discharge of its functions and programmes.

Article XI

Amendments and Withdrawal

1. Any Member may propose amendments to the Framework Agreement after expiry of one year from the commencement of the Framework Agreement.
2. Amendments to the Framework Agreement shall be adopted by the Assembly by two thirds majority of the Members present and voting. The amendments shall come into force when two thirds of the Members convey acceptance in accordance with their respective constitutional processes.
3. Any member may withdraw from the present Framework Agreement, by giving a notice of three months to the Depository in advance. Notice of such withdrawal are notified to the other Members by the Depository.

Article XII

Seat of the ISA
The seat of the ISA shall be in India.

Article XIII

Signature and Entry Into Force

1. Ratification, acceptance or approval of the Framework Agreement is effected by States in accordance with their respective constitutional processes. This Framework Agreement shall enter into force on the thirtieth day after the date of deposit of the fifteenth instrument of ratification, acceptance or approval.
2. For Members having deposited an instrument of ratification, acceptance or approval after the entry into force of the Framework Agreement, this Framework Agreement shall enter into force on the thirtieth day after the date of deposit of the relevant instrument.
3. Once the ISA is established, the International Steering Committee of the ISA ceases to exist.

Article XIV

Depositary, Registration, Authentication of the Text

1. The Government of the Republic of India is the Depositary of the Framework Agreement.
2. This Framework Agreement is registered by the Depositary pursuant to Article 102 of the Charter of the United Nations.
3. The Depositary transmits certified copies of the Framework Agreement to all Parties.
4. This Framework Agreement, of which Hindi, English and French texts are equally authentic, is deposited in the archives of the Depositary.

IN WITNESS WHEREOF the undersigned, being duly authorized thereto, have signed the Framework Agreement.
DONE at New Delhi, on this … …..day of …................2016, in the Hindi, English and French languages, all texts being equally authentic

Source: ISA, 'Framework Agreement on the establishment of the International Solar Alliance (ISA)', https://isolaralliance.org/about/framework-agreement#book5/undefined

Annex 3: ISA Prospective Member Countries and Territories

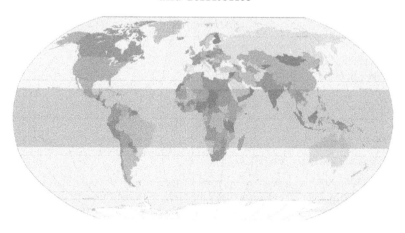

Algeria	Gabon	Papua New Guinea
Antigua and Barbuda	Gambia	Paraguay
Angola	Ghana	Peru
Argentina	Grenada	Philippines
Australia	Guatemala	Rwanda
Bahamas	Guinea	St. Lucia
Bangladesh	Guinea-Bissau	Saint Kitts and Nevis
Barbados	Guyana	Saint Vincent and the
Belize	Haiti	Grenadines
Benin	Honduras	Samoa
Bolivia	India	Sao Tome and Principe
Botswana.	Indonesia	Saudi Arabia
Brazil	Jamaica	Senegal
Brunei	Japan	Seychelles
Burkina Faso	Kenya	Sierra Leone
Burundi	Kiribati	Singapore
Cambodia	Laos	Solomon Islands
Cameroon	Liberia	Somalia
Cape Verde	Libya	South Africa
Central African Republic	Madagascar	South Sudan
Chad	Malawi	Sri Lanka
Chile	Malaysia	Sudan
China	Maldives	Suriname
Colombia	Mali	Tanzania
Comoros	Marshall Islands	Thailand
Democratic Republic	Mauritania	Timor-Leste
of Congo	Mauritius	Togo
Congo	Mexico	Tonga
Costa Rica	Micronesia	Trinidad and Tobago
Cote d'Ivoire	Mozambique	Tuvalu
Cuba	Myanmar	Uganda
Djibouti	Namibia	United Arab Emirates
Dominica	Nauru	United Kingdom
Dominican Republic	Netherlands	United States of America
Ecuador	New Zealand	Vanuatu
Egypt	Nicaragua	Venezuela
El Salvador	Niger	Vietnam
Equatorial Guinea	Nigeria	Yemen
Eritrea	Oman	Zambia
Ethiopia	Palau	Zimbabwe
Fiji	Panama	
France		

Source: Wikimedia Commons

Annex 4: ISA Member Countries and Groupings

S.No.	Country	ISA (S)	ISA (R)	G77	NAM	G20	SIS	OIF	CC
1.	Algeria	✓	✓	✓	✓				
2.	Antigua and Barbuda	✓		✓	✓		✓		✓
3.	Argentina	✓	✓			✓			
4.	Australia	✓	✓			✓			
5.	Bangladesh	✓	✓	✓	✓				
6.	Barbados	✓	✓	✓	✓		✓		✓
7.	Belize	✓	✓	✓	✓		✓		✓
8.	Benin	✓	✓	✓	✓			✓	
9.	Bolivia	✓		✓	✓				
10.	Botswana	✓	✓	✓	✓				
11.	Brazil	✓		✓		✓			
12.	Burkina Faso	✓	✓	✓	✓			✓	
13.	Burundi	✓	✓	✓	✓			✓	
14.	Cambodia	✓	✓	✓	✓			✓	
15.	Cameroon	✓	✓	✓	✓			✓	
16.	Cape Verde	✓		✓	✓		✓	✓	
17.	Chad	✓	✓	✓	✓			✓	
18.	Chile	✓		✓	✓				
19.	Comoros	✓	✓	✓	✓		✓	✓	
20.	Costa Rica	✓		✓				✓	
21.	Côte d'Ivoire	✓	✓	✓	✓			✓	
22.	Cuba	✓	✓	✓	✓		✓		
23.	Democratic Republic of Congo	✓	✓	✓	✓			✓	
24.	Denmark	✓	✓						
25.	Djibouti	✓	✓	✓	✓			✓	
26.	Dominica	✓	✓	✓	✓		✓	✓	✓
27.	Dominican Republic	✓		✓	✓		✓		
28.	Egypt	✓	✓	✓	✓			✓	
29.	El Salvador	✓	✓	✓					
30.	Equatorial Guinea	✓	✓	✓	✓			✓	
31.	Eritrea	✓		✓	✓				
32.	Ethiopia	✓	✓	✓	✓				
33.	Fiji	✓	✓	✓	✓		✓		
34.	France	✓	✓			✓		✓	
35.	Gabon	✓	✓	✓	✓			✓	
36.	Gambia	✓	✓	✓	✓				
37.	Germany	✓	✓			✓			
38.	Ghana	✓	✓	✓	✓				
39.	Greece	✓							
40.	Grenada	✓	✓	✓	✓		✓		✓
41.	Guinea	✓	✓	✓	✓			✓	

S.No.	Country	ISA (S)	ISA (R)	G77	NAM	G20	SIS	OIF	CC
42.	Guinea-Bissau	✓		✓	✓		✓	✓	
43.	Guyana	✓	✓	✓	✓		✓		✓
44.	Haiti	✓	✓	✓	✓		✓	✓	✓
45.	India	✓	✓	✓	✓	✓			
46.	Italy	✓	✓			✓			
47.	Israel	✓							
48.	Jamaica	✓	✓	✓	✓		✓		✓
49.	Japan	✓	✓			✓			
50.	Kiribati	✓	✓	✓			✓		
51.	Liberia	✓		✓	✓				
52.	Luxembourg	✓						✓	
53.	Madagascar	✓	✓	✓	✓			✓	
54.	Malawi	✓	✓	✓	✓				
55.	Maldives	✓	✓	✓	✓		✓		
56.	Mali	✓	✓	✓	✓				
57.	Marshall Islands	✓	✓	✓			✓		
58.	Mauritius	✓	✓	✓	✓		✓	✓	
59.	Morocco	✓		✓	✓			✓	
60.	Mozambique	✓	✓	✓	✓				
61.	Myanmar	✓	✓	✓	✓				
62.	Namibia	✓	✓	✓	✓				
63.	Nauru	✓	✓	✓			✓		
64.	Netherlands	✓	✓						
65.	Nicaragua	✓	✓	✓	✓				
66.	Niger	✓	✓	✓	✓			✓	
67.	Nigeria	✓	✓	✓	✓				
68.	Oman	✓	✓	✓	✓				
69.	Palau	✓					✓		
70.	Papua New Guinea	✓	✓	✓	✓		✓		
71.	Paraguay	✓		✓					
72.	Peru	✓	✓	✓	✓				
73.	Rwanda	✓	✓	✓	✓			✓	
74.	Saint Kitts and Nevis	✓		✓	✓		✓		✓
75.	Saint Vincent and the Grenadines	✓	✓	✓	✓		✓		✓
76.	Samoa	✓	✓	✓			✓		
77.	Sao Tome and Principe	✓	✓	✓	✓		✓	✓	
78.	Saudi Arabia	✓	✓	✓	✓	✓			
79.	Senegal	✓	✓	✓	✓			✓	
80.	Seychelles	✓	✓	✓	✓		✓	✓	
81.	Somalia	✓	✓	✓	✓				
82.	South Sudan	✓	✓	✓					
83.	Sri Lanka	✓	✓	✓	✓				
84.	St. Lucia	✓	✓	✓	✓		✓	✓	✓
85.	Sudan	✓	✓	✓	✓				

S.No.	Country	ISA (S)	ISA (R)	G77	NAM	G20	SIS	OIF	CC
86.	Suriname	✓	✓	✓	✓		✓		✓
87.	Sweden	✓	✓						
88.	Tanzania	✓	✓	✓	✓				
89.	Togo	✓	✓	✓	✓			✓	
90.	Tonga	✓	✓	✓					
91.	Trinidad and Tobago	✓	✓	✓	✓		✓		✓
92.	Tunisia	✓		✓	✓			✓	
93.	Tuvalu	✓	✓				✓		
94.	Uganda	✓	✓	✓	✓				
95.	United Arab Emirates	✓	✓	✓	✓				
96.	United Kingdom	✓	✓			✓			
97.	United States of America	✓				✓			
98.	Vanuatu	✓	✓	✓	✓		✓	✓	
99.	Venezuela	✓	✓	✓	✓				
100.	Yemen	✓		✓	✓				
101.	Zambia	✓		✓	✓				
102.	Zimbabwe	✓	✓	✓	✓				

ISA(S): ISA Signatory Country
ISA(R): ISA Member Country (Signed and Ratified)
G77: The Group of 77
NAM: Non-Aligned Movement
G20: The Group of 20
SIS: Alliance of Small Island States or AOSIS
OIF: Organisation Internationale de la Francophonie
CC: The Caribbean Community or CARICOM
Source: Author's own analysis

Annex 5: List of Interviewees

Interviewee	Description of role	Date	Type of interview, Place
Participant 1	Head of Research Organization	31 Jul. 2018	In person, New Delhi
Participant 2	Former Secretary, MNRE	30 Jul. 2018	In person, New Delhi
Participant 3	Former Official, United States Department of State	30 Jul. 2019	Phone, Stanford, CA
Participant 4	Head of Policy Think Tank	16 Dec. 2016; 3 Aug. 2018	In person, New Delhi

Interviewee	Description of role	Date	Type of interview, Place
Participant 5	Former Secretary, MOEFCC	26 Jul. 2018	In person, New Delhi
Participant 6	French Official	6 Sep. 2018	Skype, Stanford, CA
Participant 7	Head of Research Organization	6 Dec. 2016; 27 Jul. 2018	In person, New Delhi
Participant 8	Official, MEA	9 Aug. 2020	Phone, Stanford, CA
Participant 9	French Solar Energy Entrepreneur	14 Sep. 2020	Zoom, Stanford, CA
Participant 10	Senior Official, MEA	19 Jul. 2018	In person, New Delhi
Participant 11	Head of Government Relations, Foreign Investor	29 Jul. 2019	Phone, Stanford, CA
Participant 12	Energy Journalist	25 Jun. 2019	Phone, Stanford, CA
Participant 13	Senior Official, MNRE	8 Dec. 2016; 17 Jul. 2018	In person, New Delhi
Participant 14	Senior Official, Exim Bank of India	8 Aug. 2019	Phone, Stanford, CA
Participant 15	Official, Ministry of Finance	5 Dec.2016; 24 Jul. 2018	In person, New Delhi
Participant 16	Senior Official, MOEFCC	14 Dec. 2016; 17 Jul. 2018	In person, New Delhi
Participant 17	Former Secretary, MEA	6 Aug. 2018	In person, New Delhi
Participant 18	Senior Official, Industry Association	26 Jul. 2019	Phone, Stanford, CA
Participant 19	Former Secretary, MEA	18 Jul. 2018	In person, New Delhi
Participant 20	Senior Official, International Organization	26 Jul. 2019	Phone, Stanford, CA
Participant 21	Former Secretary, MEA	26 Jul. 2018	In person, New Delhi
Participant 22	Former Senior Official, MOEFCC	25 Jul. 2018	In person, New Delhi
Participant 23	Former Secretary, MNRE	27 Jul. 2018	In person, New Delhi
Participant 24	Indian Solar Energy Entrepreneur	6 Feb. 2017	Phone, Stanford, CA
Participant 25	Professor of International Trade Law	28 Jan. 2017	Phone, Stanford, CA
Participant 26	Former Ambassador of India to the WTO	9 Dec. 2016	In person, New Delhi
Participant 27	International Legal Adviser	16 Dec. 2016	In person, New Delhi

Interviewee	Description of role	Date	Type of interview, Place
Participant 28	Senior Expert, Policy Think Tank	12 Dec. 2016	In person, New Delhi
Participant 29	Professor of International Trade and Investment Law	13 Dec. 2016	In person, New Delhi
Participant 30	Former Secretary, MOCI	14 Dec. 2016	In person, New Delhi
Participant 31	Former Secretary, MOCI	18 Dec. 2016	In person, New Delhi
Participant 32	Former Senior Official, MOEFCC	14 Dec. 2016	In person, New Delhi
Participant 33	International Trade Lawyer	8 Dec. 2016	In person, New Delhi
Participant 34	Senior Official, MNRE	8 Dec. 2016	In person, New Delhi
Participant 35	Trade Law Expert	14 Dec. 2016	In person, New Delhi
Participant 36	Head of Research Organization	6 Dec. 2016	In person, New Delhi
Participant 37	Energy Expert	14 Dec. 2016	In person, New Delhi
Participant 38	Official, MOCI	17 Jan. 2017	Phone, Stanford, CA
Participant 39	Senior Official, MNRE	14 & 16 Dec. 2016	Phone, New Delhi
Participant 40	Former Official, USTR	27 Jan. 2017	Phone, Stanford, CA

Bibliography

Primary Sources

ISA

Framework Agreement on the establishment of the International Solar Alliance (ISA), Marrakesh (Morocco), 15 Nov. 2016, in force 6 Dec. 2017.

ISA, 'Constitution of the Interim Administrative Cell of the International Solar Alliance to facilitate establishment of ISA from de facto to de jure status', Steering Committees (29 Jan. 2016), https://isolaralliance.org/about/steering-committees, accessed 15 Dec. 2022.

ISA, 'Declaration on the occasion to launch the International Solar Alliance of countries dedicated to the promotion of solar energy' (30 Nov. 2015), https://isolaralliance.org/media/press-release, accessed 15 Dec. 2022.

ISA, 'Report of the Eighth Meeting of the Interim Administrative Cell of the International Solar Alliance', Steering Committees (New Delhi, 3 Mar. 2017), https://isolaralliance.org/about/steering-committees, accessed 15 Dec. 2022.

ISA, 'Report of the Fifth Meeting of the Interim Administrative Cell of the International Solar Alliance', Steering Committees (New Delhi, 11 May 2016), https://isolaralliance.org/about/steering-committees, accessed 15 Dec. 2022.

ISA, 'Report of the Fifth Meeting of the International Steering Committee', Steering Committees (New Delhi, 27 Sep. 2017), https://isolaralliance.org/about/steering-committees, accessed 15 Dec. 2022.

ISA, 'Report of the First Assembly of the International Solar Alliance', Governance (National Capital Region, 14 Jan. 2019), https://isolaralliance.org/governance/first-assembly, accessed 15 Dec. 2022.

ISA, 'Report of the First Meeting of the Interim Administrative Cell of the International Solar Alliance', Steering Committees (New Delhi, 10 Feb. 2016), https://isolaralliance.org/about/steering-committees, accessed 15 Dec. 2022.

ISA, 'Report of the First Meeting of the International Steering Committee', Steering Committees (Paris, 1 Dec. 2015), https://isolaralliance.org/about/steering-committees, accessed 15 Dec. 2022.

ISA, 'Report of the Fourth Meeting of the Interim Administrative Cell of the International Solar Alliance', Steering Committees (New Delhi, 18 Mar. 2016), https://isolaralliance.org/about/steering-committees, accessed 15 Dec. 2022.

ISA, 'Report of the Fourth Meeting of the International Steering Committee', Steering Committees (New Delhi, 5 Oct. 2016), https://isolaralliance.org/about/steering-committees, accessed 15 Dec. 2022.

ISA, 'Report of the Second Meeting of the Interim Administrative Cell of the International Solar Alliance', Steering Committees (17 Feb. 2016), https://isolara lliance.org/about/steering-committees, accessed 15 Dec. 2022.

ISA, 'Report of the Second Meeting of the International Steering Committee', Steering Committees (Abu Dhabi, 18 Jan. 2016), https://isolaralliance.org/about/steering-committees, accessed 15 Dec. 2022.

ISA, 'Report of the Seventh Meeting of the Interim Administrative Cell of the International Solar Alliance', Steering Committees (New Delhi, 7 Sep.2016), https://isolaralliance.org/about/steering-committees, accessed 15 Dec. 2022.

ISA, 'Report of the Sixth Meeting of the Interim Administrative Cell of the International Solar Alliance', Steering Committees (New Delhi, 14 Jun. 2016), https://isolaralliance.org/about/steering-committees, accessed 15 Dec. 2022.

ISA, 'Report of the Sixth Meeting of the International Steering Committee', Steering Committees (New Delhi, 20 Feb. 2018), https://isolaralliance.org/about/steering-committees, accessed 15 Dec. 2022.

ISA, 'Report of the Third Meeting of the Interim Administrative Cell of the International Solar Alliance', Steering Committees (New Delhi, 11 Mar. 2016), https://isolaralliance.org/about/steering-committees, accessed 15 Dec. 2022.

ISA, 'Report of the Third Meeting of the International Steering Committee', Steering Committees (New York, 21 Apr. 2016), https://isolaralliance.org/about/steering-committees, accessed 15 Dec. 2022.

ISA, 'Working Paper on International Solar Alliance', Media (30 Nov. 2015), https://isolaralliance.org/media/press-release, accessed 15 Dec. 2022.

Government of India

MEA (Government of India), 'Address by External Affairs Minister at the International Solar Alliance Founding Conference', ISA Founding Conference (11 Mar. 2018), https://meacms.mea.gov.in/ISAFoundingConference.htm, accessed 15 Dec. 2022.

MEA (Government of India), *Annual Reports*, https://meacms.mea.gov.in/annual-reports.htm?57/Annual_Reports, accessed 15 Dec. 2022.

MEA (Government of India), 'English Translation of Prime Minister's speech at Founding Conference of International Solar Alliance', ISA Founding Conference (11 Mar. 2018), https://meacms.mea.gov.in/ISAFoundingConference.htm, accessed 15 Dec. 2022.

MEA (Government of India), *Indian Treaties Database*, https://www.mea.gov.in/treaty.htm, accessed 15 Dec. 2022.

MEA (Government of India), 'List of solar projects under GOI-LOCs for announcement at ISA Founding Conference', ISA Founding Conference (11 Mar. 2018), https://meacms.mea.gov.in/ISAFoundingConference.htm, accessed 15 Dec. 2022.

MEA (Government of India), 'Solar Projects under implementation under GOI LOCs', ISA Founding Conference (11 Mar. 2018), https://meacms.mea.gov.in/ISAFoundingConference.htm, accessed 15 Dec. 2022.

MEA (Government of India), 'Transcript of Curtain Raiser Briefing on the International Solar Alliance Founding Conference', ISA Founding Conference (22 Feb. 2018), https://meacms.mea.gov.in/ISAFoundingConference.htm, accessed 15 Dec. 2022.

MEA (Government of India), 'Transcript of Media Briefing on Founding Conference of ISA', ISA Founding Conference (12 Mar. 2018), https://meacms.mea.gov.in/ISAFoundingConference.htm, accessed 15 Dec. 2022.

MOEFCC (Government of India), 'India's Intended Nationally Determined Contribution: Working Towards Climate Justice' (1 Oct. 2015), http://moef.gov.in/division/environment-divisions/climate-changecc-2/documents-publications/, accessed 15 Dec. 2022.

MOEFCC (Government of India), 'National Action Plan on Climate Change' (30 Jun. 2008), http://moef.gov.in/division/environment-divisions/climate-changecc-2/documents-publications/, accessed 15 Dec. 2022.

UNFCCC

Kyoto Protocol to the United Nations Framework Convention on Climate Change, Kyoto (Japan), 11 Dec. 1997, in force 16 Feb. 2005.

UNFCCC, 'Adoption of the Paris Agreement', FCCC/CP/2015/L.9/Rev.1 (12 Dec. 2015), https://unfccc.int/resource/docs/2015/cop21/eng/l09r01.pdf, accessed 15 Dec. 2022.

UNFCCC, 'Establishment of an Ad-Hoc Working Group on the Durban Platform for Enhanced Action', Decision 1/CP.17, FCCC/CP/2011/9/Add.1 (15 Mar. 2012), https://unfccc.int/resource/docs/2011/cop17/eng/09a01.pdf, accessed 15 Dec. 2022.

UNFCCC, 'Synthesis Report on the Aggregate Effect of the Intended Nationally Determined Contributions', FCCC/CP/2015/7 (30 Oct. 2015), http://unfccc.int/resource/docs/2015/cop21/eng/07.pdf, accessed on 15 Dec. 2022.

UNFCCC, 'The Copenhagen Accord', Decision 2/CP.15, FCCC/CP/2009/11/Add.1 (30 Mar. 2010), https://unfccc.int/resource/docs/2009/cop15/eng/11a01.pdf, accessed 15 Dec. 2022.

United Nations Framework Convention on Climate Change, Rio de Janeiro (Brazil), 4 Jun. 1992, in force 21 Mar. 1994.

Speeches

Modi, N. D., Speeches 2014–16, available on the official website of Prime Minister Narendra Modi, see https://www.pmindia.gov.in/en/tag/pmspeech/, accessed 15 Apr 2021.

Singh, M., Speeches 2008–10, available on the official website of Former Prime Minister Dr Manmohan Singh, see https://archivepmo.nic.in/drmanmohansingh/all-speeches.php, accessed 15 Dec. 2022.

Secondary Sources

Books and Reports

Ayres, A., *Our Time Has Come: How India is Making its Place in the World* (New Delhi: Oxford University Press, 2018).

Bajpai, A., *Speaking the Nation: The Oratorical Making of Secular, Neoliberal India* (New Delhi: Oxford University Press, 2018).

Bhattacharya, S., Niranjan, E., & Purushothaman, C., *India and the International Solar Alliance* (New Delhi: Institute for Defense Studies and Analyses, Mar. 2018)

Cane, P. and Kritzer, H.M., eds, *The Oxford Handbook of Empirical Legal Research* (New York: Oxford University Press, 2010).

Carl, J., Rai, V., & Victor, D.G., *Energy and India's Foreign Policy* (Stanford, CA: Program on Energy and Sustainable Development, May 2008)

Dubash, N.K., ed., *Handbook of Climate Change and India: Development, Politics and Governance* (New Delhi: Oxford University Press, 2012).

Dubash, N.K., ed., *India in a Warming World: Integrating Climate Change and Development* (New Delhi: Oxford University Press, 2019).

Fabbricotti, A., ed., *The Political Economy of International Law: A European Perspective* (Cheltenham: Edward Elgar Publishing, 2016).

Green, J., *Rethinking Private Authority: Agents and Entrepreneurs in Global Environmental Governance* (Princeton, NJ: Princeton University Press, 2014).

Hajer, M.A., *The Politics of Environmental Discourse: Ecological Modernization and the Policy Process* (New York: Oxford University Press, 1995)

Hansel, M., Khan, R., & Levaillant, M., eds, *Theorizing Indian Foreign Policy* (London: Routledge, 2017).

Jaishankar, D., *Survey of India's Strategic Community* (New Delhi: Brookings India, Mar. 2019).

Jakobsen, S., *India's Position on Climate Change from Rio to Kyoto: A Policy Analysis* (Copenhagen: Centre for Development Research, Jan. 1998)

Joshi, S. & Powell, L., *India: Energy Geo-Politics* (New Delhi: Observer Research Foundation, Oct. 2018).

Kuntze, J. & Moerenhout, T., *Local Content Requirements and the Renewable Energy Industry—A Good Match?* (Geneva: International Centre for Trade and Sustainable Development, 2013)

Legrain, A. & Pham-Ba, J., *Well Below Two Cents* (Paris: Terrawatt Initiative, Jun. 2020).

Malone, D.M., Mohan, C.R., & Raghavan, S., eds, *The Oxford Handbook of Indian Foreign Policy* (Oxford: Oxford University Press, 2015).

Merry, S.E., *Human Rights and Gender Violence: Translating International Law into Local Justice* (Chicago: University of Chicago Press, 2006).

Michael, D. & Pandya, A., eds, *Indian Climate Policy: Choices and Challenges* (Washington, DC: The Henry L. Stimson Center, Nov. 2009)

Modi, N.D., *Convenient Action: Continuity for Change* (Gurgaon: Lexis Nexis, 2015).

Mohan, C.R., *Modi's World: Expanding India's Sphere of Influence* (New Delhi: Harper Collins India, 2015).

Nachiappan, K., *Does India Negotiate?* (New Delhi: Oxford University Press, 2019).

Narlikar, A. & Narlikar, A., *Bargaining with a Rising India: Lessons from the Mahabharata* (New Delhi: Oxford University Press, 2014).

Noronha, L. & Sudarshan, A., eds, *India's Energy Security* (Oxford: Routledge, 2009)

Pant, H.V., *Indian Foreign Policy* (Manchester: Manchester University Press, 2016).

Patel, B.N., *State Practice of India and the Development of International Law: Dynamic Interplay between Foreign Policy and Jurisprudence* (Leiden: Brill, 2016).

Plagemann, J., Destradi, S., & Narlikar, A., eds, *India Rising: A Multilayered Analysis of Ideas, Interests and Institutions* (New Delhi: Oxford University Press, 2020).

Polinsky, A.M. & Shavell, S., eds, *Handbook of Law and Economics: Volume 1* (Amsterdam: Elsevier Science Publishing, 2007).

Posner, E.A. & Skyes, A.O., *Economic Foundations of International Law* (Cambridge, MA: Harvard University Press, 2012).

Rajan, M.G., *Global Environmental Politics: India and the North–South Politics of Global Environmental Issues* (New Delhi: Oxford University Press, 1997)

Rana, K.S., *Asian Diplomacy: The Foreign Ministries of China, India, Japan, Singapore and Thailand* (Washington, DC: Woodrow Wilson Center Press, 2009).

Saran, S., *How India Sees the World: Kautilya to the 21st Century* (New Delhi: Juggernaut, 2017).

Saran, S. & Jones, A., *India's Climate Change Identity: Between Reality and Perception* (New Delhi: Springer, 2016).

Sidhu, W.P.S., Mehta, P.B., & Jones, B., eds, *Shaping the Emerging World: India and the Multilateral Order* (Washington, DC: Brookings Institution Press, 2013).

Simmons, B., *Mobilizing for Human Rights: International Law in Domestic Politics* (New York: Cambridge University Press, 2009).

Stein, J.C., ed., *Getting to the Table: The Process of International Prenegotiation* (Baltimore, MD and London: Johns Hopkins University Press, 1989).

Stephenson, S., *Addressing Local Content Requirements in a Sustainable Energy Trade Agreement* (Geneva: International Centre for Trade and Sustainable Development, 2013)

Van de Graaf, T. et al., eds, *Handbook on the International Political Economy of Energy* (London: Palgrave Macmillan, 2016).

Victor, D.G., *The Case for Climate Clubs* (Geneva: International Centre for Trade and Sustainable Development and World Economic Forum, 2015)

Victor, D.G., *Global Warming Gridlock: Creating More Effective Strategies for Protecting the Planet* (New York: Cambridge University Press, 2011).

Wilke, M., *Feed-in Tariffs for Renewable Energy and WTO Subsidy Rules: An Initial Legal Review* (Geneva: International Centre for Trade and Sustainable Development, 2011).

Wilkins, D.B., Khanna, V.S., & Trubek, D.M., eds, *The Indian Legal Profession in the Age of Globalization: The Rise of the Corporate Legal Sector and its Impact on Lawyers and Society* (Cambridge: Cambridge University Press, 2017).

Yin, R.K., *Case Study Research and Applications: Design and Applications* (6th edition, Los Angeles: Sage Publications Inc., 2018).

Zidar, A. & Gauci, J., eds, *The Role of Legal Advisers in International Law* (Leiden: Brill, 2017).

Book Chapters

Agarwal, A. & Narain, S., 'Global Warming in an Unequal World: A Case of Environmental Colonialism', in N.K. Dubash, ed., *India in a Warming World: Integrating Climate Change and Development* (New Delhi: Oxford University Press, 2019), 81–91.

Chawla, K., 'Drivers, Apparatus, and Implications of India's Renewable Energy Ambitions', in D. Scholten, ed., *The Geopolitics of Renewables* (The Netherlands: Springer, 2018), 203–27.

Criekemans, D., 'Geopolitics of the Renewable Energy Game and Its Potential Impact upon Global Power Relations', in D. Scholten, ed., *The Geopolitics of Renewables* (The Netherlands: Springer, 2018), 37–73.

Dasgupta, C., 'Present at the Creation: The Making of the Framework Convention on Climate Change', in N.K. Dubash, ed., *India in a Warming World: Integrating Climate Change and Development* (New Delhi: Oxford University Press, 2019), 142–56.

Debiel, T. & Wulf, H., 'More than a Rule Taker: The Indian Way of Multilateralism', in M. Hansel, R. Khan, & M. Levaillant, eds, *Theorizing Indian Foreign Policy* (London: Routledge, 2017), 49–68.

Dubash, N.K., 'An Introduction to India's Evolving Climate Change Debate: From Diplomatic Insulation to Policy Integration', in N.K. Dubash, ed., *India in a Warming World: Integrating Climate Change and Development* (New Delhi: Oxford University Press, 2019), 1–28.

Dubash, N.K., 'Of Maps and Compasses: India in Multilateral Climate Negotiations', in W.P.S. Sidhu, P.B. Mehta, & B. Jones, eds, *Shaping the Emerging World: India and the Multilateral Order* (Washington, DC: Brookings Institution Press, 2013), 261–79.

Dubash, N.K. & Ghosh, S., 'National Climate Policies and Institutions', in N.K. Dubash, ed., *India in a Warming World: Integrating Climate Change and Development* (New Delhi: Oxford University Press, 2019), 329–48.

Dubash, N.K. & Rajamani, L., 'Multilateral Diplomacy on Climate Change', in D.M. Malone, C.R. Mohan, & S. Raghavan, eds, *The Oxford Handbook of Indian Foreign Policy* (Oxford: Oxford University Press, 2015), 663–77.

Fabbricotti, A., 'Introduction', in A. Fabbricotti, ed., *The Political Economy of International Law: A European Perspective* (Cheltenham: Edward Elgar Publishing, 2016), 1–8.

Ghosh, A., 'Making Sense on its Own Terms: India in the HFC and Aviation Negotiations', in N.K. Dubash, ed., *India in a Warming World: Integrating Climate Change and Development* (New Delhi: Oxford University Press, 2019), 230–49.

Ginsburg, T. & Shaffer, G., 'How Does Inter National Law Work?', in P. Cane and H.M. Kritzer, eds, *The Oxford Handbook of Empirical Legal Research* (New York: Oxford University Press, 2010), 753–84.

Hughes, V., 'The Role of the Legal Adviser in the World Trade Organization', in A. Zidar & J. Gauci, eds, *The Role of Legal Advisers in International Law* (Leiden: Brill, 2017), 237–54.

Jogesh, A., 'A Change in Climate? Trends in Climate Change Reportage in the Indian Print Media', in N.K. Dubash, ed., *Handbook of Climate Change and India: Development, Politics and Governance* (New Delhi: Oxford University Press, 2012), 266–86.

Jogesh, A., 'Looking Out, Looking In: The Shifting Discourse on Climate Change in the Indian Print Media', in N.K. Dubash, ed., *India in a Warming World: Integrating Climate Change and Development* (New Delhi: Oxford University Press, 2019), 301–25.

Lavasa, A., 'Reaching Agreement in Paris: A Negotiator's Perspective', in N.K. Dubash, ed., *India in a Warming World: Integrating Climate Change and Development* (New Delhi: Oxford University Press, 2019), 169–86.

Madan, T., 'Officialdom: South Block and Beyond', in D.M. Malone, C.R. Mohan, & S. Raghavan, eds, *The Oxford Handbook of Indian Foreign Policy* (Oxford: Oxford University Press, 2015), 232–44.

Madan, T., 'What in the World Is India Able to Do? India's State Capacity for Multilateralism', in W.P.S. Sidhu, P.B. Mehta, & B. Jones, eds, *Shaping the Emerging World: India and the Multilateral Order* (Washington, DC: Brookings Institution Press, 2013) 96–114.

Mathur, A., 'India and Paris: A Pragmatic Way Forward', in N.K. Dubash, ed., *India in a Warming World: Integrating Climate Change and Development* (New Delhi: Oxford University Press, 2019), 222–9.

Mathur, U. & Varughese, G.C., 'From "Obstructionist" to Leading Player: Transforming India's International Image', in D. Michael & A. Pandya, eds, *Indian Climate Policy: Choices and Challenges* (Washington, DC: The Henry L. Stimson Center, 2009), 43–48.

McCosker, S., 'The Intersecting Professions of the International Law Adviser and Diplomat in Rising Asia: Australia, India and Malaysia', in A. Zidar & J. Gauci, eds, *The Role of Legal Advisers in International Law* (Leiden: Brill, 2017), 96–127.

McNollgast, 'The Political Economy of Law', in A.M. Polinsky & S. Shavell, eds, *Handbook of Law and Economics: Volume 1* (Amsterdam: Elsevier Science Publishing, 2007), 1651–738.

Mehta, P.S. & Chatterjee, B., 'India in the "International Trading System"', in D.M. Malone, C.R. Mohan, & S. Raghavan, eds, *The Oxford Handbook of Indian Foreign Policy* (Oxford: Oxford University Press, 2015), 636–49.

Michael, A., 'India and multilateralism: Concepts, New Trajectories and Theorizing', in H.V. Pant, ed., *New Directions in India's Foreign Policy: Theory and Praxis* (Cambridge: Cambridge University Press, 2019), 149–71.

Mistry, D., 'Domestic and International Influences on India's Energy Policy', in S. Ganguly, ed., *Engaging the World: Indian Foreign Policy since 1947* (New Delhi: Oxford University Press, 2016), 425–47.

Norhona, L., 'Emerging Economy Resources Needs and Climate Concerns: Policy Pressures and Innovations', in E. Fritz, ed., *Developing Country, Emerging Country, Global Player: India's Route to Responsibility* (Germany: ATHENA, 2010), 187–207.

Partington, M., 'Empirical Legal Research and Policy Making', in P. Cane and H. M. Kritzer, eds, *The Oxford Handbook of Empirical Legal Research* (New York: Oxford University Press, 2010), 1025–44.

Rajamani, L., 'Understanding the 2015 Paris Agreement', in N. K. Dubash, ed., *India in a Warming World: Integrating Climate Change and Development* (New Delhi: Oxford University Press, 2019), 205–21.

Saran, S., 'India's contemporary plurilateralism', in D. M. Malone, C. R. Mohan, & S. Raghavan, eds, *The Oxford Handbook of Indian Foreign Policy* (Oxford: Oxford University Press, 2015), 623–35.

Saran, S., 'One Long Day in Copenhagen', in N.K. Dubash, ed., *India in a Warming World: Integrating Climate Change and Development* (New Delhi: Oxford University Press, 2019), 157–68.

Scott, D., 'India and the Indo-Pacific Discourse', in H.V. Pant, ed., *New Directions in India's Foreign Policy: Theory and Praxis* (Cambridge: Cambridge University Press, 2019), 195–214.

Sengupta, S., 'Deciphering India's Foreign Policy on Climate Change: Role of Interests, Institutions and Ideas', in J. Plagemann, S. Destradi, & A. Narlikar, eds, *India Rising: A Multilayered Analysis of Ideas, Interests and Institutions* (New Delhi: Oxford University Press, 2020), 166–94.

Sengupta, S., 'India's Engagement in Global Climate Negotiations from Rio to Paris', in N.K. Dubash, ed., *India in a Warming World: Integrating Climate Change and Development* (New Delhi: Oxford University Press, 2019), 114–41.

Sengupta, S., 'International Climate Negotiations and India's Role', in N.K. Dubash, ed., *Handbook of Climate Change and India: Development, Politics and Governance* (New Delhi: Oxford University Press, 2012), 101–17.

Shaffer, G. et al., 'Equalizing Access to the WTO: How Indian Trade Lawyers Build State Capacity', in D.B. Wilkins, V.S. Khanna, & D.M. Trubek, eds, *The Indian Legal Profession in the Age of Globalization: The Rise of the Corporate Legal Sector and its Impact on Lawyers and Society* (Cambridge: Cambridge University Press, 2017), 631–71.

Stein, J.C., 'Getting to the Table: The Triggers, Stages, Functions and Consequences of Prenegotiation', in J.C. Stein, ed., *Getting to the Table: The Process of International Prenegotiation* (Baltimore. MD and London: Johns Hopkins University Press, 1989), 239–68.

Sykes, A.O., 'International Law', in A.M. Polinsky & S. Shavell, eds, *Handbook of Law and Economics: Volume 1* (Amsterdam: Elsevier Science Publishing, 2007), 757–826.

Van Aaken, A. & Trachtman, J.P., 'Political Economy of International Law: Towards a Holistic Model of State Behaviour', in A. Fabbricotti, ed., *The Political Economy of International Law: A European Perspective* (Cheltenham: Edward Elgar Publishing, 2016), 9–43.

Van de Graaf, T. et al., 'States, Markets and Institutions: Integrating International Political Economy and Global Energy Politics', in T. Van de Graaf et al., eds, *Handbook on the International Political Economy of Energy* (London: Palgrave Macmillan, 2016), 3–44.

Webley, L., 'Qualitative Approaches to Empirical Legal Research', in P. Cane and H.M. Kritzer, eds, *The Oxford Handbook of Empirical Legal Research* (New York: Oxford University Press, 2010), 926–50.

Wu, M., 'Indian Corporations, the Administrative State, and the Rise of Indian Trade Remedies', in D.B. Wilkins, V.S. Khanna, & D.M. Trubek, eds, *The Indian Legal Profession in the Age of Globalization: The Rise of the Corporate Legal Sector and its Impact on Lawyers and Society* (Cambridge: Cambridge University Press, 201), 672–704.

Zartman, W., 'Prenegotiation: Phases and Functions', in J.C. Stein, ed., *Getting to the Table: The Process of International Prenegotiation* (Baltimore, MD and London: Johns Hopkins University Press, 1989), 1–17.

Journal Articles

Abbott, K.W. & Snidal, D., 'Hard and Soft Law in International Governance', *International Organization*, 54/3 (2000), 421–56.

Atteridge, A. et al., 'Climate Policy in India: What Shapes International, National and State Policy?', *Ambio*, 41/1 (2012), 68–77.

Bodansky, D., 'The Legal Character of the Paris Agreement', *Review of European, Comparative and International Environmental Law*, 25/2 (2016) 142–50.

Bodansky, D. & Rajamani, L., 'Issues that Never Die', *Carbon and Climate Law Review*, 12/3 (2018), 184–90.

Brunnee, J., 'COPing with Consent: Law-making under Multilateral Environmental Agreements', *Leiden Journal of International Law*, 15/1 (2002), 1–52.

Burley, A.S., 'International Law and International Relations Theory: A Dual Agenda', *American Journal of International Law*, 87/2 (1993), 205–39.

Cassese, A., 'The Role of Legal Advisers in Ensuring that Foreign Policy Conforms to International Legal Standards', *Michigan Journal of International Law*, 14 (1992), 139–217.

Chatterjee-Miller, M., 'India's Feeble Foreign Policy: A Would-Be Great Power Resists its Own Rise', *Foreign Affairs*, 92/3 (2013), 14–19.

Chatterjee-Miller, M., 'The Un-Argumentative Indian?: Ideas About the Rise of India and Their Interaction With Domestic Structures', *India Review*, 13/1 (2014), 1–14.

Chaudhary, A., Krishna, C., & Sagar, A., 'Policy Making for Renewable Energy in India: Lessons from Wind and Solar Power Sectors', *Climate Policy*, 15/1 (2014), 58–87.

Colgan, J.D., 'The Emperor Has No Clothes: The Limits of OPEC in the Global Oil Market', *International Organization*, 68/3 (2014), 599–632.

Dubash, N.K, 'From Norm Taker to Norm Maker? Indian Energy Governance in Global Context', *Global Policy*, 2 (2011), 66–79.

Dubash, N.K., 'the Politics of Climate Change in India: Narratives of Equity and Cobenefits', *WIREs Climate Change*, 4/3 (2013), 191–201.

Dubash, N.K., 'Safeguarding Development and Limiting Vulnerability? India's Stakes in the Paris Agreement', *WIREs Climate Change*, 8/2 (2017), e444.

Dubash, N.K. & Joseph, N.B., 'Evolution of Institutions for Climate Policy in India', *Economic & Political Weekly*, 51/3 (2016), 45–54.

Florini, A. & Dubash, N.K., 'Introduction to the Special Issue: Governing Energy in a Fragmented World', *Global Policy*, 2/s1 (2011), 1–5.

Florini, A. & Dubash, N.K., 'Mapping Global Energy Governance', *Global Policy*, 2/s1 (2011), 6–18.

Florini, A., 'The International Energy Agency in Global Energy Governance', *Global Policy*, 2/s1 (2011), 40–50.

Ghosh, A., 'Governing Clean Energy Subsidies: Why Legal and Policy Clarity is Needed', *BioRes*, 5/3 (2011), 2–4.

Ghosh, A., 'Seeking Coherence in Complexity? The Governance of Energy by Trade and Investment Institutions', *Global Policy*, 2/s1 (2011), 106–19.

Gonsalves, E., 'India in a Future World: Reflections of an Indian Diplomat', *India Quarterly*, 71/4 (2015), 287–99.

Guttergide, J., 'Foreign Policy and the Government Legal Adviser', *Georgia Journal of International and Comparative Law*, 2 (1972), 71–75.

Guzman, A.T., 'The Design of International Agreements', *European Journal of International Law*, 16/4 (2005), 579–612.

Hall, I., 'Narendra Modi and India's Normative Power', *International Affairs*, 93/1 (2017), 113–31.

Helfer, L.R., 'Regime Shifting: The TRIPS Agreement and New Dynamics of International Intellectual Property Lawmaking', *Yale Journal of International Law*, 29/1 (2004), 1–83.

Hopewell, K., 'Recalcitrant Spoiler? Contesting Dominant Accounts of India's Role in Global Trade Governance', *Third World Quarterly*, 39/3 (2018), 577–93.

Hughes, L. & Lipscy, P.Y., 'The Politics of Energy', *Annual Review of Political Science*, 16 (2013), 449–69.

Hurrell, A. & Sengupta, S., 'Emerging Powers, North–South Relations and Global Climate Politics', *International Affairs*, 88/3 (2012), 463–84.

Jasanoff, S., 'India at the Crossroads in Global Environmental Policy', *Global Environmental Change*, 3/1 (1993), 32–52.

Jernnäs, M. & Linnér, B., 'A Discursive Cartography of Nationally Determined Contributions to the Paris Climate Agreement', *Global Environmental Change*, 55 (2019), 73–83.

Jha, V., '"Soft Law in a Hard Shell": India, International Rulemaking and the International Solar Alliance', *Transnational Environmental Law*, 10/3 (2021), 1–25.

Jha, V., 'India's Twin Concerns over Energy Security and Climate Change: Revisiting India's Investment Treaties through a Sustainable Development Lens', *Trade, Law and Development*, 5/1 (2013), 109–49.

Jha, V., 'Sunny Skies Ahead? Political Economy of Climate, Trade and Solar Energy in India', *Trade, Law and Development*, 9/2 (2017), 255–304.

Kandlikar, M. & Sagar, A., 'Climate Change Research and Analysis in India: An Integrated Assessment of a South–North Divide', *Global Environmental Change*, 9/2 (1999), 119–38.

Kennedy, D., 'Law and the Political Economy of the World', *Leiden Journal of International Law*, 26 (2013), 7–48.

Keohane, R.O., 'International Agencies and the Art of the Possible: The Case of the IEA', *Journal of Policy Analysis and Management*, 1/4 (1982), 469–81.

Leal-Arcas, R. & Filis, A., 'The Fragmented Governance of the Global Energy Economy: A Legal-Institutional Analysis', *The Journal of World Energy Law & Business*, 6/4 (2013), 348–405.

Lewis, J.I., 'The Rise of Renewable Energy Protectionism: Emerging Trade Conflicts and Implications for Low Carbon Development', *Global Environmental Politics* 14/4 (2014), 10–35.

Lipson, C., 'Why are Some International Agreements Informal?', *International Organization*, 45/4 (1991), 495–538.

Michaelowa, K. & Michaelowa, A., 'India as an Emerging Power in International Climate Negotiations', *Climate Policy*, 12 (2012), 575–90.

Mohan, A. & Wehnert, T., 'Is India Pulling Its Weight? India's Nationally Determined Contribution and Future Energy Plans in Global Climate Policy', *Climate Policy*, 19/3 (2019), 275–82.

Mohan, A., 'From Rio to Paris: India in Global Climate Politics', *Rising Powers Quarterly*, 2/3 (2017), 39–61.

Mukherjee, R. & Malone, D.M., 'From High Ground to High Table: The Evolution of Indian Multilateralism', *Global Governance*, 17 (2011), 311–29.

Narlikar, A., 'India Rising: Responsible to Whom?', *International Affairs*, 89/3 (2013), 595–614.

Narlikar, A., 'India's Role in Global Governance: A Modification?', *International Affairs*, 93/1 (2017), 93–111.

Narlikar, A., 'Introduction: Negotiating the Rise of New Powers', *International Affairs*, 89/3 (2013), 561–76.

Narlikar, A., 'Peculiar Chauvinism or Strategic Calculation? Explaining the Negotiating Strategy of a Rising India', *International Affairs*, 82/1 (2006), 59–76.

Overland, I. & Reischl, G., 'A Place in the Sun? IRENA's Position in the Global Energy Governance Landscape', *International Environmental Agreements*, 18 (2018), 335–50.

Plagemann, J. & Prys-Hansen, M., ' "Responsibility", Change, and Rising Powers' Role Conceptions: Comparing Indian Foreign Policy Roles in Global Climate Change Negotiations and Maritime Security', *International Relations of the Asia-Pacific* 20/2 (2020), 275–305.

Rajamani, L., 'Ambition and Differentiation in the 2015 Paris Agreement: Interpretative Possibilities and Underlying Politics', *International and Comparative Law Quarterly*, 65/2 (2016), 493–514.

Rajamani, L., 'Ambition and Differentiation in the 2015 Paris Agreement: Interpretative Possibilities and Underlying Politics', *International and Comparative Law Quarterly*, 65/2 (2016), 493–514.

Rajamani, L., 'India and Climate Change: What India Wants, Needs, and Needs to Do', *India Review*, 8/3 (2009) 340–74.

Rajamani, L., 'India's Approach to International Law in the Climate Change Regime', *Indian Journal of International Law*, 57/2 (2017), 1–23.

Rajamani, L., 'The 2015 Paris Agreement: Interplay between Hard, Soft, and Non-Obligations', *Journal of Environmental Law*, 28/2 (2016), 337–58.

Rajamani, L., 'The Durban Platform for Enhanced Action and the Future of the Climate Regime', *International and Comparative Law Quarterly*, 61/2 (2012), 501–18.

Rajamani, L., 'The Warsaw Climate Negotiations: Emerging Understandings and Battle Lines on the Road to the 2015 Climate Agreement', *International and Comparative Law Quarterly*, 63/3 (2014), 721–40.

Rastogi, N.P, 'Winds of Change: India's Emerging Climate Strategy', *The International Spectator*, 46/2 (2011), 127–41.

Raustiala, K., 'Form and Substance in International Agreements', *American Journal of International Law*, 99/3 (2005), 581–614.

Rimmer, M., 'Beyond the Paris Agreement: Intellectual Property, Innovation Policy, and Climate Justice', *Laws*, 8/1 (2019), 1–24.

Sabel, R., 'Role of Legal Adviser in Diplomacy', *Diplomacy and Statecraft*, 8/1 (1997), 1–9.

Shaffer, G., Nedumpara, J., & Sinha, A., 'State Transformation and the Role of Lawyers: The WTO, India, and Transnational Legal Ordering', *Law and Society Review*, 49/3 (2015), 595–629.

Sharma, M.S. & Bhogal, P., 'India and Global Trade Governance: Re-Defining Its "National" Interest', *Rising Powers Quarterly*, 2/3 (2017), 125–46.

Shidore, S. & Busby, J.W., 'One More Try: The International Solar Alliance and India's Search for Geopolitical Influence', *Energy Strategy Reviews*, 26 (2019), 100385.

Shidore, S. & Busby, J.W., 'What Explains India's Embrace of Solar? State-Led Energy Transition in a Developmental Policy', *Energy Policy*, 129 (2019), 1179–89.

Späth, P., 'Understanding the Social Dynamics of Energy Regions—The Importance of Discourse Analysis', *Sustainability*, 4 (2012), 1256–73.

Sprinz, D.F. et al., 'The Effectiveness of Climate Clubs under Donald Trump', *Climate Policy*, 18/7 (2018), 828–38.

Stewart, R. et al., 'Building Blocks for Global Climate Protection', *Stanford Environmental Law Journal*, 32 (2013), 341–92.

Thaker, J. & Leiserowitz, A., 'Shifting Discourses of Climate Change in India', *Climatic Change*, 123/2 (2014), 107–19.

Urpelainen, J. & Van de Graaf, T., 'The International Renewable Energy Agency: A Success Story in Institutional Innovation?', *International Environmental Agreements: Politics, Law and Economics*, 15/2 (2015), 159–77.

Van de Graaf, T. & Colgan, J., 'Global Energy Governance: A Review and Research Agenda', *Palgrave Communications*, 2/15047 (2016), 1–12.

Van de Graaf, T., 'Fragmentation in Global Energy Governance: Explaining the Creation of IRENA', *Global Environmental Politics*, 13/3 (2013), 14–33.

Van de Graaf, T., 'Obsolete or Resurgent? The International Energy Agency in a Changing Global Landscape', *Energy Policy*, 48 (2012), 233–41.

Vihma, A., 'India and the Global Climate Governance: Between Principles and Pragmatism', *The Journal of Environment & Development*, 20/1 (2011), 69–94.

Wu, M. & Salzman, J., 'The Next Generation of Trade and Environment Conflicts: The Rise of Green Industrial Policy', *Northwestern Law Review*, 108 (2014), 401–74.

Young, M.K., 'The Role of the Attorney-Adviser in the U.S. Department of State: Institutional Arrangements and Structural Imperatives', *Law and Contemporary Problems*, 61/2 (1998), 133–53.

Newspapers and Periodicals

Agencies, 'India Should Take Initiatives to Form League Like OPEC: Narendra Modi', *The Indian Express* (19 Apr. 2012), https://indianexpress.com/article/news-arch ive/web/india-should-take-initiatives-to-form-league-like-opec-narendra-modi/ , accessed 15 Dec. 2022.

Bagchi, I. & Sethi, N., 'Saran is PM's Envoy on Climate Change', *The Economic Times* (12 Mar. 2008), https://economictimes.indiatimes.com/news/environment/glo bal-warming/saran-is-pms-envoy-on-climate-change/articleshow/2856831. cms?from=mdr, accessed 15 Dec. 2022.

Chawla, K., 'The International Solar Alliance: From Promise to Action', *India Global Business* (15 Nov. 2018), https://www.indiaglobalbusiness.com/igb-archive/the-international-solar-alliance-from-promise-to-action-india-global-business, ac cessed 15 Dec. 2022.

DNA Correspondent, 'Asia's Largest Solar Park Inaugurated in Patan', *DNA* (31 Dec. 2010), https://www.dnaindia.com/india/report-asia-s-largest-solar-park-inau gurated-in-patan-1488351, accessed on 15 Dec. 2022.

ET Bureau, 'Ministry of Environment and Forests Undergoes a Nomenclature Change; Government Serious to Tackle Climate Change', *The Economic Times* (28 May 2014), https://economictimes.indiatimes.com/news/economy/policy/minis try-of-environment-and-forests-undergoes-a-nomenclature-change-governm ent-serious-to-tackle-climate-change/articleshow/35651292.cms,   accessed   15 Dec. 2022.

Express News Service, 'India, France warm up to solar alliance', *The Indian Express* (26 Jan.   2016),   https://indianexpress.com/article/india/india-news-india/india-fra nce-warm-up-to-solar-alliance/, accessed on 15 Dec. 2022.

FWire, 'India Should Take Initiatives to Form League Like OPEC: Modi', *Firstpost* (19 Apr. 2012), https://www.firstpost.com/fwire/india-should-take-initiatives-to-form-league-like-opec-modi-281550.html, accessed 15 Dec. 2022.

Goswami, U.A., 'Reactive No More, India Gets Proactive on Climate Change', *The Economic Times* (10 Nov. 2015), https://economictimes.indiatimes.com/blogs/ GreyMatters/reactive-no-more-india-gets-proactive-on-climate-change/?sou rce=app&frmapp=yes, accessed 15 Dec. 2022.

HT Correspondent, 'Kalam to Release Modi's Book on Climate Change', *The Hindustan Times* (21 Dec. 2010), https://www.hindustantimes.com/books/kalam-to-release-modi-s-book-on-climate-change/story-a2M5P48BiAWYvrT8d3JYrM. html, accessed 15 Dec. 2022.

IANS, 'France Pledges 500 Million Euros More to ISA', *Business Standard* (14 Mar. 2019),   https://www.business-standard.com/article/news-ians/france-pledges-500-million-euros-more-to-isa-119031401268_1.html, accessed on 15 Dec. 2022.

IANS, 'PM Narendra Modi Pushes Grand Global Solar Alliance before G20', *NDTV* (15 Nov. 2015), https://www.ndtv.com/india-news/pm-narendra-modi-pushes-grand-global-solar-alliance-before-g20-1243705, accessed 15 Dec. 2022.

Jai, S., '70% Duty on Solar Imports: How Serious Is China Dominance in Indian Market?', *Business Standard* (12 Jan. 2018), https://www.business-standard.com/ article/economy-policy/70-duty-on-solar-imports-how-serious-is-china-domina nce-in-indian-market-118011100565_1.html, accessed 15 Dec. 2022.

Jai, S., 'CEO Masayoshi Son Offers Free Power from Softbank's Solar Plants in India', *Business Standard* (4 Oct. 2018), https://www.business-standard.com/article/ companies/ceo-masayoshi-son-offers-free-power-from-softbank-s-solar-plants-in-india-118100400071_1.html, accessed 15 Dec. 2022.

Jai, S., 'One Sun, One World, One Grid: All You Need to Know about Mega Solar Plan', *Business Standard* (15 Aug. 2020, https://www.business-standard.com/article/curr ent-affairs/one-sun-one-world-one-grid-all-you-need-to-know-about-solar-strat egy-120081500417_1.html, accessed 15 Dec. 2022.

Koundal, A., 'India's Renewable Power Capacity Is the Fourth Largest in the World, Says PM Modi', *The Economic Times* (26 Nov. 2020), https://energy.economictimes. indiatimes.com/news/renewable/indias-renewable-power-capacity-is-the-fou rth-largest-in-the-world-says-pm-modi/79430910, accessed 15 Dec. 2022.

Laha, R., 'SoftBank Chief Masayoshi Son to Offer Free Solar Power to India', *Fortune India* (4 Oct. 2018), https://www.fortuneindia.com/macro/softbank-chief-masayo shi-son-to-offer-free-solar-power-to-india/102542, accessed 15 Dec. 2022.

Landler, M., 'U.S. and China Reach Climate Accord after Months of Talks', *The New York Times* (11 Nov. 2014), https://www.nytimes.com/2014/11/12/world/ asia/china-us-xi-obama-apec.html, accessed 15 Dec. 2022.

Mathew, L. & Shah, A., 'Narendra Modi Makes Election History as BJP Gets Majority on Its Own', *Mint* (17 May 2014), https://www.livemint.com/Politics/vGyzihx

gQEuYmzRmyRA1vN/Election-results-2014-Counting-begins-as-Narendra-Modi-eyes.html, accessed 15 Dec. 2022.

Mazumdar, R., 'Trade: A Dark Spot in the Solar World', *The Hindu Business Line* (8 Mar. 2018), https://www.thehindubusinessline.com/opinion/trade-a-dark-spot-in-the-solarworld/article22985420.ece, accessed 15 Dec. 2022.

Modi, N., 'The Rich Must Take Greater Responsibility for Climate Change', *Financial Times* (29 Nov. 2015), https://www.ft.com/content/03a251c6-95f7-11e5-9228-87e603d47bdc, accessed 15 Dec. 2022.

Mukhopadhyay, A., 'India Only G20 Nation Doing Its 'Fair Share' to Meet 2 Degree Goal—Report', *DW* (19 Nov. 2020), https://www.dw.com/en/india-only-g20-nation-doing-its-fair-share-to-meet-2-degree-goal-report/a-55657420, accessed 15 Dec. 2022.

Oza, M., 'Interview with Upendra Tripathy, Director General, International Solar Alliance', *Energetica India* (1 Apr. 2019), https://www.energetica-india.net/power ful-thoughts/online/upendra-tripathy, accessed 15 Dec. 2022.

Parikh, K., 'It's Time for India to Turn to the Sun', *Hindustan Times* (30 Dec. 2010), https://www.hindustantimes.com/delhi/it-s-time-for-india-to-turn-to-the-sun/story-A5SoH6aPSC5VwPlhnpryrO.html, accessed 15 Dec. 2022.

Patel, T. & Nicola, S., 'Engie Buys Solairedirect for $222 Million in Renewables Push', *Bloomberg* (1 Jul. 2015), https://www.bloomberg.com/news/articles/2015-07-01/engie-buys-solairedirect-for-222-million-in-renewables-push, accessed on 15 Dec. 2022.

Power for All, 'Multi-Billion Dollar Africa–India Partnership Aims to Eradicate Electricity Poverty', *Medium* (13 Jun. 2017), https://medium.com/energy-access-india/multi-billion-dollar-afro-india-partnership-aims-to-eradicate-electricity-poverty-298ec3b95525, accessed 15 Dec. 2022.

PTI, 'India Elected Non-Permanent Member of UN Security Council for 2-Year Term', *Business Standard* (18 Jun. 2020), https://www.business-standard.com/arti cle/current-affairs/india-elected-non-permanent-member-of-un-security-coun cil-for-2021-22-term-120061800081_1.html, accessed 15 Dec. 2022.

PTI, 'India Gifts Solar Panels to UN, One Each for 193 Member States', *The Economic Times* (13 Sep. 2019), https://economictimes.indiatimes.com/news/politics-and-nation/india-gifts-solar-panels-to-un-one-each-for-193-member-states/articles how/71117091.cms, accessed 15 Dec. 2022.

PTI, 'India on Track to Meet NDC Goals under Paris Agreement: Survey', *The Economic Times* (31 Jan. 2020), https://economictimes.indiatimes.com/news/econ omy/policy/india-on-track-to-meet-ndc-goals-under-paris-agreement-survey/articleshow/73809685.cms?from=mdr, accessed 15 Dec. 2022

Rana, N. 'India on Track to Meet 175 GW Renewable Energy Targets by 2022', *The Economic Times* (16 Feb. 2021), https://economictimes.indiatimes.com/indus try/energy/power/india-on-track-to-meet-175-gw-renewable-energy-targets-by-2022-etilc-members/articleshow/80976846.cms?from=mdr, accessed 15 Dec. 2022.

Rowlatt, J., 'Can Paris Climate Talks Overcome the India Challenge?', *BBC News* (26 Nov. 2015), https://www.bbc.com/news/world-asia-india-34929578, accessed 15 Dec. 2022.

Sevastopulo, D. & Clark, P., 'Paris Climate Deal Will Not Be a Legally Binding Treaty', *Financial Times* (11 Nov. 2015), https://www.ft.com/content/79daf872–8894-11e5–90de-f44762bf9896, accessed 15 Dec. 2022.

Times News Network, 'Macron Announces Extra €700m for Green Energy, Hails "Solar Mamas"', *The Economic Times* (12 Mar. 2018), https://energy.economicti mes.indiatimes.com/news/renewable/macron-announces-extra-700m-for-green-energy-hails-solar-mamas/63262680, accessed on 15 Dec. 2022.

Press Releases

Engie, *Launch of the Terrawatt Initiative Aimed at Meeting the International Solar Alliance's Objective of 1TW of Additional Solar Capacity by 2030* [media release] (1 Dec. 2015), https://www.engie.com/en/journalists/press-releases/terrawatt-initiat ive-international-solar-alliances-objective-2030, accessed 15 Dec. 2022.

FICCI, *ISA Constituted Global Leadership Task Force of Corporates on Innovation Meets in Delhi* [media release] (29 Apr. 2018), http://www.ficci.in/pressrelease-page.asp?nid=3101, accessed 15 Dec. 2022.

MEA (Government of India), *Universalization of the Membership of the International Solar Alliance (ISA)* [media release] (31 Jul. 2020), https://www.mea.gov.in/press-releases.htm?dtl/32866/Universalization_of_the_Membership_of_the_Internati onal_Solar_Alliance_ISA, accessed 15 Dec. 2022.

PIB, *'Make in India' Programme* [media release] (24 Jul. 2015), http://pib.nic.in/news ite/PrintRelease.aspx?relid=123724, accessed 15 Dec. 2022.

PIB, *Executive Committee on Climate Change Constituted* [media release] (31 Jan. 2013), https://archivepmo.nic.in/drmanmohansingh/press-details.php?nodeid= 1568, accessed 15 Dec. 2022.

PIB, *Government Reconstitutes the Prime Minister's Council on Climate Change* [media release] (5 Nov. 2014), https://pib.gov.in/newsite/printrelease.aspx?relid= 111090, accessed 15 Dec. 2022.

PIB, *India Designated as Chair to the Ninth Meeting of the International Renewable Energy Agency (IRENA)* [media release] (10 Apr. 2015), https://pib.gov.in/newsite/ PrintRelease.aspx?relid=118146, accessed on 15 Dec. 2022.

PIB, *International Solar Alliance will Be the First International and Inter-Governmental Organisation of 121 Countries to Have Headquarters in India with United Nations as Strategic Partner* [media release] (25 Jan. 2016), https://pib.gov.in/newsite/print release.aspx?relid=135794, accessed 15 Dec. 2022.

PIB, *ISA to Become a Treaty-Based International Intergovernmental Organization Tomorrow* [media release] (5 Dec. 2017), http://pib.nic.in/newsite/PrintRelease. aspx?relid=174097, accessed 15 Dec. 2022.

PIB, *PM's Council on Climate Change Constituted* [media release] (5 Jun. 2007), https://archivepmo.nic.in/drmanmohansingh/press-details.php?nodeid=575, ac-cessed 15 Dec. 2022.

PIB, *Prime Minister Announces Coalition for Disaster Resilient Infrastructure at UN Climate Action Summit 2019* [media release] (24 Sep. 2019), https://pib.gov.in/ Pressreleaseshare.aspx?PRID=1586051, accessed 15 Dec. 2022.

PIB, *Prime Minister to Launch 'Make in India' Initiative* [media release] (24 Sep. 2014), http://pib.nic.in/newsite/PrintRelease.aspx?relid=109953, accessed 15 Dec. 2022

PIB, *Prime Minister's Council on Climate Change Constituted* [media release] (5 Jun. 2007), http://www.pib.nic.in/newsite/erelease.aspx?relid=28457, accessed 15 Dec. 2022.

PIB, *Revision of Cumulative Targets under National Solar Mission* [media release] (17 Jun. 2015), http://pib.nic.in/newsite/PrintRelease.aspx?relid=122566, accessed 15 Dec. 2022.

PMO, *PM Council on Climate Change Constituted* [media release] (5 Jun. 2007), https://archivepmo.nic.in/drmanmohansingh/press-details.php?nodeid=575, accessed 15 Dec. 2022.

Online Sources

IISD, 'How to Make Hybrid Meetings Work', *Earth Negotiations Bulletin* (22 Apr. 2021), https://enb.iisd.org/articles/how-make-hybrid-meetings-work, accessed 15 Dec. 2022.

IRENA, *Country Rankings*, https://www.irena.org/Statistics/View-Data-by-Topic/Capacity-and-Generation/Country-Rankings, accessed 15 Dec. 2022.

ISA, 'Corporate Partners', *Partners and Collaborations*, https://isolaralliance.org/partners/corporate, accessed 15 Dec. 2022.

ISA, 'Member Countries', *Membership*, https://isolaralliance.org/membership/countries, accessed 15 Dec. 2022.

ISA, 'Partner Organizations', *Partners and Collaborations*, https://isolaralliance.org/partners/organisations, accessed 15 Dec. 2022.

ISA, *Background*, https://isolaralliance.org/about/background, accessed 15 Dec. 2022.

ISA, *Governance*, https://isolaralliance.org/governance/first-assembly, accessed 15 Dec. 2022.

M. Wood & O. Sender, 'State Practice', *Oxford Public International Law* (Jan. 2017), http://opil.ouplaw.com/view/10.1093/law:epil/9780199231690/law-9780199231690-e1107, accessed 15 Dec. 2022.

Make in India (Government of India), 'FDI Policy', *Renewable Energy*, https://www.makeinindia.com/sector/renewable-energy, accessed 15 Dec. 2022.

MEA (Government of India), 'Lok Sabha Unstarred Question No. 1557 Infrastructure Development in African Countries: Answer by V. Muraleedharan, Minister of State in the Ministry of External Affairs' (10 Feb. 2021), https://www.mea.gov.in/lok-sabha.htm?dtl/33496/question+no1557+infrastructure+development+in+african+countries, accessed on 15 Dec. 2022.

MEA (Government of India), 'Lok Sabha Unstarred Question No. 3893 Completion of Projects: Answer by V. Muraleedharan, Minister of State in the Ministry of External Affairs' (11 Dec. 2019), https://www.mea.gov.in/lok-sabha.htm?dtl/32190/question+no3893+completion+of+projects, accessed on 15 Dec. 2022.

MEA (Government of India), 'Rajya Sabha Unstarred Question No. 1817 Development Cooperation with Foreign Countries: Answer by V. Muraleedharan, Minister of State in the Ministry of External Affairs' (3 Jul. 2019), https://www.mea.gov.in/lok-sabha.htm?dtl/31525/question+no1817+development+cooperation+with+foreign+countries, accessed on 15 Dec. 2022.

MEA (Government of India), 'Rajya Sabha Unstarred Question No. 460 Development Cooperation with Foreign Countries: Answer by Gen. (Dr.) V.K. Singh, Minister of

State in the Ministry of External Affairs' (7 Feb. 2019), https://www.mea.gov.in/rajya-sabha.htm?dtl/31007/question+no460+development+cooperation+with+foreign+countries, accessed on 15 Dec. 2022.

MOP (Government of India), 'Total Installed Capacity', *Power Sector at a Glance: All India (31. Jan. 2021),* https://powermin.nic.in/en/content/power-sector-glance-all-india, *accessed* 15 Dec. 2022.

UNFCCC, 'International Solar Energy Alliance Launched at COP21', *Newsroom* (30 Nov. 2015), https://newsroom.unfccc.int/news/international-solar-energy-alliance-launched-at-cop21, accessed 15 Dec. 2022.

UNFCCC, 'Mission Innovation—Clean Energy', *Newsroom* (30 Nov. 2015), https://unfccc.int/news/mission-innovation-clean-energy, accessed 15 Dec. 2022.

World Bank, *Solar Risk Mitigation Initiative*, https://www.worldbank.org/en/topic/energy/brief/srmi, accessed 15 Dec. 2022.

Index

Milton Keynes UK
Ingram Content Group UK Ltd.
UKHW010618050224
437282UK00001B/2